D0115328

A PLUME BOOK

HOW TO SURVIVE
THE END OF THE WORLD
AS WE KNOW IT

JAMES WESLEY, RAWLES is the founder and editor of SurvivalBlog .com, the Internet's most popular blog on family preparedness. He is a world-renowned expert on a wide range of preparedness topics, including food storage, fuel storage, self-defense, communications, retreat security, "bug out" bags, survival vehicles, retreat architecture, gardening for self-sufficiency, small livestock, and a wide variety of traditional pioneer and self-sufficiency skills.

The author is a former U.S. Army Intelligence officer. His preparedness consulting clients have included Fortune 500 executives, clergy, entrepreneurs, and fund managers. An influential figure in the modern preparedness movement, Rawles not only talks the talk, but he walks the walk: He and his family live at a well-stocked and fully self-sufficient retreat that is nestled in a mountain range "somewhere west of the Rockies."

Rawles is also the author of *Patriots: A Novel of Survival in the Coming Collapse*, which has been described as "a survival manual, dressed neatly as fiction." Two sequels are forthcoming from Simon & Schuster.

HOW TO SURVIVE
THE END OF THE WORLD
AS WE KNOW IT

Tactics, Techniques, and Technologies
for Uncertain Times

James Wesley, Rawles

A PLUME BOOK

PLUME
Published by Penguin Group
Penguin Group (USA) Inc., 375 Hudson Street, New York, New York 10014, U.S.A.
Penguin Group (Canada), 90 Eglinton Avenue East, Suite 700, Toronto, Ontario, Canada M4P 2Y3 (a division of Pearson Penguin Canada Inc.)
Penguin Books Ltd., 80 Strand, London WC2R 0RL, England
Penguin Ireland, 25 St. Stephen's Green, Dublin 2, Ireland (a division of Penguin Books Ltd.)
Penguin Group (Australia), 250 Camberwell Road, Camberwell, Victoria 3124, Australia (a division of Pearson Australia Group Pty. Ltd.)
Penguin Books India Pvt. Ltd., 11 Community Centre, Panchsheel Park, New Delhi – 110 017, India
Penguin Books (NZ), 67 Apollo Drive, Rosedale, North Shore 0632, New Zealand (a division of Pearson New Zealand Ltd.)
Penguin Books (South Africa) (Pty.) Ltd., 24 Sturdee Avenue, Rosebank, Johannesburg 2196, South Africa

Penguin Books Ltd., Registered Offices: 80 Strand, London WC2R 0RL, England

First published by Plume, a member of Penguin Group (USA) Inc.

First Printing, October 2009
20 19 18 17 16

Ⓟ REGISTERED TRADEMARK—MARCA REGISTRADA

LIBRARY OF CONGRESS CATALOGING-IN-PUBLICATION DATA

Rawles, James Wesley.
  How to survive the end of the world as we know it : tactics, techniques, and techhnologies for uncertain times / James Wesley Rawles.
    p. cm.
  Includes index.
  ISBN 978-0-452-29583-4
  1. Survival skills. 2. Survivalism. 3. reparedness. 4. Disasters—Social aspects. I. Title.
  GF86.R39 2009
  613.6'9—dc22   2009028617

Printed in the United States of America
Set in Iowan Old Style
Designed by Chris Welsh

Contents

Acknowledgments

My sincere thanks to the more than 135,000 SurvivalBlog readers. Thank you for sharing your tremendous knowledge and insights.

Special thanks to the Memsahib for her tremendous support.

Thanks also to Michael Z. Williamson and to my Penguin Books editor, Becky Cole, for her patience and her eagle eye.

INTRODUCTION

An Extremely Fragile Society

We live in a time of relative prosperity. Our health care is excellent, our grocery-store shelves bulge with a huge assortment of fresh foods, and our telecommunications systems are lightning fast. We have cheap transportation, with our cities linked by an elaborate and fairly well-maintained system of roads, freeways, rails, canals, seaports, and airports. For the first time in human history, the majority of the world's population now lives in cities.

But the downside to all this abundance is overcomplexity, overspecialization, and overly long supply chains. In the First

World, less than 2 percent of the population is engaged in agriculture or fishing. Ponder that for a moment: Just 2 percent of us are feeding the other 98 percent. The food on our tables often comes from hundreds if not thousands of miles away. Our heating and lighting are typically provided by power sources hundreds of miles away. For many people, even their tap water travels that far. Our factories produce sophisticated cars and electronics that have subcomponents that are sourced from three continents. The average American comes home from work each day to find that his refrigerator is well-stocked with food, his lights come on reliably, his telephone works, his tap gushes pure water, his toilet flushes, his paycheck has been automatically deposited to his bank, his garbage has been collected, his house is a comfortable seventy degrees, his televised entertainment is up and running 24/7, and his Internet connection is rock solid. We've built a very Big Machine that up until now has worked remarkably well, with just a few glitches. But that may not always be the case. As Napoleon found out the hard way, long chains of supply and communication are fragile and vulnerable. Someday the Big Machine may grind to a halt.

Let me describe just one set of circumstances that could cause that to happen:

Imagine the greatest of all influenza pandemics, spread by casual contact—a virus so virulent that it kills more than half of the people infected. And imagine the advance of a disease so rapid that it makes its way around the globe in less than a week. (Isn't modern jet air travel grand?) Consider that we have global news media that is so rabid for "hot" news that they can't resist showing pictures of men in respirators, rubber gloves, goggles, and Tyvek coveralls wheeling gurneys out of houses, laden with body bags. These scenes will be repeated so many times that the majority of citizens decides "I'm *not* going to go to work tomorrow, or the day after, or in fact until after things get better." But by not going to work, some important cogs will be missing from the Big Machine.

What will happen when the Big Machine is missing pieces? Orders won't get processed at the Walmart distribution center. The 18-wheelers won't make deliveries to groceries stores. Gas stations will run out of fuel. Some policemen and firemen won't show up for work, having decided that protecting their own families is their top priority. Power lines will get knocked down in windstorms, and there will be nobody to repair them. Crops will rot in the fields and orchards because there will be nobody to pick them, or transport them, or magically bake them into Pop-Tarts, or stock them on your supermarket shelf. The Big Machine will be *broken*.

Does this sound scary? Sure it does, and it should. The implications are huge. But it gets worse: The average suburban family has only about a week's worth of food in their pantry. Let's say the pandemic continues for weeks or months on end—what will they do when that food is gone and there is no reasonably immediate prospect of resupply? Supermarket shelves will be stripped bare. Faced with the prospect of staying home and starving or going out to meet Mr. Influenza, millions of Joe Americans will be forced to go out and "forage" for food. The first likely targets will be restaurants, stores, and food-distribution warehouses. As the crisis deepens, not a few "foragers" will soon transition to full-scale looting, taking the little that their neighbors have left. Next, they'll move on to farms that are in close proximity to cities. A few looters will form gangs that will be highly mobile and well armed, ranging deeper and deeper into farmlands, running their vehicles on surreptitiously siphoned gasoline.

Eventually their luck will run out and they will all die of the flu, or of lead poisoning. But before the looters are all dead they will do a tremendous amount of damage. You must be ready for a coming crisis. Your life and the lives of your loved ones will depend on it.

The New World and You

If and when the flu pandemic—or terrorist attack, or massive currency devaluation, or some other unthinkable crisis—occurs, things could turn very, very ugly all over the globe. Think through all of the implications of disruption of key portions of our modern technological infrastructure. You need to be able to provide water, food, heating, and lighting for your family. Ditto for law enforcement, since odds are that a pandemic will be YOYO (You're on your own) time.

You'll need to get your beans, bullets, and Band-Aids squared away, pronto. Most important, you'll need to be prepared to hunker down for three or four months, with minimal outside contact. That will take a lot of logistics, as well as plenty of cash on hand to pay your bills in the absence of a continuing income stream.

The Great Unraveling

As this book goes to press in the summer of 2009, we are witnessing a global economy in deep, deep trouble. Artificially low interest rates and artificially high residential real estate prices in many First World nations fueled a worldwide credit bubble.

That bubble burst in 2007, and the full effects of the credit collapse are just now being felt. The resulting recession might turn into an economic depression that could last more than a decade.

The collapse of the credit default swaps (CDS) casino is indicative of much larger systemic risk. These exotic hedges are just one small part of the more than six-hundred-trillion-dollar global derivatives market. There are other derivatives that are just as dangerous. Veteran investor Warren Buffett called derivatives "a ticking time bomb." I concur.

All of the recent bad economic news and the advent of the H1N1 flu call into question some of the basic assumptions about living in a modern industrialized society. We are forced to ask ourselves: How much stress can a society take before it begins to unravel? How safe will our cities be in another year, or in five years? Will supermarket shelves continue to be well stocked with such a tremendous abundance and such a wide assortment of goods?

With the information contained in this book, you can prepare yourself to live independently ("off the grid") for an extended period of time. Self-sufficiency is the bottom line.

Please note that I make reference to some useful Web sites throughout this book. If you aren't on the Internet at home, you can access these sites from free Internet terminals at most public libraries. If any of these URLs are obsolete, then do Web searches for their new URLs or comparable Web sites. For the sake of brevity, I have used the SnipURL.com service to truncate the longer URLs for Web sites mentioned in the book. These short URLs will make it quick and easy for you to reference the Web sites mentioned herein.

Also for the sake of brevity, I use a lot of acronyms in my writings. Each acronym is spelled out the first time it is used, and in this book's glossary.

This book provides both a challenge and a response: Are you truly ready for TEOTWAWKI? If not, then herein is what you'll need to know.

Read this book. Give it some prayer. Then get busy!

PUBLISHER'S NOTE

Every effort has been made to ensure that the information contained in this book is complete and accurate. However, neither the publisher nor the author is engaged in rendering professional advice or services to the individual reader. The ideas, procedures, and suggestions contained in this book are not intended as a substitute for consulting with your physician. All matters regarding your health require medical supervision. Neither the author nor the publisher shall be liable or responsible for any loss or damage allegedly arising from any information or suggestion in this book.

Regarding finances, this publication is designed to provide accurate and authoritative information in regard to the subject matter covered. It is sold with the understanding that the publisher is not engaged in rendering legal, accounting, or other professional services. If you require legal advice or other expert assistance, you should seek the services of a competent professional.

Furthermore, outdoor activities are by their very nature potentially hazardous. All participants in such activities must assume the responsibility for their own actions and safety. If you have any health problems or medical conditions, consult with your physician before undertaking any outdoor activities. The information contained in this guidebook cannot replace sound judgment and good decision making, which can help reduce risk exposure, nor does the scope of this book allow for disclosure of all the potential hazards and risks involved in such activities.

Learn as much as possible about the outdoor recreational activities in which you participate, prepare for the unexpected, and be cautious. The reward will be a safer and more enjoyable experience.

Finally, accordingly nothing in this book is intended as an express or implied warranty of the suitability or fitness of any product, service, or design. The reader wishing to use a product, service, or design discussed in this book should first consult a specialist or professional to ensure suitability and fitness for the reader's particular lifestyle and environmental needs.

HOW TO SURVIVE
THE END OF THE WORLD
AS WE KNOW IT

1

THE SURVIVAL MIND-SET FOR LIVING IN UNCERTAIN TIMES

A Very Bad Day . . .

There has been a power failure. It is a minor annoyance at first. You've awoken late on a winter morning because your alarm clock didn't go off. The house is chilly, and even though you have a natural-gas furnace, the digital thermostat is not working, so there is no electricity for the heater fan to push the air through the ducts. Then you realize that with nighttime lows in the single digits and daytime highs in the twenties, if the power isn't restored by the time you get home from work, it will be very cold in the house. You surmise that freezing rain must have knocked down some power lines.

For breakfast, you have cold cereal and juice instead of scrambled eggs and hot coffee. When will that power come back on? You muse about how long the food in the freezer will last. You skip shaving because you are running late for work and your electric razor won't work without power anyway. Then your car won't start. The car radio doesn't work either. You notice that one of your neighbors is poking and prodding around under the hood of his car. The cold weather must have killed his battery too. You hear what must be a truck backfiring far in the distance. At least somebody got theirs started.

You go into the house and turn on your transistor radio. It won't work either, which is odd, since it is both AC and battery operated. Your kid must have switched the batteries with dead ones from his digital camera. Finally, you dig out your spare transistor radio from the battered ammo can that you use as a fishing tackle box—the one you take on your fly-fishing trips. You scan through the AM and FM bands—there is mostly static. There is only one radio station broadcasting. A frantic news announcer says something about a "high-altitude electromagnetic pulse [EMP] over the Midwest" and the power grids being down all over the United States, Mexico, and Canada.

You are startled to hear loud, rapid-fire gunshots. They are very close by—right near your neighborhood. This is going to be a very bad day . . .

The scenario that I just described is just one of dozens that could cause The End of the World as We Know It (TEOTWAWKI) in the near future.

But for what other reasons should you prepare? Here are just a few terrifying possibilities (in no particular order):

- Hyperinflationary depression
- Deflationary depression
- Terrorist nuclear, biological, or chemical warfare
- Nation-state nuclear, biological, or chemical warfare
- A third World War
- An oil embargo on the First World nations
- Martial law
- Invasion
- Climate change
- Major volcanic and/or earthquake events
- Major asteroid or comet strike

Suffice it to say, we live in an increasingly dangerous world, with a fragile and highly interdependent infrastructure. In recent years we have witnessed accelerating threats of terrorism and economic instability. It is prudent to prepare. In this book, I will focus on specific criteria for choosing the location for a place to live, and once you have it—or even if you decide to prepare right where you are—how to stock up and equip for self-sufficiency. With the right preparation, you can protect your family from numerous threats—so you can not only survive, but *thrive*.

Because I strongly believe that you will stand the best chance of survival if you are able to live in a retreat location year-round, most of the information in this book is geared toward that ideal scenario. It may sound extreme, but When the Schumer Hits the Fan (WTSHTF), you will thank me. There is no single ideal retreat location, because everyone's needs are different. For some, their work requires that they be near a major airport or university. Others, for example, might have chronic health conditions that require proximity to a specialized medical center. So everything that I put forth herein must be tempered by your own particular requirements.

The Golden Horde

Because of the urbanization of the U.S. population, if the entire eastern or western power grid goes down for more than a week, the cities will rapidly become unlivable. I foresee that there could be an almost unstoppable chain of events:

Power Failures, followed by
Municipal Water Supply Failures, followed by
Disruption of Food Distribution, followed by
Collapse of Law and Order, followed by
Fires and Full-Scale Looting, followed by
Massive "Golden Horde" Out-Migration from Major Cities

As the comfort level in the cities rapidly drops to nil, there will be a massive outpouring from the big cities and suburbs into the hinterboonies. This is the phenomenon that my late father, Donald Rawles—a career physics research administrator at Lawrence Livermore National Laboratory, in California—half-jokingly called "the Golden Horde." He was of course referring to the Mongol horde of the thirteenth century, but in a modern context. (The Mongol rulers were chosen from the "Golden Family" of Temujin. Hence the term Golden Horde.)

The Thin Veneer

In my lectures on survival topics I often mention that there is just a thin veneer of civilization on our society. What is underneath is not pretty, and it does not take much to peel away that veneer. You take your average urbanite or suburbanite and get him excessively cold, wet, tired, hungry, and/or thirsty and take away his television, beer, drugs, and other pacifiers, and you will soon see the savage within. It is like peeling the skin off an onion—remove a couple of layers and it gets very smelly.

Here is a mental exercise: Put yourself in the mind-set of Mr. Joe Six-pack, a hypothetical but fairly typical suburbanite. Visualize him in or near a big city close to where you live. He is unprepared for a crisis. He has less than one week's food in his kitchen. He has a 12-gauge pump-action shotgun that he hasn't fired in years, and just half a tank of gas in his minivan and maybe a gallon or two more in a can that he keeps on hand for his lawn mower. Then TEOTWAWKI hits. The power grid is down, his job is history, the toilet doesn't flush, and water no longer magically comes cascading from the tap. His wife and kids are panicky. The supermarket shelves have been stripped bare. There are riots beginning in his city. The local service stations have run out of gas. The banks have closed. Now he is suddenly *desperate*. Where will he go? What will he do?

Odds are Joe will think: "I've gotta go find a vacation cabin somewhere, up in the mountains, where some rich dude only goes a couple of times each year." So vacation destinations like Lake Tahoe, Lake Arrowhead, and Squaw Valley, California; Prescott and Sedona, Arizona; Hot Springs, Arkansas; Vail and Steamboat Springs, Colorado; and the other various rural ski, spa, Great Lakes, and coastal resort areas will get swarmed.

Or, Joe will think: "I've got to go to where they grow food." So places like the Imperial Valley, the Willamette Valley, and the Red River Valley will similarly get overrun. There will be so many desperate Joe Six-packs arriving all at once that these areas will degenerate into free-fire zones. It will be an intensely ugly situation and will not be safe for anyone.

The Linchpin: The Power Grids

The level of severity for any survival scenario will be tremendously greater if the power grid goes down ("grid down") for a period of more than a week. Consider the following:

If there is an extended grid-down scenario . . .

- Most towns and cities will be without municipal (utility) drinking water.
- There will likely be huge outflows of refugees from cities.
- There will possibly be mass prison escapes.
- Virtually all communications will go down. Telephone-company central offices (COs) do have battery backup. These are huge banks of two-volt deep-cycle floating batteries. But those batteries will last only about a week. Backup generators were not installed at most COs, because no situation that would take the power grid down for more than seventy-two hours was ever anticipated. (Bad planning, Ma Bell!) Thus, if and when the grid goes down, hard-wired phones, cell phones, and the Internet will all go down. When both the power grid and phone systems go down, law and order will likely disintegrate. There will be no burglar alarms, no security lighting or cameras, and no reliable way to contact police or fire departments, and so forth.
- There will be no power for kidney-dialysis machines or ventilators for respiratory patients, no resupply of oxygen bottles for people with chronic lung conditions, no resupply of insulin for diabetics, etc. Anyone with a chronic health problem may die.
- Most heaters with fans won't work, even if you can bypass the thermostat. And pellet stoves won't work at all.

- Piped-natural-gas service will be disrupted in all but a few small areas near wellheads.
- There will be no 911 to call, no backup, no "cavalry coming over the hill" in the nick of time. You, your family, and your neighbors will have to handle any lawlessness that comes your way.
- Sanitation will be problematic in any large town or city. Virtually everyone will be forced to draw water from open sources, and meanwhile their neighbors will be inadvertently fouling those same sources. With the grid down and city water disrupted, toilets won't flush and most urbanites and suburbanites will not dig outhouse or garbage pits. A grid-down condition could be a public-health nightmare within a week in metropolitan regions.

Chains of Supply: Lengthy and Fragile

When I give lectures or do radio interviews, I'm often asked for proof that we live in a fragile society. Here is one prime example: The *kanban* or "just-in-time" inventory system was developed in Japan and became popular in America starting in the 1970s. It is now ubiquitous in nearly every industry. The concept is simple: Through close coordination with subcontractors and piece part suppliers, a manufacturer can keep its parts inventory small. *Kanban* is a key element of lean manufacturing. Manufacturers order batches of parts only as needed, sometimes ordering as frequently as twice a week. Companies now hire Six Sigma consultants and *Kaizen* gurus, they buy sophisticated data-processing systems, and they hire extra purchasing administrators, and these expenses actually save them money at the bottom line.

Just-in-time inventory systems have several advantages: less warehouse space, less capital tied up in parts inventory, and less risk of parts obsolescence.

The downside is that lean inventories leave companies vulnerable to any disruption of supply. If transportation gets snarled, or if communications get disrupted, or a parts vendor has a strike or a production problem, then assembly lines grind to halt. Just one missing part means that no finished products go out the door.

The *kanban* concept has also been taken up by America's retailers, most notably its grocery sellers. In the old days—say, twenty years ago—grocery stores had well-stocked back rooms, with many extra cases of dry goods. But now in most stores the back room has been replaced with just a pallet-break-down area. Merchandise comes in from distribution centers and it *all* goes immediately to the consumer shelves out front. Thus, what you see on the grocery-store shelf is all that the store has on hand. What you see is what you get. The bar-code scanners at the checkout counters feed a complex reordering system. If Mrs. Jones buys three jars of pasta sauce, that could trigger a reorder for three more jars. As long as communications and transportation work smoothly, then the entire system hums along like a Swiss watch. But what happens when the transportation infrastructure gets disrupted?

Panic buying can clean out supermarket shelves in a matter of hours. The important lesson in all this is to get prepared in advance. DO NOT count on being able to buy anything to provide for your family on or after TEOTWAWKI Day. So stock up.

Consider the fact that there are only about fifteen large long-term-storage food packers in the country, and even fewer firms that sell non-hybrid (heirloom) gardening seed. How long do you think their inventories will last once there is news that there is a lethal, easily transmissible, human-to-human strain of flu? Prices are currently low and inventories are plentiful. It is better to be a year too early than a day too late.

This book will help you get started with your preparations for WTSHTF.

Just How Rawlesian Are You?

Before we begin, let me tell you a bit about my background. I grew up in the Bomb Shelter era of the 1960s. I was born in raised in Livermore, California, the home of Lawrence Livermore National Laboratory. Living there, with one of the highest per-capita numbers of home fallout shelters in the nation, gave me an appreciation for global threats that had personal implications. I have a bachelor's degree in journalism, and minor degrees in history, military science, and military history. I'm also a former U.S. Army Intelligence officer, where I worked at both the tactical and strategic levels. As an intelligence officer, I monitored the global geopolitical situation very closely. This study helped me appreciate just how fragile all societies can be. I observed that economic and sociopolitical tipping points don't happen often, but when they do come, they are dramatic and often appear to occur overnight. I also observed that it was refugees who became casualties, so I vowed never to be a refugee.

Even as a teenager, I decided that through training and prudent preparation, I could greatly increase my chances for surviving traumatic times. More recently, as a novelist and as a blogger, I've been given a bully pulpit, with the opportunity to encourage hundreds of thousands of people to get prepared. It is my hope that my writings will convince you to substantively increase your preparedness. You, too, can beat the odds and avoid being a mere statistic.

The folks who read my blog, SurvivalBlog.com, regularly refer to themselves as Rawlesian survivalists. To fully understand Rawlesian survivalism, it is important to distinguish it from the numerous quasi-survivalist schools of thought. Some pundits overemphasize primitive wilderness and outdoor survival, while others overemphasize high-tech gadgets. Still others dismiss any planning for self-defense. And many don't give any thought to charity and assisting your neighbors in the aftermath of a disaster. The following is a general summary of my survivalist philosophy, in addition to the tenets I've already discussed:

Lightly Populated Areas Are Safer Than High-Density Areas

With a few exceptions, lower population means fewer problems. WTSHTF, there will be a mass exodus from the cities. Think of it as an army that is spreading out across a battlefield: The wider they are spread, the less effective they are. The inverse-square law hasn't been repealed.

Show Restraint, But Always Have Recourse to Lethal Force

My father often told me, "It is better to have a gun and not need it than to need a gun and not have it." I urge readers to use less than lethal means when safe and practicable, but at times there is not a satisfactory substitute for well-aimed lead going down range at high velocity.

There Is Strength in Numbers

Rugged individualism is all well and good, but it takes more than one man to defend a retreat. Effective defense necessitates having at least two families to provide 24/7 perimeter security.

But of course every individual added means having another mouth to feed. Unless you have an unlimited budget and an infinite larder, you will need to strike a balance when deciding the size of a retreat group.

There Are Moral Absolutes

The foundational morality of the civilized world is best summarized in the Ten Commandments. Moral relativism and secular humanism are slippery slopes. The terminal moraine at the base of these slopes is a rubble pile consisting of either despotism and pillage, or anarchy and the depths of depravity. I believe that it takes both faith and friends to survive perilous times.

Racism Ignores Reason

People should be judged as individuals. Anyone who makes blanket statements about other races is ignorant of the fact that there are both good and bad individuals in all groups.

Skills Beat Gadgets and Practicality Beats Style

The modern world is full of pundits, poseurs, and mall ninjas. Preparedness is not just about accumulating a pile of stuff. You need practical skills, and those come only with study, training, and practice. Any armchair survivalist with a credit card can buy a set of stylish camouflage fatigues and an "M4gery" carbine encrusted with umpteen accessories. Style points should not be mistaken for genuine skills and practicality.

Plentiful Water and Good Soil Are Crucial

Modern mechanized farming, electrically pumped irrigation, chemical fertilizers, and pesticides can make deserts bloom. But when the grid goes down, deserts and marginal farmland will revert to their natural states. The most viable places to survive in the midst of a long-term societal collapse will be those with reliable summer rains and rich topsoil.

Tangibles Trump Conceptuals

Modern fiat currencies are generally accepted, but have essentially no backing. Because they are largely a by-product of interest-bearing debt, modern currencies are destined for inflation. In the long run, inflation dooms fiat currencies to collapse. The majority of your assets should be invested in productive farmland and other tangibles such as useful hand tools. After you have your key logistics squared away, anything extra should be invested in silver and gold.

Governments Tend to Expand Their Power to the Point That They Do Harm

In SurvivalBlog, I often warn of the insidious tyranny of the Nanny State. (There is a predominant trend in First World countries to regulate nearly every aspect of daily life. These regulations have become so pervasive and annoying that the "Nanny State" moniker was developed to describe it.) If the state where you live becomes oppressive, then don't hesitate to relocate. Vote with your feet!

There Is Value in Redundancy

A common saying of my readers is: "Two is one, and one is none." You must be prepared to provide for your family during a protracted period of societal disruption. That means storing essential "beans, bullets, and Band-Aids" in quantity. If commerce is disrupted by a disaster, at least in the short term you will have only your own logistics to fall back on. The more you have stored, the more you will have available for barter and charity. Just as important as redundancy are the attributes of versatility and flexibility. For example, a Rawlesian survivalist who is wealthy likely owns as many as four vehicles: one powered by gasoline, one by diesel, one by propane, and one that is electric. The same individual probably owns a tri-fuel backup power generator that can run on gasoline, propane, or utility natural gas. But even folks on a modest budget can have considerable multi-fuel versatility by making their one and only vehicle a diesel. (I'll talk more about that in Chapter 12.)

A Deep Larder Is Essential

Food storage is key. Even if you have a fantastic self-sufficient garden and pasture ground, you must always have food storage that you can fall back on in the event that your crops fail due to drought, disease, or infestation.

Tools Without Training Are Useless

Owning a gun doesn't make someone a "shooter" any more than owning a surfboard makes someone a surfer. With proper training and practice, you will be miles ahead of the average citizen. Get advanced medical training (MedicalCorps.org). Get the best firearms training that you can afford, at a place like Gunsite or

Thunder Ranch. Learn about amateur radio from your local affiliated American Radio Relay League (ARRL) club. Practice raising a vegetable garden each summer. Learn how to weld, and buy your own oxyacetylene rig. Some skills are perfected only over a period of years.

Old Technologies Are Appropriate Technologies

In the event of a societal collapse, nineteenth-century (or earlier) technologies such as the blacksmith's forge, the treadle sewing machine, and the horse-drawn plow will be far easier to reconstruct than modern technologies.

Charity Is a Moral Imperative

As a Christian, I feel morally obligated to assist others who are less fortunate. Following the Old Testament laws of tzedakah (charity and tithing), I believe that my responsibility begins with my immediate family and expands in successive rings to supporting my immediate neighborhood and church, to my community, and beyond, as resources allow. My philosophy is to give until it hurts in times of disaster.

Buy Life Assurance, Not Life Insurance

Self-sufficiency and self-reliance are multifaceted. You need to systematically provide for water, food, shelter, fuel, first aid, communications, and, if need be, the tools to enforce Rule 308 (lethal force).

Exploit Force Multipliers

Night-vision gear, intrusion detection sensors, and radio-communications equipment are key force multipliers. Because these devices use high technology, they cannot be depended upon in a long-term collapse, but in the short term they can provide a big advantage. Some low technologies such as barbed wire and defensive road cables also provide advantages and can last for several decades.

Invest Your Sweat Equity

Even if some of you have a millionaire's budget, you need to learn how to do things for yourself, and be willing to get your hands dirty. In a societal collapse, the division of labor will be reduced tremendously. Odds are that the only "skilled craftsmen" available to build a shed, mend a fence, shuck corn, repair an engine, or pitch manure will be you and your family. A by-product of sweat equity is muscle tone and proper body weight.

Choose Your Friends Wisely

Associate yourself with skilled doers, not "talkers." Seek out people who share your outlook and morality. Living in close confines with other families is sure to cause friction, but that will be minimized if you share a common religion and norms of behavior. You can't learn every skill yourself. Assemble a team that includes members with medical knowledge, tactical skills, electronics experience, and traditional practical skills.

There Is No Substitute for Mass

Mass stops bullets. Mass stops gamma radiation. Mass stops (or at least slows down) bad guys from entering a home and depriving its residents of life and property. Sandbags are cheap, so buy plenty of them. When planning your retreat house, think: medieval castle.

Always Have a Plan B and a Plan C

Regardless of your pet scenario and your personal grand plan of survival, you need to be flexible and adaptable. Situations and circumstances change. Always keep a Get out of Dodge (G.O.O.D.) kit handy, even if you are fortunate enough to live at your retreat year-round.

Be Frugal

I grew up in a family that still remembered both our pioneer history and the more recent lessons of the Great Depression. One of our family mottoes is: "Use it up, wear it out, make do, or do without."

Some Things Are Worth Fighting For

I encourage my readers to avoid trouble, most importantly via relocation to safe areas where trouble is unlikely to visit. But there may come an unavoidable day when you have to make a stand to defend your own family or your neighbors. Furthermore, if you value your liberty, then be prepared to fight for it, both for yourself and for the sake of your progeny.

The Best Defense: Live at Your Retreat Year-Round

An eleventh-hour Get Out of Dodge (G.O.O.D.) is a bad idea. Even if you have 90 percent of your gear pre-positioned at your retreat, there is the prospect of never making it there safely. Or if you arrive days or weeks late, on foot, you may find your retreat occupied by armed squatters who are gleefully eating from your carefully planned deep larder. Being forced to abandon a vehicle and travel on foot is a dicey proposition, at best. I strongly recommend that readers live at their retreats year-round—even if it means giving up a high-paying big-city job.

It is best if you can get away from urban regions fairly quickly and then take secondary or tertiary back roads. For those who are forced by circumstances or family obligations to live a long distance from their intended retreat, I recommend doing some detailed map studies and then some test-drives with a GPS receiver in hand, to establish five or more G.O.O.D. routes—some quite circuitous—to stay away from high-population regions and expected refugee lines of drift. Needless to say, always, *always* have enough fuel on hand to make the drive from your home to your retreat without buying any.

Depending on the fire code in your town, that might necessitate caching some fuel along your route (ideally with relatives or friends). Along with that comes the further complication of systematically rotating that cached fuel. In this regard, diesel is best, because it is much safer to store and has a much longer storage life than gasoline.

If and when The Day comes, do not hesitate. You need to get out of town well ahead of the Golden Horde, while roads are still passable. It is better to be ultracautious and run the risk of burning up some of your hard-earned vacation hours in the event of a few false alarms than to be complacent and thereby end up stuck in traffic, staring at the taillights of the linear parking lot created by the people who left town ahead of you. (Just ask the folks who tried leaving the Gulf Coast cities immediately before Hurricane Katrina arrived. It was a monumental traffic jam.)

Picking a retreat that is at least three hundred miles from a major metropolitan center and that is away from channelized areas or refugee lines of drift will drastically reduce your chances of ever having uninvited visitors.

Nothing Happens by Chance

You are holding this book in your hands for a reason. Nothing happens entirely by chance. I trust that you will soon be ready to embark on an adventure that will result not only in greater logistical preparedness but also in learning valuable skills that you can use throughout your life. These skills will build your self-confidence. When combined with acquiring the requisite tools, it will help you develop genuine self-reliance—regardless of the adversities that you might someday face. By being well prepared and well trained, you'll also be in a position to share your skills and some of your extra supplies with less prudent relatives, neighbors, and friends.

2

PRIORITIES

Your List of Lists

First Things First

Survival isn't about stuff. It is about skills. If you have time and just a bit of money, then you can get some very well-rounded training in skills that are quite applicable to post-TEOTWAWKI living. In my experience, the most cost-effective training opportunities in the United States include:

- American Red Cross first aid and CPR classes
- Local community college, park district, and adult education classes. They offer courses in metal shop, auto shop, wood shop, leather crafting, ceramics, baking, gardening, welding, and so forth.

- RWVA Appleseed rifle matches and clinics. These are held all over the nation. They offer great training for very little money.
- Reserve Officers' Training Corps (ROTC) classes and camps
- FEMA/CERT classes (classroom and Internet courses, some with team commitment)
- LDS (Mormon) cannery classes/canning sessions. Many wards have their own canneries, which are generally open to non-Mormons.
- ARRL amateur-radio classes
- Species-specific and breed-specific livestock and pet clubs
- NRA and State Rifle and Pistol Association training and shooting events
- Fiber guilds (spinning and weaving) and local knitting clubs
- Mountain Man/Rendezvous clubs (black-powder shooting, flint knapping, soapmaking, rope making, etc.)
- University/county agricultural extension and Cattlemen's Club classes on livestock, gardening, weed control, canning, etc.
- Medical Corps (medicalcorps.org) small group classes. They offer great training—including advanced lifesaving topics that the American Red Cross doesn't teach—at very reasonable cost.
- Volunteer Fire Department (VFD) classes (usually with some commitment)
- Candle and soapmaking clubs/conventions
- Boy Scouts and 4-H. Informal, unenrolled ("straphanger") training is available for adults—just take your kids to the meetings and *don't leave*. Consider becoming a scout leader.

Start with a "List of Lists"

You should start your family-preparedness stocking effort by first composing a List of Lists, then draft prioritized lists for each subject on separate sheets of paper. (Or in a spreadsheet if you are a techno-nerd like me. Just be sure to print out a hard copy for use when the power grid goes down!)

It is important to tailor your lists to suit your particular geography, climate, and population density as well as your peculiar needs and likes/dislikes. Someone setting up a retreat in a coastal area is likely to have a far different list than someone living in the Rockies.

Distinguishing Wants from Needs in Preparedness Planning

My consulting clients often ask me for advice on their preparedness purchasing programs. Some of the items that I've seen them purchase in the name of preparedness make me wonder. For example, a family that recently relocated from Michigan to Idaho's Clearwater River Valley purchased matching snowmobiles for every member of the family. But they now live in a climate where in some years they only have snow that sticks for two or three weeks. In most years they will have to put their snow machines *on trailers* to get up to the high country to use them.

Most of my consulting clients take a methodical, well-balanced approach to their planning and procurement. It is the people who are clever, methodical, and hardworking who are better prepared than the wealthy few who just throw money at the problem. Do your best to make a purchasing plan and stick to it.

Don't go overboard in one area at the expense of another. Preparedness takes balance: food storage, gardening supplies, canning supplies, medical gear, communications gear, reliable vehicles, fuel storage, field gear, cold-weather gear, night-vision equipment, and so forth. Maintaining that balance takes both focused planning and self-control.

The TEOTWAWKI Weekend Experiment

A great way to create truly commonsense preparedness lists is to take a three-day TEOTWAWKI Weekend Experiment with your family. When you come home from work on Friday evening, turn off your main circuit breaker, turn off your gas main (or propane tank), and shut your main water valve (or turn off your well pump). Spend that weekend in primitive conditions. Practice using only your storage food, preparing it on a woodstove (or camping stove).

A TEOTWAWKI Weekend Experiment will surprise you. Things that you take for granted will suddenly become labor intensive. False assumptions will be shattered, but as you regroup and tailor your plan, your family will grow closer and more confident. Some of the most thorough lists that you will ever make will be those written by candlelight.

Your List of Lists Should Include:

- Water List
- Food-Storage List
- Food-Preparation List
- Personal List
- First-Aid/Minor-Surgery List

- Chem/Nuke-Defense List
- Biological-Warfare- and Pandemic-Defense List
- Gardening List
- Hygiene/Sanitation List
- Hunting/Fishing/Trapping List
- Power/Lighting/Batteries List
- Fuels List
- Firefighting List
- Tactical-Living List
- Security—General
- Security—Firearms
- Communications/Monitoring List
- Tools List
- Sundries List
- Survival-Bookshelf List
- Barter and Charity List

Specific Recommendations for Developing Your Lists

Water List (For details, see Chapter 4.)

- **House downspout conversion sheet metal work and barrels.**
- Think through how you'll draw water from open sources. Buy extra containers. Don't buy big barrels. **Five-gallon food-grade buckets** are the largest size that most people can handle without back strain.
- For transporting water if and when gas is too precious to waste, buy a couple of **heavy-duty two-wheel garden carts**—convert the wheels to foam-filled "no-flats" tires.

You will find lots of other uses for those carts around your retreat, such as hauling (of hay, firewood, manure, etc.).

- Treating water. Buy plain **Clorox hypochlorite bleach**. A little goes a long way. Buy some extra half-gallon bottles for barter and charity. If you can afford it, buy a **"Big Berky" British Berkefeld ceramic water filter**.

Food-Storage List (For details, see Chapter 5.)

Lay in an honest one-year supply of storage food for your family:

- Start by increasing the quantities of canned foods that you use on a regular basis.
- Buy some short-term **Get out of Dodge foods** that don't require adding water, such as military-specification **Meals, Ready To Eat (MRE).**
- Build a large supply of **wheat, rice, beans, honey, and salt,** in five- or six-gallon food-grade buckets.
- Rotate your storage food consistently, using the First-In, First-Out (FIFO) inventory methodology.
- Store extra food for charity and barter.

Food-Preparation List

- Having more people under your roof will necessitate having an **oversize skillet** and a **huge stew pot.** You will want to buy **several huge kettles,** because odds are you will have to heat water on your woodstove for bathing, dish washing, and clothes washing.
- You will need even more **kettles, barrels, and five- or six-gallon PVC buckets**—for water hauling, rendering, soap-making, and dying. They will also make great barter or

charity items. To quote my mentor Dr. Gary North: "Nails: Buy a barrel of them. Barrels: Buy a barrel of them!"
- Don't overlook **skinning knives**, **gut-buckets**, **gambrels**, and **meat saws**.

Personal List

Make a separate personal list for each family member.

- **Spare glasses**
- Prescription and nonprescription **medications**
- **Birth control**

Fitness List

- Keep dentistry up to date.
- Any elective surgery that you've been postponing
- Work off that gut.
- Stay in shape.
- Back strength and health—particularly important given the heavy manual tasks required for self-sufficiency
- "Comfort" items to help get through high-stress times (books, games, CDs, chocolate, etc.)

First-Aid/Minor-Surgery List (For details, see Chapter 8.)

When tailoring this list, consider your neighborhood going for many months without power, extensive use of open flames, and sentries standing picket shifts exposed to the elements. Then consider axes, chain saws, and tractors being wielded by newbies, and a greater likelihood of gunshot wounds. With all of this, add the possibility of no access to doctors or high-tech medical diagnostic equipment.

- Put a strong emphasis on **burn-treatment first-aid supplies**.
- Don't overlook do-it-yourself dentistry. (**Oil of cloves, temporary-filling kit, extraction tools**, etc.)
- Buy a **full minor-surgery outfit** containing inexpensive Pakistani stainless steel instruments, even if you don't know how to use them all yet. You may have to learn, or you will have the opportunity to put them in the hands of someone experienced who needs them.

Chem/Nuke-Defense List

- **Dosimeter, rate meter, and charger**
- **Radiac meter** (handheld Geiger counter)
- **Rolls of sheet plastic** (for isolating airflow to air-filter inlets and for covering window frames in the event that windows are broken due to blast effects)
- **Duct tape**
- **HEPA filters** (and spares) for your shelter
- **Potassium iodate** (KIO_3) tablets to prevent thyroid damage
- **Outdoor shower rig** for just outside your shelter entrance.

Biological-Warfare- and Pandemic-Defense List (For details, see Appendix C.)

- **Disinfectants**
- **Hand sanitizer**
- **N95 respirator masks**
- **Steam vaporizer**
- **Expectorant**
- **Antibiotic and antiviral medications**

Gardening List (For details, see Chapter 7.)

- One important item for your gardening list is a very tall deer-proof and rabbit-proof **fence**. Under current circumstances, a raid by deer on your garden is probably just an inconvenience. After the balloon goes up, it could mean the difference between eating well and starvation.
- **Topsoil/Amendments/Fertilizers**
- **Gardening tools** and spares for barter/charity
- Long-term-storage non-hybrid (open-pollinated) **seed**. Non-hybrid heirloom seed assortments tailored to different climate zones are available from The Ark Institute.
- **Herbs**: Get started with medicinal herbs such as aloe vera (for burns), echinacea (purple cone flower), valerian, etc.

Hygiene/Sanitation List

- Sacks of **powdered lime** for the outhouse
- **TP** in quantity
- **Soap** in quantity (hand soap, dish soap, laundry soap, cleansers, etc.) I have used four-ounce squeeze bottles of Dr. Bronner's peppermint castile soap for many years, mostly on backpacking trips. A little bit goes a long way.
- **Bottled lye** for soapmaking
- **Feminine-hygiene supplies**
- **Toothpaste** (or powder)
- **Floss**
- **Fluoride rinse**
- Sunscreen

Livestock List

- Hoof rasp, hoof nippers, hoof pick, horse brushes, hand sheep shears, styptic, carding combs
- Goat-milking stand, teat dip, udder wash, Bag Balm, elastrator and bands
- Swat fly repellent, nail clippers (various sizes), Kopertox
- Leads, leashes, collars, halters
- Hay hooks, hay fork, manure shovel, feed buckets, bulk grain, and C.O.B. sweet feed (store in galvanized trash cans with tight-fitting lids to keep the mice out)
- Various tack and saddles, tack-repair tools, etc.
- If your region has selenium-deficient soil (ask your local agricultural extension office), then be sure to get selenium-fortified salt blocks rather than plain white salt blocks—at least for those you are going to set aside strictly for your livestock.

Hunting/Fishing/Trapping List

- "Buckshot" Bruce Hemming has produced an excellent series of videos on trapping and making improvised traps.
- **Night-vision gear, spares, maintenance, and battery charging**
- **Salt.** Post-TEOTWAWKI, don't go hunting. That would be a waste of effort. Have the game come to you. Buy twenty or more salt blocks.
- Sell your fly-fishing gear (all but perhaps a few flies) and buy practical **spin-casting equipment.**
- Extra tackle may be useful for barter, but probably only in a very long-term crunch.
- Buy some **frog gigs** if you have bullfrogs in your area. Buy some **crawfish traps** if you have crawfish in your area.

- Learn how to rig trot lines and make fish traps for non-labor-intensive fishing WTSHTF.

Power/Lighting/Batteries List (For details, see Chapter 6.)

- In the event of a grid-down situation, if you are the only family in the area with power, it could turn your house into a "come loot me" beacon at night. Make plans and buy materials in advance for making blackout screens or **fully opaque curtains** for your windows.
- When possible, buy **low self-discharge (LSD) nickel-metal hydride batteries.**
- If your home has propane appliances, get a **"tri-fuel" generator**—with a carburetor that is selectable between gasoline, propane, and natural gas. If you heat your house with home-heating oil, then get a **diesel-burning generator.** And plan on getting at least one diesel-burning pickup and/or tractor.
- Kerosene lamps; plenty of extra wicks, mantles, and chimneys

Fuels List

- Buy the **largest propane, home-heating-oil, gas, or diesel tanks that your local ordinances permit and that you can afford.** Always keep them at least two-thirds full.
- For privacy concerns, ballistic-impact concerns, and fire concerns, underground tanks are best if you local water table allows it. In any case, do not buy an aboveground fuel tank that would be visible from any public road or navigable waterway.

- Buy plenty of **extra fuel**. Don't overlook buying ample **kerosene**.
- Stock up on **firewood or coal**.
- Get the best quality **chain saw** you can afford. I prefer Stihl and Husqvarna, but you might want to buy your regional favorite, to have better availability of spare parts. If you can afford it, buy two of the same model. Buy extra chains, critical spare parts, and plenty of two-cycle oil.
- Get a pair of **Kevlar chain saw safety chaps.** They are expensive but they might save you a trip to the emergency room. Always wear **gloves, goggles, and earmuffs**. Wear a **logger's helmet** when felling.

Firefighting List

- You should be ready for uncontrolled brush or residential fires, as well as the greater fire risk associated with greenhorns who have just arrived at your retreat working with wood stoves and kerosene lamps.
- Upgrade your retreat with a **fireproof metal roof.**
- **Two-inch diameter water line** from your gravity-fed storage tank to provide large water volume for firefighting
- **Firefighting rig** with an adjustable stream/mist head
- **Smoke and CO detectors**

Tactical-Living List

- Gradually adjust your wardrobe toward sturdy **earth-tone clothing.**
- **Dyes.** Stock up on some boxes of green and brown cloth

dye. With dye, you can turn most light-colored clothes into semi-tactical clothing on short notice.

- Two-inch-wide **burlap strip material** in green and brown. This burlap is available in large spools from Numrich Gun Parts Corporation. Even if you don't have time now, stock up so that you can make camouflage ghillie suits post-TEOTWAWKI.
- Save those **wine corks**. Burned cork makes quick and cheap face camouflage.
- **Cold-weather and foul-weather gear**—buy plenty, since you will be doing more outdoor chores, hunting, and standing guard duty.
- Don't overlook **ponchos and gaiters**.
- **Mosquito repellent**
- Synthetic double-bag (modular) **sleeping bags** for each person at the retreat, plus a couple of spares. The Flexible Temperature Range Sleep System (FTRSS), made by Wiggy's, of Grand Junction, Colorado, is highly recommended.
- **Night-vision gear and IR floodlights** for your retreat house
- **Subdued flashlights and penlights**
- Noise, light, and litter discipline

Security—General List

- **Locks, intrusion detection/alarm systems,** exterior obstacles: fences, gates (five-eighths-inch diameter or larger), locking road cables, rosebush plantings, "decorative" ponds (moats), ballistic protection (personal and residential), anti-vehicular ditches/berms, anti-vehicular concrete "planter boxes," razor wire, etc.

- **Starlight electronic light-amplification scopes** are critical tools for retreat security. A starlight scope (or goggles, or a monocular) amplifies low ambient light by up to 100,000 times, turning nighttime darkness into daylight—albeit a green and fuzzy view.

- **Range cards and sector sketches.** If you live in the boonies, piece together nine of the **USGS 15-minute maps,** with your retreat property on the center map. Mount that map on an oversize map board. Draw in the property lines and owner names of all of your surrounding neighbors' parcels in at least a five-mile radius. Get boundary line and current owner name info from your county recorder's office. Study and memorize both the terrain and the neighbors' names. Make a phone number/e-mail list that corresponds to all of the names marked on the map, plus city and county office contact numbers for quick reference, and tack it up right next to the map board.

Security—Firearms List (For details, see Chapter 11.)

- **Guns, ammunition**
- **Web gear**
- **Eye and ear protection**
- **Cleaning equipment, carrying cases, scopes, magazines, spare parts, gunsmithing tools, targets and target frames,** etc.
- Each rifle and pistol should have at least six top-quality (original military contract or original manufacturer) full-capacity **spare magazines.**

Communications/Monitoring List (For details, see Chapter 9.)

- When selecting **radios**, buy only models that will run on twelve-volt DC power or rechargeable nickel-metal hydride battery packs (which can be recharged from your retreat's twelve-VDC power system without having to use an inverter).
- As a secondary purchasing goal, buy **spare radios** of each type if you can afford them. Keep your spares in sealed metal boxes to protect them from EMP.
- If you live in a far-inland region, I recommend buying two or more twelve-VDC marine band radios. These frequencies will probably not be monitored in your region, leaving you an essentially private band to use.

Tools List

- **Gardening tools**
- **Auto-mechanics tools**
- **Welding equipment and supplies**
- **Bolt cutters**—the indispensable "universal key"
- **Woodworking tools**
- **Gunsmithing tools**
- Emphasis on hand-powered tools
- **Hand-crank or treadle-powered grinding wheel**
- Plenty of extra **work gloves** in earth-tone colors

Sundries List

- Systematically list the things that you use on a regular basis, or that you might need if the local hardware store were ever to disappear: **wire** of various gauges, **duct tape**, reinforced strapping tape, chain, nails, nuts and bolts, weather stripping, abrasives, twine, white glue, cyano-acrylate glue, etc.

Survival-Bookshelf List (For details, see Appendix B.)

- You should probably have nearly every book on my blog's Bookshelf page.

Barter and Charity List (For details, see Chapter 13.)

For your barter list, acquire primarily items that are durable, nonperishable, and either in small packages or easily divisible. Concentrate on the items that other people are likely to overlook or have in short supply.

- **Ammunition**
- **Feminine-hygiene supplies**
- **Salt.** Buy lots of cattle blocks and one-pound canisters of iodized table salt.
- Two-cycle **engine oil**
- **Gas stabilizer**
- **Diesel antibacterial additive**
- Fifty-pound sacks of **lime** for use in outhouses
- One-ounce bottles of **military-rifle-bore cleaner** and Break-Free (or similar) lubricant
- Waterproof **duffel bags** in earth-tone colors (white-water-rafting "dry bags")
- Thermal **socks**
- **Semi-waterproof matches** from military rations
- Military **web gear.** Lots of folks will suddenly need pistol belts, holsters, magazine pouches, etc.

- Pre-1965 silver dimes
- One-gallon cans of **kerosene**
- Rolls of olive-drab **parachute cord**
- Rolls of olive-drab **duct tape**
- Spools of monofilament **fishing line**
- Rolls of ten-mil Visqueen (or similar) **sheet plastic** for replacing windows, isolating air spaces for nuke scenarios, etc.
- **Strike-anywhere matches.** Dip the heads in paraffin to make them waterproof.
- **Playing cards**
- Cooking **spices**. Do a Web search for reasonably priced bulk spices.
- **Rope and string**
- **Sewing supplies**
- **Candle wax and wicking**
- Lastly, any supplies necessary for operating a home-based business. Some that you might consider are leather crafting, small-appliance repair, gun repair, locksmithing, etc. Every family should have at least one home-based business (preferably two) that they can depend on in the event of an economic collapse.
- Stock up on additional items to dispense to refugees as charity.

As time goes on you'll have the opportunity to expand and refine your lists. But don't get too caught up in just the planning. There is the risk of planning endlessly and accomplishing nothing.

3

THE SURVIVAL RETREAT

Your First Big Decision: A Demographic Dilemma

Probably the most important decision you'll make in your preparations for a crisis is the location of your retreat. The best choice is a dedicated safe haven—a family survival retreat. A retreat is not just "a cabin in the mountains." Rather, it is a well-prepared and defensible redoubt with well-planned logistics. A proper survival retreat is in effect a modern-day castle able to provide for its inhabitants and protect them from any outside danger. You will have to weigh your options carefully as you decide whether to try to establish your retreat in your current home or whether you should consider relocating. I realize this may sound extreme, but my goal in this book is to provide you and your family the best chance for survival should the worst happen.

Ideally, a survival retreat is located in a region with most or all of the following characteristics:

- A long growing season
- Geographic isolation from major population centers
- Sufficient year-round precipitation and surface water
- Rich topsoil
- A diverse economy and agriculture
- Away from interstate freeways and other channelized areas
- Low taxes
- Nonintrusive scale of government
- Favorable zoning and inexpensive building permits
- Minimal gun laws
- No major earthquake, hurricane, or tornado risks
- No flooding risk
- No tidal-wave risk (at least two hundred feet above sea level)
- Minimal forest-fire risk
- A lifestyle geared toward self-sufficiency
- Plentiful local sources of wood or coal
- No restrictions on keeping livestock
- Defendable terrain
- Not near a prison or large mental institution
- Inexpensive insurance rates (home, auto, health)
- Upwind from major nuclear-weapons targets

This list should help you to narrow your search for potential retreat regions. You should also keep in mind that in troubled times fewer people means fewer problems. In the event of a social upheaval, rioting, urban looting, etc., being west of the Missouri River will mean a statistically much lower chance of coming face-to-face with lawless rioters or looters WTSHTF. Look at a population-density of map of the United States, or the "Satellite Photo of Earth at Night" images available on the Internet (snipurl.com/hokhx). The difference in population density in the western United States is immediately apparent.

Americans live in a highly urbanized society. Roughly 90 percent of the population is crammed into 5 percent of the land area. And most of that is within sixty miles of the coastlines. But there are large patches of the West with population densities of less than ten people per square mile—particularly in the Great Basin region that extends from the eastern slope of the Sierra Nevada mountains to Utah and Eastern Oregon. The average population density in this region is less than two people per square mile. It is essentially an empty quarter of the continental United States.

If you are an eastern urbanite you might come to the conclusion that you need to buy "a cabin in upstate New York " or "a brick house in New Jersey's Pine Barrens," but this would be a mistake. A rural area that is *within* an overall heavily populated region is *not* truly rural. It lacks real isolation from the basic problem—population. You will need to be at least one tank of gas away from the big cities—preferably no less than three hundred miles, if possible.

The northeastern states depend on nuclear power plants for 47 percent of their electricity. (South Carolina is similarly dependent.) This is an unacceptable level of high-technology-systems dependence, particularly in light of the emerging terrorist threat. You must also consider that virtually all of the eastern states are downwind of major nuclear targets—most notably the U.S. Air Force missile fields in the Dakotas, Wyoming, and Colorado. If for one reason or another you are stuck in the

Northeast, then consider New Hampshire or Vermont. They are both gun friendly and have a more self-sufficient lifestyle. But unless you have a very compelling reason to stay in the East, I most strongly encourage you to Go West!

As an example of the low population density in the West, I often like to cite Idaho County, Idaho: This one county measures 8,485 square miles—bigger than Connecticut and Rhode Island combined. But it has a population of just 15,400. And of those residents, roughly 3,300 people live in Grangeville, the county seat. Who lives in the rest of the county? Nary a soul. There are far more deer and elk than there are people. The population density of the county is 1.8 people per square mile. The county has more than 3 million acres of U.S. Forest Service land, BLM land, and designated federal wilderness areas. Now *that* is elbow room!

Channelization and Lines of Drift

Most primary routes out of major cities will be very dangerous places to be in the event of a massive involuntary urban exodus. Imagine the situation WTSHTF in small towns on either side of the Snoqualmie Pass in Washington, or near I-80 across the Donner Pass in California, or along the Columbia River Gorge (dividing Oregon and Washington), or virtually every other stretch of interstate freeway that is within 150 miles of a metropolitan region. These channelized areas (also called "refugee lines of drift" by military-police war-game planners) should be studiously avoided.

Conversely, there are areas between lines of drift that will likely be bypassed by refugees and looters, due to poor access (constrained by small winding mountainous roads, water obstacles, intervening canyon lands, etc.). Some of these bypassed zones may be fairly close to urban areas. It is a dangerous gamble, but if you must live near a city, I suggest that you carefully search for what may be a largely bypassed zone for your retreat and/or home.

High Fuel Costs and Retreat Locales

The substantially higher fuel costs that we've seen in the past few years will likely change the way you look at your retreat, and where it is located. Remote properties will seem even more remote when gas tops five dollars per gallon. If you are retired, self-employed, or a telecommuter, the impact won't be nearly so great. As fuel prices spike, you can simply adapt your lifestyle to make trips into town less often. But if you have a daily job in town, then the impact could be substantial.

If you have *not yet* bought a retreat, then you might want to make the new fuel-cost paradigm a more important part of your locale-selection process. If you do some concerted searching, you may be able to find a piece of land with a low-volume natural-gas well, or a surface coal seam. Another possibility is finding property with a large year-round stream and sufficient change in elevation ("fall"), allowing installation of a micro-hydro system. You should consider buying a retreat that is close to a community in a truck farming region—someplace that is expected to be self-sufficient in the event of chronic gas and diesel shortages. There are of course security trade-offs, so such a decision will be a momentous one to make.

Precipitation and Growing Season
as Retreat-Locale Criteria

I have always recommended that readers do detailed study of microclimates before relocation. Start with state and regional climate data books and Web sites, then do detailed climate and soil studies using data from the NWS, NRCS, and various online resources.

My general guidance is to avoid areas that require irrigation, with the exception of the very few locales that are serviced by an end-to-end gravity-fed irrigation infrastructure. If and when the power grids go down, many parts of the western United States will quickly revert to *desert*. Hence, my preference is for reliable-rain or dryland-farming regions where crops can be grown with regular spring and summer rains. But here is the rub: Many of those regions are heavily populated and might not be safe in the event of a major societal disruption. So your choices will be narrowed to a subset of a subset.

When you are traveling in search of potential retreat properties, observe the native vegetation on the nonirrigated hillsides. What you see is what you'll get when the grid goes down.

In-Town Versus Isolated Retreats

There are two distinct modes of fixed-location survival retreats: "In town" and "isolated." The former depends on some local infrastructure while the latter is designed to be almost entirely self-sufficient and self-contained. Isolated retreats are also often termed "remote" retreats.

Not everyone is suited to tackling the tasks required for self-sufficiency. Advanced age, physical handicaps, lack of trustworthy family or friends, or chronic health conditions could rule out total self-sufficiency. If that is your situation, then you will probably want to establish an inconspicuous in-town retreat rather than an isolated "stronghold" retreat.

If opting for in town, carefully select a town with a small population—somewhere between 1,000 and 3,000 if it has a true end-to-end gravity-fed water supply, or from 200 to 1,000 if the water system is in any way dependent on the power grid. A population of more than 1,000 presents additional sanitation problems. Towns larger than 3,000 people lack a cohesive sense of community, and any town with a population smaller than 200 lacks a sufficient mix of skills and the manpower required to mount an adequate defense in the event of a true worst case. At some point over the 3,000-inhabitant threshold, it could be every man for himself. It is therefore best to avoid larger towns.

The late Mel Tappan wisely opined that if your house is at the dead end of a road at the edge of town with no nearby neighbors, then it might just as well be five or ten miles out of town—since it will be psychologically outside of the invisible ring of protection that will constitute "in town." If you are in town you will benefit from what I call a Neighborhood Watch on Steroids. Make sure that your retreat is either clearly in town or not. A property that is in between will have none of the advantages and all of the disadvantages.

Tappan championed the concept of small-town retreating: owning a mini-farm that is physically and psychologically inside an existing small community. This approach has several advantages. Before making your decision, consider the following pro and con lists.

Advantages of In-Town Retreats:

- Better for a slow-slide scenario or a "grid-up" depression wherein the local agricultural and industrial payrolls may still be viable
- You will be a member of the community.
- You will benefit from local security arrangements.
- Ready access to local barter economy
- Ready access to local skills and medical facilities

Disadvantages of In-Town Retreats:

- Privacy is very limited. Transporting bulky logistics must be done at odd hours to minimize observation by neighbors.
- Fuel storage is severely limited. (Consult the local ordinances on storage before you buy a home.)
- Poor sanitation in the event of a grid-down situation, unless your town has a truly end-to-end gravity-fed water system
- You can't test-fire and zero your guns at your own property.
- You can't set up elaborate antenna arrays, because your house will look out of place.
- You probably can't hunt on your own land, except perhaps some small game and pests, and then only with an air rifle.
- You can't keep livestock other than perhaps a few rabbits. (Consult the local ordinances before you buy a home.)
- You can't make substantial ballistic and anti-vehicular barrier retreat upgrades.
- Greater risk of communicable diseases
- Greater risk of burglary
- Greater risk of having your supplies confiscated

Advantages of Isolated Retreats:

- More room for gardening, pasturing, and growing row crops
- Lower house and land prices
- Better for a total-wipeout grid-down scenario in which virtually everyone will be out of work
- You can stock up in quantity with less fear of the watchful eyes of nosy neighbors.
- You can test-fire and zero your guns at your own property.
- You can build with nontraditional architecture (earth sheltered, for example).
- You can set up more elaborate antenna arrays—and other things that would look odd in town.
- Better sanitation in the event of a grid-down situation
- You can hunt on your own land.
- You can cut your own firewood.
- You can keep livestock.
- You can make ballistic and anti-vehicular upgrades.
- A "dog run" chain-link fence around your house won't look too out of place.
- Virtually unlimited fuel storage. (Consult your county and state laws before ordering large gas, diesel, heating-oil, and propane-fuel tanks.)
- Much lower risk of communicable diseases

Disadvantages of Isolated Retreats:

- Difficult for just one family to maintain and defend
- Cannot depend on much help from neighbors or law enforcement if your home is attacked by looters or in the event of fire or medical emergency. You will likely be entirely on your own to resolve those situations.

- Isolation from day-to-day barter/commerce
- A longer commute to your day job, shopping, and church

A careful analysis of the preceding lists should lead you to conclude which approach is right for you, given your family situation, your stage in life, and your own view of the potential severity of events to come. Pray about it, mull it over, before making a decision of this gravity.

The Best Retreats

A retreat situated in a hilly or mountainous region is preferable to one on the plains in the event of a worst case. Why? Towns on plains simply have too many vehicular access points, and more access points means more potential intruders. Hill or canyon towns, by comparison, are limited by terrain to having just a few accesses.

When shopping for a home that would make a good retreat, look for a masonry house with a fireproof roof on an oversize lot—or a wood-frame construction if you live in earthquake country. Buy a house with at least one more bedroom than you currently need, preferably with a full basement. (Proviso: A basement only if the local water-table level will allow this without aid of an electric sump pump. The basement must be "dry and tight.")

The following chapters in this book will go into greater detail about essentials for surviving TEOTWAWKI, but here is a brief overview of what you will need to do at your retreat:

- Stock up on extra tools, sturdy clothes, food, guns, web gear, and necessities for family and friends, who will surely show up on your doorstep on TEOTWAWKI+1.

- Put in an oversize vegetable garden, preferably out of line of sight from the street. Ring the garden with flower beds and some tall flowering shrubs to make the garden look more decorative than practical to the casual observer.
- Get a big, quiet, mean-looking (but obedient) guard dog. I tend toward Airedales (the largest of the terriers) and Rhodesian Ridgebacks. Both are fairly large breeds with loyal and highly territorial temperaments.
- Plant several rosebushes or thorny bougainvillea vines beneath each window. Bush roses and climbing varieties can be used in various ways to defend your home. You'll need to keep scraps of carpeting or heavy blankets handy so that your family members can use bedroom windows as escape routes in the event of fire or a home invasion.
- Buy defensive wire (military-surplus concertina wire or civilian razor wire). Keep it stored discreetly and out of sight in your garage and put it up only in the event of a true worst-case situation, in which the town must be barricaded. When you donate that wire to the local security committee you will be looked at as a forward-thinking lifesaver, not a wacko.
- Replace all of your exterior doors with sturdy steel ones in steel frames. If your house has a connecting garage, pay particular attention to beefing up the door between it and the house. Turn your garage into a mini-warehouse, with lots of heavy-duty shelving.
- Buy vehicles that will blend in day-to-day but will be eminently practical WTSHTF. See Chapter 12 for more details.
- Buy a low-profile camper shell that can be removed quickly in a pinch. Winches front and back may look cool, but they really aren't worth the weight and expense. You are better off spending some money on heavy-duty front and rear

bumpers. Recommended bumper modifications include: large crash bars in the front, a removable cable cutter post that is as tall as your truck's cab, and ten or more sturdy towing attachment J hooks (front and rear center and all four corners). Buy two or three come-alongs (ratchet cable hoists), and a couple of forty-eight-inch Hi-Lift jacks. Carry two spare inflated tires mounted on rims. That plus shovels, a pick, an ax, a couple of rugged tow chains, some shorter "tree-wrapper" choker chains, and a pair of American-made thirty-six-inch bolt cutters will get you through virtually any obstacle, given enough time.

- Determine the amount of fuel required to get to your retreat using the slowest possible route with a maximum load of gear. Add 10 percent to that figure for good measure, and be sure to always have that amount of fuel on hand. Regardless of the fuel capacity of your rig, buy at least six additional jerry cans to keep at home. (First consult your local fire-code regulations.) Keep those cans filled with fuel and rotate them regularly.

- If there won't be somebody who is extremely trustworthy living at your retreat at all times to secure it, buy a twenty-four-foot or larger Conex steel shipping container, and have an extra lock shroud flange welded on. Ideally, your trailer should be custom built (or rebuilt) to use the same rims and tires as your primary vehicle. That way, with two spare tires carried on your vehicle and one more on the front of your trailer, you will have three spares available for either your trailer or your pickup.

- Most important: Pre-position the vast majority of your gear, guns, and groceries at your retreat! Make sure to store plenty of fuel there. Buy a utility trailer, but leave it at your retreat to use for wood and hay hauling, or in case you need to bug out a second time. You may have only one trip out of the big city, and messing with a trailer in heavy traffic or on snowy or muddy roads could lead to your own personal disaster within a disaster.

Your Survival Community

I've observed that survivalists tend to fall into two schools of thought: those who are loners and those who are community minded. The loners would prefer to disappear into the wilds—somewhere they can lie low, while things sort themselves out back in civilization. In my opinion, this is both a naive and self-ish starting point for preparedness. It is not realistic to expect that you can find a remote rural property where you'd have no contact with outsiders for an extended period of time. We live in the era of Google Earth, when there are few truly secret hide-aways. Even Mel Gibson couldn't buy total privacy. His private island in Fiji was "outed." Even if you live off-grid, if there is a road leading to your house, eventually someone will find you.

Furthermore, you should discard any fantasies that you might have about strapping on a backpack and disappearing into a nearby national forest to "live off the land." That is an invitation for disaster. Too many things can go wrong: You will lack suffi-cient shelter. You will not be able to carry enough food reserves. Once lost or broken, your one rifle, your one pistol, and your one ax will leave you vulnerable and unable to provide for your sustenance or self-defense. Any illness or injury could be life threatening. Even just a dunking in a stream in midwinter could cost your life. Also, consider how many thousands of urbanites will probably try to do the same thing. Even if you manage to avoid encounters with them, all those legions of people foraging at once will quickly deplete the available wild game in many re-gions. For countless reasons, playing "Batman in the Boondocks" just won't work. So forget about the one-pack solution, other than as a last resort.

If you are planning a remote retreat, plan ahead to double up or even triple up with other families to provide the manpower needed for 24-hour, 7-day-a-week, 360-degree security if things go truly worst-case with a complete breakdown of law and order. One family on its own cannot both provide security and handle the many chores required to operate a self-sufficient retreat—particularly in summer and fall, with gardening and food-storage tasks. The physical and emotional toll of manning twelve-on/twelve-off security shifts would bring most people to the breaking point in just a few weeks. As a former U.S. Army officer, I can at-test to the terrible drain that continuous operations create—even upon physically fit, twentysomething soldiers. Lesser security will leave your retreat vulnerable to being overrun. Manning an iso-lated retreat will take a bare minimum of four adults, and ideally six. (Typically, three couples, plus their kids.) This will mean buy-ing a five- or six-bedroom house with a full basement.

Most of us will have retreats on a recognizable road, and we will have neighbors. Having neighbors generally necessitates being neighborly. From the perspective of disaster preparedness, one of the positive aspects is the community-mindedness that can arise. I have long been an advocate of setting up small cov-enant communities inhabited by like-minded people, so when you're preparing for disaster, spend time thinking about whom you want on your crisis-preparedness team.

Hunkering Down in the Big City?

I've been asked many times over the years if it would be possible to ride out a major societal collapse by keeping hidden in a major metropolitan area. Frankly, I do not think that it is realistic. Your chances of survival would probably be low—certainly much lower than Getting Out of Dodge to a lightly populated area at the onset of a crisis. Undoubtedly, in a total societal collapse there will be some stay-put urbanites who survive by their wits supplemented by plenty of providential fortune, but the vast majority would perish. I wouldn't want to play those odds. Here are a few things to keep in mind if you're considering hunkering down in an urban area:

Water

Even with extreme conservation measures you will need at least one gallon of water per day. That one gallon will provide just enough water for one adult for drinking and cooking, and none for washing. If you run out of water you will be forced to go out and forage for it, putting yourself at enormous risk. And even then, you will have to treat the water that you find with chlorine, iodine (such as Polar Pure—now very scarce), or a top-quality water filter such as a Katadyn Pocket.

Food

You will need a large amount of food in order to survive. Work out a daily menu and budget for an honest six-month supply of food with a decent variety and sufficient caloric intake. See Chapter 5 for more details. Don't overlook vitamin supplements to make up for the lack of fresh fruit and vegetables. Sprouting is also a great option to provide vitamins and minerals, as well as aid digestion.

Sanitation

Without water for flushing toilets, odds are that people in neighboring apartments will dump raw sewage out their windows, causing a public-health nightmare on the ground floor. Since you will not want to alert others to your presence by opening your window, and no doubt the apartment building's septic-system stack will be clogged in short order, you will need to make plans to store your waste in your apartment. I suggest five-gallon buckets and a large supply of powdered lime to cut down on the stench before each bucket is sealed. Since you won't have water available for washing, you should also lay in a supply of baby wipes.

Space Heating

In midwinter you could freeze to death in your apartment without supplemental heat. A small heater or just a few candles can keep the air temperature above freezing. I strongly recommend installing a quality wood or coal stove. But even apartment dwellers can use a kerosene heater (such as one from Kero-Sun), with proper ventilation.

Ventilation

If you are going to use any source of open flame, you will need lots of additional ventilation. Asphyxiation from lack of oxygen or slow carbon-monoxide (CO) poisoning is the alternative. Unfortunately, increased ventilation required to mitigate these hazards can pose a security risk—as a conduit for the smell of food or fuel, as a source of light that can be seen from outside the apartment, and as an additional point of entry for robbers.

Security

The main point of entry for miscreants will probably be your front door. Odds are that you have a traditional solid-core wood door. It is best to replace wooden apartment doors with steel ones. Merely bracing a wood door will not suffice. Furthermore, if you have an exterior window with a fire escape or access to a shared balcony, then those are also points of entry for the bad guys. How could you effectively barricade a large expanse of windows?

If you live in a ground-floor apartment or an older apartment with exterior metal fire escapes, then I recommend that you move as soon as possible to a third-, fourth-, or fifth-floor apartment that is in a modern apartment building of concrete construction, preferably without balconies, with steel entry doors, and with interior fire-escape stairwells.

Self-defense

To fend off intruders, or for self-defense when you eventually emerge from your apartment, you will need to be well armed. Preferably you should also be teamed with at least two other armed and trained adults. Look into local legalities for large-volume pepper-spray dispensers. These are marketed primarily as bear repellent, with brand names like Guard Alaska, Bear Guard, and 17% Streetwise. If they are indeed legal in your jurisdiction, then buy several of the big one-pound dispensers, first making sure that they are at least a 12 percent oleoresin-capsicum (OC) formulation.

If you can get a firearms permit, then I recommend that you get a Remington, Winchester, or Mossberg 12-gauge pump-action shotgun with a SureFire flashlight fore-end. The best load for defense in an urban environment where over-penetration (into neighboring apartments) is an issue is #4 buckshot (not to be confused with the much smaller #4 bird shot). But if getting a firearms permit proves too daunting, there is a nice exemption in even New York City's firearms laws for muzzle loaders and pre-1894 manufactured antique guns that are chambered for cartridges that are no longer commercially made. It is not difficult to find a Winchester Model 1876 or a Model 1886 rifle in a serial-number range that distinguishes it as pre-1894 production. You will be limited to chamberings like .40-65 and .45-90. You can have a supply of ammunition custom loaded. Be sure to select rifles with excellent bores and in nice mechanical condition.

For an antique handgun, I would recommend a Smith and Wesson double-action top-break revolver chambered in .44 S&W Russian, with semi-custom extra-mild loads.

Firearms training from a quality school is crucial.

Fire Detection and Contingency Bugout

A battery-powered smoke detector is an absolute must. Even if you are careful with candles, lanterns, and cookstoves, your neighbors may not be. There is a considerable risk that your apartment building will catch fire, whether by accident or by others' intentions. Therefore, you need to have a "Bugout" back-pack (BOB) ready to grab at a moment's notice.

Although they are no proper substitutes for a fireman's compressed-air breathing rig, a commercially made egress smoke hood or a military-surplus gas mask might allow you to escape your building in time.

Fuel Storage

Bulk fuel storage has three problematic issues: 1) safety (fire hazard); 2) security (odors that could attract robbers); and 3) legality. Most urban fire codes would not allow you to have more than a week's worth of propane on hand, and they completely prohibit keeping more than just one small container of kerosene or Coleman fuel. From the standpoint of both safety and minimizing detectable odors, propane is probably the best option. But of course consult both your local fire code and your apartment lease agreement to determine the maximum allowable quantity to keep on hand.

Odds are that there will be no limit on the number of candles that you can store. If that is the case, then lay in a large supply of unscented jar candles designed for long burning (formulated high in stearic acid). I suggest the tall, clear-glass-jar-enclosed devotional candles manufactured in large numbers for the Catholic market. You can even heat individual servings of food over these if you construct a stand with a wide base out of stout wire. Watch for these candles at discount and closeout stores.

Cooking Odors

In addition to the smell of fuel, cooking food will produce odors. I recommend that you store only foods with minimal spices. In a situation in which you are surrounded by starving people, just frying foods with grease or heating up a can of spicy chili con carne could be a death warrant.

Firefighting

Buy at least two large multipurpose (ABC) chemical fire extinguishers.

Noise and Light Discipline

If you make noise or if you have any source of light in your apartment, it could make your presence known. In an extended power blackout, it will become obvious to looters within a couple of weeks who has lanterns or large supplies of candles and/or flashlight batteries, and I predict that it will be the apartments that are still lit up that will be deemed the ones worth robbing. So if you are going to have a light source, you must systematically black out all of your windows. But sadly these efforts will be in direct conflict with your need for ventilation for your heating and/or cooking.

Heat

With the aforementioned restrictions on fuel storage, heating your apartment for more than just a few days will probably be impossible. Buy an expedition-quality sleeping bag—preferably a two-bag system such as a Wiggy's brand Flexible Temperature Range Sleep System (FTRSS). To maximize your chances for survival, construct a small room-within-a-room—perhaps under a large dining-room table, or by setting up a camping tent inside your home—to hoard heat. Even if the rest of your home drops to twenty-five or thirty degrees Fahrenheit, your body heat alone will keep your demi-room in the forties. Burning just one candle will raise the temperature another five or ten degrees. For the greatest efficiency retaining heat, your demi-room should be draped with two layers of Mylar space blankets.

Exercise

While you are hunkered down, you will need to maintain muscle tone. Get some quiet exercise equipment, such as a pull-up bar and some large elastic straps. Perhaps, if your budget allows in the future, also purchase or construct your own quiet, stationary-bicycle-powered generator (snipurl.com/hotd5). This would provide both exercise and battery charging.

Sanity

Hunkering down solo in silence for an extended period would be a supreme challenge, both physically and mentally. Assuming that you can somehow tackle all of the aforementioned problems, you also need to plan to stay sane. Have lots of reading materials on hand.

When one considers the preceding long list of dependencies and complexities, it makes staying put in a worst case very unattractive. In less inimical circumstances, it is certainly feasible, but in a grid-down situation with utilities disrupted, the big city is no place to live.

Mobile Retreats

"Land-mobile" retreating in a recreational vehicle (RV) is another invitation for disaster. In a TEOTWAWKI situation, a fixed-location retreat is vastly superior to going mobile. If you choose to go entirely vehicle-mobile you will eventually lose a battle—most likely in a roadblock ambush—or your RV will break down. Or it will run out of fuel—with some likelihood that it will be on exposed terrain in an untenable situation. Also, since the logistics that you can carry will be limited, you will start out with an inherent disadvantage compared with fixed-location retreats. This also creates the prospect that once your food supplies are depleted you will be tempted to take what you need from others.

A live-aboard sailboat or motor cruiser is another frequently touted retreat option. Unless you are an experienced blue-water yachtsman with many years of experience, I cannot recommend "sea-mobile" retreating.

Mobile approaches to retreating have too many drawbacks to recommend them, except perhaps in a few cases for those with a huge budget. Pragmatically, you will need a fixed location with a deep larder, tools, weapons, barter goods, and friends you can count on. In essence, the only tenable mobile approach is for the very short term: a reliable vehicle that gets you to a well-provisioned and defendable fixed retreat.

Just One Trip Outta Dodge

It is essential to pre-position the vast majority of your logistics at your retreat. The following chapters will help you to determine what supplies you'll need and what preparations you'll want to make in advance. Of course, these preparations will be useless if you cannot reach your retreat WTSHTF.

Circumstances may dictate that you can make only one trip to your retreat before roads are unusable or unsafe to use. It would be tragic to have to pick and choose what portion of your gear to take in that one trip, so it makes sense to pre-position most of your gear. It is wise to do a "test load" once every two years to insure that those items that you keep in your home will fit in that one trip. And, needless to say, plan multiple routes using secondary roads in case the freeways are clogged. Have a Plan A, Plan B, Plan C, and a Plan D. The latter may be on mountain bikes or on foot.

For detailed information on your G.O.O.D. vehicles, see Chapter 12.

If family or work circumstances dictate that you can't live locally at your retreat, then at least look like a local. If your retreat is across a state line, then carry the driver's license of the state where you have your retreat (with the town nearest your retreat listed as your home address), and get dual registration for all of your G.O.O.D. vehicles. To get past roadblocks you will want to look like you are obviously headed "home" to your retreat. Paying a little extra each year for dual registration could save your life.

If you have a great salary and can afford to buy a retreat but can't telecommute, you will need a caretaker. Just watering and pruning the dozens of fruit and nut trees is a big chore. Finding a trustworthy caretaker for a retreat can be problematic. When selecting a caretaker, it is important to find someone committed to staying long term, someone you can trust with certainty, and someone who has practical skills and is not afraid to get his hands dirty or paint-stained. Make each party's rights and responsibilities perfectly clear from the outset. In many states, if you charge any form of rent, then that person is a renter and has all the legal rights of such under the law including the right to privacy—which might preclude your showing up at the door of your own retreat WTSHTF. If you're charging rent, consult with a real estate lawyer to make sure you're not stranded on your own doorstep.

One compromise approach is to leave your retreat house unoccupied and rent a commercial storage space in the town nearest your retreat. This constitutes pitiful operational security (OPSEC), but it is better than leaving valuable gear unattended and vulnerable to burglary. This approach also makes it difficult to practice using your gear, or to rotate your storage food or establish a garden and livestock between now and TEOTWAWKI, but it might be the best option for many of you.

G.O.O.D. Backpack

Put together a Get Out of Dodge backpack. This is especially important if you don't live year-round at your retreat. The pack is intended only for a very short period—to get you *to* your retreat—in the event that for whatever reason a vehicle is not available. You should dread ever having to *use that pack* when you are overrun and forced to abandon a well-stocked retreat and taking off on foot to fend for yourself.

Recommended G.O.O.D. Backpack Contents

Tailor this list to meet your personal and regional requirements. Obviously, if you live in Florida, your list will be much different than if you live in Maine.

- Sleeping bag
- Jacket
- Gloves
- Boots
- Poncho
- Small tarp (six feet by eight feet)
- Financial and personal papers
- Cash and a roll of quarters for making phone calls
- Road maps
- First-aid kit
- Insect repellent
- Fire-starting kit
- Leatherman-type multipurpose tool with knife and pliers

- Utility knife
- Ten to fifteen MRE entrées
- Extra socks and underwear
- Two canteens or a CamelBak hydration pack
- Broad-brim hat
- LED flashlight with extra lithium batteries
- Firearms or other weapons (depending on your local laws)
- Cell phone
- GPS
- Brunton SolarPort (www.brunton.com/product.php?id=280) or similar compact photovoltaic-panel charger, with cabling and/or battery trays for all of your electronic gear

Add-on Kits:
- **Note:** These are usually too heavy or bulky to carry in your backpack, but can be carried in your vehicle. Store these in plastic tote bins to keep everything together and handy to load quickly.

Camp-Kitchen Kit:

- Stainless steel eating utensils
- Reusable plastic plates
- Cups and bowls
- Small grill to place over rocks
- Coffee pot
- Several large serving spoons
- Spatulas
- Kitchen knives
- Roll of heavy-duty aluminum foil
- Plastic wrap

- Half-gallon Ziploc bags
- Box of strike-anywhere matches
- Long neck lighter
- Bar soap
- Small bottle of dish soap
- Washcloth
- Hand towel
- Steel wool and scrub pads
- Paper towels
- Coffee filters
- Paper plates
- Dutch oven with lid and a lid-lifting handle
- Cast-iron skillet
- Salt, pepper, and other spices

Field Food Kit

- A tote bin (or bins) filled with camping foods. These can be the usual soup, chili, canned meats, rice, beans, noodles, MREs, and freeze-dried food.
- PowerBars, Gatorade, and whatever else you prefer for quick field meals

Shelter and Camp Kit

- In a waterproof white-water-rafting bag:
    - ~ full-size camping tent
    - ~ all of the tent's poles and stakes
    - ~ rope
    - ~ cloth ground tarp
    - ~ two or three tarps of various sizes

- Extra rope
- Sewing kit
- Collapsing four-gallon water container
- Entrenching tool
- Miner's (short-handle) axe

4

WATER

The Key Resource

Water is *the* key resource for family-preparedness planning. Plentiful fresh water for drinking, cooking, washing, and gardening is the most critical resource for all societies. You can improvise a lot of things, but you can't improvise water. (Well, actually, you *can* now buy a machine that will suck water out of the atmosphere, but it's an expensive, high-maintenance power hog.)

The vast majority of the residents of First World countries are dependent on grid power to supply their water. When the grid goes down for more than a few days, water towers will quickly be drained and huge numbers of people will be forced to draw water from open sources. Thankfully, there are streams, rivers, lakes, and ponds within walking distance of most homes. Rain-water from roof downspouts can also be used, but for many, especially in areas with only seasonal precipitation, the logistics of hauling water will be a challenge.

Once you've found water, you will need to *treat* all that water, or face infection. Most families don't own a water filter. Boiling water is an option, but only if you have natural-gas, propane, or wood cooking stoves, since electric ranges don't work without grid power. Even folks with well water will face difficulties, unless you have a backup generator or a fully capable alternative energy system.

This chapter will cover water sources and how to filter and treat water so that it is potable.

Plan Ahead

It is important that every prepared family make plans in advance for exactly how they will handle their water supply in the event of a long-term grid-down situation. Buy the gear. Test it extensively. Also locate primary, secondary, and even tertiary sources of water in your area.

If you are unfortunate enough to live in a region that lacks open water sources that are available in every month of the year and within walking distance, then you ought to seriously consider relocating to a region with more plentiful water.

As space permits, apartment dwellers should store lightly chlorinated water in used two-liter plastic bottles. I recommend using two-liter bottles because they are relatively lightweight (easily transportable) and compact (can be stored under beds), and remarkably sturdy. They are even earthquake-proof. Once that supply is expended, it is crucial that you have previously located a nearby open water source such as a lake or reservoir, and that you have both containers to haul water and water-purification and filtration equipment, as discussed later in this chapter.

Sources of Water

Springwater

Gravity-fed springwater is the ideal water supply for a rural retreat. There is no need for power, installation expense is relatively low, it's low maintenance, and there is little risk of frozen pipes. But unfortunately very few properties are blessed with a spring that is situated to provide gravity flow to a house. When I advise my consulting clients, I urge them to make gravity-fed springwater a top priority when they are evaluating properties for relocation.

Well Water

Grid-powered well pumps are problematic, since most wells use just a small pressure tank. Whenever there is a power failure, the water pressure drops to nil in just a short time. Photovoltaically pumped well water is a good solution, albeit with a fairly high installation cost. With a large cistern that is positioned to supply gravity flow to your house (typically thirty-five to sixty feet of "head"), you can skip putting a battery bank in your system. When the sun shines, it pumps, and when the sun sets, it stops. Simple. A float switch on the cistern will insure that you prevent needless wear and tear on your pump.

Water from Downspouts

I find it amazing that so many people allow copious rainwater from their roof downspouts to go to waste in the midst of a civic water crisis. They just don't have the survival mind-set. At the very least, they could be using rainwater for clothes washing, bathing, and toilet flushing. With a water filter, they could also use rainwater for drinking and cooking.

You should of course never reuse something like a fuel tank or a toxic-chemical tank for a water barrel. See Chapter 5 for instructions on finding food-grade plastic buckets.

The three questions that the readers of SurvivalBlog most often ask me about rainwater, well water, and springwater are:

Is well or springwater safe to drink?
> Generally, yes. And because it is not fluoridated, it is probably much healthier than public-utility-provided "city" water.

Do I have to worry about pesticides, methyl tertiary butyl ether (MTBE), or heavy-metal contaminants in well or springwater?
> Yes, and you should have the water tested before you buy a property that has a well. Any certified lab will test for these contaminants, as well as bacteria. Do a Web search for your state's Department of Environmental Quality (DEQ) or its equivalent. The DEQ Web site should list some approved/ certified commercial laboratories that do water testing. In some states, spring- and well-water testing is also handled by state universities. The good news is that you will have to do this only once, unless you hear about some drastic change in local water conditions.

Do I need to chlorinate my well or springwater?

In most cases, no. It is possible that your well might get contaminated by a flood, or seasonally contaminated with coliform bacteria from rainwater runoff. The best solution is to use a UV sterilizer year-round so that you don't have to worry about it. Alternatively, if you know that there has been a contamination, you could add a calculated quantity of plain hypochlorite liquid bleach solution down your well shaft, but if there is continual bacterial contamination of your well or spring, then, again, the best solution is to use a UV sterilizer year-round.

Treating Water

Water from open sources must always be treated before use. Typical chlorine concentrations will kill bacteria but not all viruses, so I recommend a three-step approach to treating water from open sources (however, keep in mind no filter system is 100 percent effective at removing herbicides and pesticides. For that, you would need either a distillation or a reverse-osmosis system, which are far more complex and have large power requirements):

Pre-filtering. This removes particulate matter. Pouring water though a couple of thicknesses of T-shirts or tightly woven bath towels works fine. The water that comes through will still look like tea, but at least you will have removed the crud and larger particles. By pre-filtering, you will also extend the life of your water filter, because you'll avoid clogging the microscopic pores in the filter media.

Chlorinating. This can be accomplished following the chlorine-concentration guidelines discussed on page 72.

Filtering. I recommend the large Katadyn or British Berkefeld filters. Some filter elements available for Katadyn and British Berkefeld filters can even remove chlorine. Complete filter systems and spare filter elements are available from Ready MadeResources.com, SafecastleRoyal.com, and other Internet vendors.

Ultraviolet Treatment

Ultraviolet (UV) treatment is an interesting innovation that was first embraced by fish farmers and koi-pond enthusiasts. The UV technology is quite promising for anyone with a shallow well or spring that has an unacceptable bacteria count, which typically happens during a flood or seasonally with heavy rains that increase surface water that can get into a well or spring. The UV method of treatment is growing in popularity in the United States and Canada, because there is no need for chemicals. Ultraviolet light rays—just like those from the sun that produce sunburn, only stronger—alter the DNA of bacteria, viruses, molds, and parasites so that they cannot reproduce. They are not killed, but are merely rendered sterile. Thus, they safely pass through your digestive tract, but are unable to reproduce—which is otherwise the cause of intestinal illness.

The compact UV sterilizer that I recommend for field use is sold under the brand name SteriPEN. For year-round use at home, I recommend the Crystal Quest Ultraviolet Water Sterilizer. Note that these are normally powered with an AC power cube. If and when you set up an alternate home-power system with a battery bank, the power cube can be removed, and the UV wand can be powered directly with DC power.

Compact Water Filters

I am often asked about compact water filters for backpacking, hunting trips, and Get Out of Dodge/Bugout situations. For this, Katadyn makes an excellent compact water filter/pump called a Pocket filter. The volume of water that the Pocket can process is limited, but it is perfect for its intended purpose. Another option is the recently introduced Hydro Photon SteriPEN— a compact, battery-powered UV sterilizer. This is a miniature version of a home water UV sterilizer. Very clever! SteriPENs are available from Safecastle, Ready Made Resources, and several other Internet vendors. I recommend stocking up.

Water-Pasteurization Indicators and Heating Water

Water-pasteurization indicators (WAPIs) are now commonly used in the Third World to save fuel and time when treating drinking water. Water that is heated to 149 degrees for a short time is free from living microbes. Water does not have to be "boiled for ten minutes," as some have erroneously suggested in the past. A WAPI is a simple, small, and low-cost tube with a special soy wax that indicates when water has reached a safe pasteurization temperature.

Alternatively, you can heat your water, using a dairy thermometer to be sure the water reaches 149 degrees. You can also use a kitchen or roasting thermometer, but since they are notoriously inaccurate, add ten degrees, just to be on the safe side.

Pool Shock: The Low-Cost Lifesaver

Pool-shock chlorination tablets can be bought in a five-gallon pail—enough to treat many thousands of gallons of water. Calcium hypochlorite (sold as pool shock) may be used to make your own bleach solution. Here is the information in a nutshell:

Use one heaping teaspoon of granular calcium hypochlorite (approximately .25 ounce) for each 2 gallons of water; dissolve in a plastic or glass container. (Don't use a metal container, or it may react with the hypochlorite.) This will produce a strong "stock chlorine" solution of approximately 500 milligrams per liter, since the calcium hypochlorite has available chlorine equal to 70 percent of its weight. To disinfect water, add the chlorine solution in the ratio of 1 part chlorine solution to each 100 parts water to be treated. This is roughly equal to adding 1 pint (16 ounces) of stock chlorine to each 12.5 gallons of water to be disinfected.

Note: You must be absolutely certain to get the variety of pool shock that **contains only calcium chlorite**. The other types of chlorine, tri-chlor and di-chlor, are *not* suitable for this. Make sure that there are no antifungal or clarifier additives! Also, be advised that calcium hypochlorite is a powerful oxidizer, and should be stored in a dry container, sealed from moisture. It can also catch fire violently if put in contact with brake fluid and similar substances, so be careful.

With some planning, you should be able to distribute water-purification supplies as charity. Make some photocopies of directions for using hypochlorite tablets. If you distribute plastic ziplock bags of hypochlorite tablets (roughly six ounces per bag) along with direction sheets, you could save hundreds of lives in a public-health emergency such as a flood, or any other situation that disrupts utility water-distribution systems.

A Budget Water Filter: Constructing a Big Berky Clone

Every family should own a water filter. The problem is that high-volume ceramic filters such as the Big Berky are quite expensive. One considerably less expensive option is to make your own filter. In my experience, the field-expedient sand and clay filters touted by wilderness and bushcraft survival experts are effective only for use as a prefilter. Their output still has a brown-tinged pond-water look to it, and since the filter media is so coarse, they do not remove all harmful bacteria, so their output still has to be treated either chemically or by heating to 149 degrees Fahrenheit.

You can buy Berkefeld white ceramic-filter elements by themselves from a number of vendors including Ready Made Resources and Lehman's. With these elements, you can build your own bargain-basement "Berky clone." This consists of a pair of food-grade plastic buckets stacked one above the other. The top bucket has one or more holes drilled into it, to accept the Berky spare-filter elements. Each element by itself costs around forty dollars. To get decent volume production from your filter, I recommend that you buy at least two elements. In my experience, getting a set of four filter elements is best, unless you are very patient.

Materials:

- 4 food-grade HDPE food-storage buckets (3- to 6-gallon capacity), with lids
- 1 to 4 Berkefeld white ceramic-filter elements

Construction:

- Drill one to four half-inch-diameter holes near the bottom center of the upper bucket (the same number of holes as you have filter elements). Space the holes at least two inches apart and no closer than one-and-a-half inches from the edge of the bucket. With clean hands (to avoid contaminating the filter pores), insert the filters into the holes, screwing down their nuts on the bottom of the bucket. The nuts are plastic, so do not overtighten them, but they must be tight enough to compress the O-ring seal, or the seal may leak—and this would be a contaminating leak. The filters must point *upward* into the upper bucket, to avoid damage and to allow for periodical cleaning.

- Using a jigsaw, cut a seven-and-a-half-inch-diameter hole in the center of the lid of the lower bucket.
- A third bucket is used to carry water. The fourth bucket is used as a prefilter. This has a piece of tightly woven cloth that is wired or taped over the top. Since the cloth will be saturated and will drip over the edge, the pre-filtering step is best done outdoors or in a large laundry sink. If treating river, stream, or pond water, be sure to use a prefilter. Just using a couple of thicknesses of T-shirt material will greatly extend the useful life of your secondary filter element(s).

Use:
- Set the bucket with the hole in the lid on a low, stable surface. Stack the bucket with the filter element(s) on top of it. *Gently* pour pre-filtered water into the upper bucket, until the bucket is nearly full. Note: Be very careful not to spill any water down the exterior of the upper bucket, or you will contaminate the water in the bucket beneath. This is a slow filtering process, so be patient. Even with four filter elements, it will take a considerable time to filter six gallons.

Well "Torpedo" or "Bullet" Bucket Construction Plans

If you live on a property with well water but don't own a backup generator, or if you anticipate a situation that will outlast your stored fuel for your generator, then you should learn how to construct a well torpedo. This is a PVC tube with a flapper valve at the bottom, which, when sent down the well shaft, hits the water and causes the tube to fill and then sink. When you pull on the rope, the flapper valve closes, sealing in the water for you to pull up the well shaft.

For any readers who aren't familiar with them, narrow-shaft well buckets—also sometimes called "bullet buckets" or "torpedo buckets"—are designed for manually drawing water from modern small-diameter wells that are more than twenty feet deep. Shallow wells (less than twenty-foot depth) are much more efficiently accessed with a hand pump, such as a traditional pitcher-type cistern pump (available from Lehmans.com) or a home-fabricated PVC design by Keith Hendricks, as shown at the Perma Pak Web site (snipurl.com/honqb). Deeper wells require a sucker-rod actuated pump.

Have a deep well but you can't afford a manual pump or you don't foresee anything but short-term emergency need to draw water? A bucket will do. The following method works, but you will first have to pull out the pump, wiring, and its draw pipe before you can use an emergency bucket. Most modern wells have four- or six-inch-diameter casings. Well buckets can be made from PVC pipe and some fittings available at nearly any hardware store. The only hard-to-find item is the foot valve. Use a four- or five-foot length of three-inch-diameter white PVC pipe if your well has a four-inch casing, or four-inch-diameter pipe if your well has a six-inch casing.

Assembling the Bucket:

- For the top cap, drill a hole in the center and insert a threaded eyebolt with lock washer and nut to hold the lifting/lowering rope. Use PVC cement to attach the pipe cap. Be sure to use sturdy nylon rope. Recovering a bucket if the rope breaks would be problematic, to say the least. In the bottom cap, drill a centered hole and install a foot valve. This will be open when floating and allow water into the bucket. The valve will automatically close when the bucket is pulled up. Foot valves (also called "check valves") are available in PVC construction as well as brass and cast iron. Depending on the type of valve you buy, you will probably have to screw a threaded pipe adapter (male-to-male short coupling) into the top of the valve and then glue it into the appropriate-size hole that you have drilled into the end cap. Needless to say, you need to be sure that the valve's flapper is oriented in the right direction before you attach it to the bottom cap. You need the bucket valve to *hold* rather than release water when the bucket is raised!

For anyone who would rather buy a commercially made well bucket, they are available from ReadyMadeResources.com (search for "well bucket") and from Lehmans.com (search for "galvanized well bucket").

Transporting Water

You need to plan ahead for transporting your water, even if fuel for vehicles is not available. Think in terms of a two-wheel garden cart or a bicycle cargo trailer with "Slimed" tires—or better yet, foam-filled "airless" tires (available from PerformanceBike

.com or Nashbar.com). A cart or trailer can be loaded with five- or six-gallon plastic buckets or water cans. Each five-gallon water can will weigh about forty-two pounds, so you'll want a cart or trailer with at least two-hundred-pound capacity. Oh yes, and if times get really bad, then you'll need to plan for a security detail to protect the water detail. This is starting to get complicated, isn't it? All the more reason to get started right now!

5

THE DEEP LARDER

Your Family's Food Storage

Getting Started

TEOTWAWKI will certainly mean a disruption in food production and distribution. As you prepare, plan to have enough food stored for your family to last a year, and much longer if you can afford it. It may seem excessive, but you won't regret it when you are able to live with a full stomach WTSHTF. Keeping a deep larder has numerous advantages. By buying in bulk, you will be eating less expensively, and you will be able to provide for your family during a crisis. Just imagine how much extra food you will need to dispense as charity to your head-in-the-sand relatives, neighbors, friends, fellow church members, and refugees, so store *lots* of extra food, especially wheat, rice, beans, and honey. These items are cheap now, but may be very expensive later.

When storing foods, moderation and variety are the keys. Your staples will be dried goods such as corn, wheat, rice, and beans, but you will also need to stock up on canned fruits and vegetables, powdered milk, and lots and lots of salt. Include plenty of different foods to keep your bowels moving properly. This is a serious issue. Constipation that progresses to fecal impaction can be lethal, particularly in situations in which strong physical exertion is required.

As you plan for your larder, it will be important for you to calculate precisely how much food you will need for each member of your family for one year. In the following list, I provide recommended quantities, but you may want to do more specific calculations based on your family's situation. While I do not share the religious beliefs of the LDS (Mormon) church, I commend them for their food-storage philosophy, practice, and infrastructure. Your local LDS ward probably has a dry-pack cannery, and they will let non-LDS members use it on a space-available basis. Members are usually on hand to train newbies on how to operate the equipment.

The real key to self-sufficiency is having both storage foods and the ability to grow your own grains and vegetables. If you are worried about nutritional value, then *nothing* beats freshly grown. You should consider storing non-hybrid seed of equal or perhaps greater importance than food storage. Growing a garden and raising livestock are the main things that will provide our sustenance in a very long-term grid-down scenario. See Chapter 7 for more details.

What to Keep in Your Larder

Your larder should consist of three basic categories: dried foods, canned foods, and supplementary foods. For canned goods, consistently use FIFO (First In, First Out) rotation. Always place the newest cans at the back of the shelf and move the older cans forward. Eat the oldest foods first. It's a good idea date all of your storage foods. I use a medium-point Sharpie pen. If you have a lot of canned goods to mark, then use a date stamp. To stay current, keep a multi-year rotation calendar.

In addition to the items mentioned in Chapter 2, here are a few more things you'll want in your larder:

- Canning lids and rings. Buy plenty of extras for barter.
- Salt. Stock up in quantity, particularly if your retreat is more than thirty miles inland.
- Sulfur for drying fruit
- Vinegar. Buy a couple of cases of one-gallon bottles.
- Spices
- Baking soda
- Yeast
- Food-storage (freezer and vacuum) bags
- Aluminum foil. Buy lots—there are 101 uses, including making improvised solar ovens.
- Deer bags

The Top Ten Essentials

1. **Salt:** Salt is important to store, both for flavoring and preserving food and as a practical means to attract wild game. In many locales, natural salt licks are off-limits to hunters, since hunting there is too easy and hence not considered sporting.

That ought to tell you something. I recommend that you store several times more salt than you think you'll ever need.

Unless you live next to a salt lick or salt marsh, I cannot overemphasize the importance of storing salt. Salt is cheap and plentiful now, but in the event of TEOTWAWKI it will be a scarce and valuable commodity in most inland regions. Salt also has a virtually unlimited shelf life. Do some research on natural salt deposits near your intended retreat. That could be quite valuable knowledge in the event of TEOTWAWKI.

Lay in a supply of ten pounds of salt per member of your family. This figure may sound high, but, again, it includes extra for attracting wild game. The portion for cooking and table salt should be iodized.

2. Rice: I prefer brown rice for its nutritional benefits, even though its storage life is shorter than that of white rice. The combined weight should be about thirty pounds per adult, per year. Storage life is around eight years.

3. Wheat (or substitute grains, for celiacs): Grain storage is a crucial aspect of family preparedness. Grain may soon no longer be cheap or plentiful, so stock up. Buy 220 pounds per adult, per year. (Part of this can be in the form of pasta.) Storage life is thirty or more years. I also recommend buying plenty of extra for barter and charity.

I do not recommend storing flour, since it keeps for only two or three years. Whole wheat stores for thirty-plus years, maintaining 80 percent or more of its nutritional value. Buy whole grains and a hand wheat grinder.

Don't overlook the easiest preparation method of all: soaked wheat berries. By simply soaking for twenty-four to thirty-six hours, whole grain wheat plumps and softens into "berries." When then heated, wheat berries make a nutritious breakfast cereal.

4. Corn: Whole corn stores much longer than cracked corn or cornmeal, so store whole corn and grind your own. Get fifty pounds per adult, per year. The storage life of whole corn is eight to twelve years, but cracked or ground corn stores only eighteen to thirty-six months.

5. Oats: Lay in a supply of twenty pounds per adult, per year. The storage life of oats is three to seven years, depending on variety and packing method.

6. Fats and Oils: I recommend storing primarily olive oil (frozen, in plastic bottles), mayonnaise, canned butter, and peanut butter. The combined weight of these should be about ninety-six pounds per adult, per year. (Four gallons is about twenty-four pounds.) The canned products must be continuously rotated, or else donated to charity biannually. The frozen oil should also be rotated, or donated to charity once every four years.

7. Powdered Milk: Buy the nonfat variety. Store about twenty pounds per adult, per year. For the longest storage life, it is best to buy nitrogen-packed dry milk from a storage-food vendor. That type has a shelf life of five or more years.

8. Canned Fruit and Vegetables: It is most economical (and good practice) to can your own. As long as you rotate continuously, you should lay in a two-year supply per family member. Quantities will depend on the ratio of fruit and vegetables in your preferred diet.

9. Canned Meats: Again, you must rotate continuously, and don't store more than you would use in two years. I like the DAK brand canned hams.

10. Sugars: I prefer honey (except of course for infants), but depending on your taste, you will also want to lay in a supply of sugar, molasses, sorghum, maple syrup, and various jams and jellies. The combined weight of these should be about fifty pounds per adult, per year.

Nitrogen Packing

Nitrogen packing is good for roughly eight to ten years for most foods, and much longer for whole grains. I recommend buying commercially nitrogen-packed cans only for the items that don't store well otherwise, e.g., dehydrated peas, powdered milk, peanut-butter powder, and textured vegetable protein (TVP).

Other Musts for Your Larder

Retort-Packaged Ultrahigh-Temperature Pasteurized Milk

For a short-term supply (up to six months), UHT (ultrahigh-temperature) pasteurized retort-packaged milk makes a lot of sense. For longer term, you should store nitrogen-packed canned powdered nonfat milk from a competent and reliable vendor such as Ready Made Resources or Walton Feed (waltonfeed .com). I have found that the nonfat variety stores the best because it is the butterfat in whole milk that goes rancid, significantly shortening the shelf life.

Rice and soy "milks" store even longer than cow milk. Like any other storage food, be sure to store retort-packaged "bricks" in the coolest (but not ever below freezing) part of your house, and away from vermin. Never stack individual retort bricks horizontally more than five bricks high, or vertically more than seven bricks high. Or, if storing them in their original factory shipping cardboard cases (of vertical bricks) no more than five cases high.

Multivitamins and Other Food Supplements

You should plan to supplement your foodstuffs with a good-quality double-encapsulated multivitamin, a good-quality B-complex tablet, and a five-hundred-milligram vitamin C tablet. See Vitacost .com for some of the least expensive vitamins and nutritional supplements available via the Internet. Unconsumed vitamins should be replaced at least every three years. Store them in a cool, very dark place. Light kills vitamins quickly.

Store as many vitamins as you can rotate without exceeding expiration dates (roughly three to four years' worth, unless you have an ultracold medical freezer). My only strong proviso is to avoid overdosing any of the fat-soluble vitamins (vitamins A, D, E, and K—best mnemonically memorized with the word *KADE*.)

Natural Laxatives

Your diet may shift heavily toward meat, and this could cause problems. Plan ahead. Bulk Metamucil is one option.

Vitamin C

Vitamin C is crucial for healing following trauma, and it minimizes trauma-induced bruising. There is little harm in megadosing vitamin C, since any excess that the body does not need is passed through the urinary tract. Cumulatively, however, if megadosing is done frequently it might be hard on the kidneys, so be careful.

Peanut Butter

There are few sources of protein that are more compact for use in a Get Out Of Dodge (G.O.O.D.) bag than peanut butter. Survival Blog reader H. Hunter mentioned, "In a 40-ounce jar (typical large jar from a grocery store) of reduced-fat peanut butter there are 6,100 calories. Of course full-fat varieties would have more (about 7,000 calories). Beans, in the same container, would contain 1,200–2,000 calories. That makes peanut butter a very calorie-dense food. It doesn't require hours and hours of prep time as beans do, and a jar can easily be thrown in your Bugout bag. The reduced-fat variety has a stamped shelf life of a little over two years."

One other important proviso involves digestion. A diet that is heavy in peanut butter or meat is likely to induce constipation, so, again, vary your diet.

Blue-Green-Algae Tablets

This is both a primary food and a vitamin/mineral supplement. It is one of the most compact forms of storage food for a short-term Bugout bag.

Sprouts

Lay in a supply of three pounds of sprouting seed per adult. Before you buy in quantity, try several varieties to see which you like.

Coffee

There is no perfect way to store coffee long-term and still maintain connoisseur's taste quality, but for the purposes of average coffee drinkers, the vacuum-packed "bricks" of ground coffee beans store fairly well. Just be sure to protect them from vermin.

Special Considerations for Infants

Breast milk is best, and of course obviates the storage-life issues with formula. But if formula is used, it must be rotated like any other storage food. Transitional baby foods can be stored in moderate quantities, but my general advice is to buy a baby-food grinder and simply transition your infant to normal kitchen-table foods very gradually.

Special Considerations for Pets

Stock up on food for your pets, and rotate it religiously. Date-mark every can and bag. Bagged dog and cat food can be bucket-packed, just like human foods. (Use the same vermin-proof packing-methods available for bulk grains.) Keep in mind that the lower the fat content, the longer the shelf life for dry dog and cat food. Hence, low-oil kibble-type foods are best, but be sure to test a small quantity first to see if you can transition your pet's diet. You can supplement with a bit of your canned butter or other stored fats and oils.

Additional Storage-Food Details

Hard Red Wheat Versus Soft White Wheat for Storage and Baking

I'm often asked the difference between varieties of wheat, particularly hard wheat and soft wheat. Soft white wheat has a lower nutritive value (protein) than hard red winter wheat. Although they are both categorized as hard grains, the hard wheat varieties store better than the soft wheats (thirty or more years versus fifteen to twenty years for soft white wheat). For both of these reasons, **hard red winter wheat is better for home food-storage programs.** The following is a quote from the excellent wheat article at the Walton Feed Web site:

> The hard wheats generally contain smaller kernels and are harder than soft wheat kernels. They contain high protein and gluten levels primarily designed for making bread flours. Depending on variety and growing conditions, hard wheats can have vastly different protein levels. For bread making, your wheat should have a minimum of 12 percent protein. The hard varieties of wheat can have protein levels up to 15 or 16 percent. Generally speaking for bread making, the higher the protein content the better. Hard white wheat is a relative newcomer that tends to produce a lighter colored, more spongy loaf of bread and because of this, it is gaining quick popularity among home bread makers. However, we have talked with bread makers who prefer the hard red wheat for its more robust flavor and more traditional textured loaf of bread it makes.

Whole Grains Versus Milled Grains for Storage

Once they are ground, wheat, corn, and other grains begin to lose their nutritive value almost immediately, and their shelf life is shortened drastically. Once the outer kernel (bran) of a grain is penetrated and the inner germ is exposed, the inevitable degradation begins. Here are some rough storage-life figures to consider:

Whole corn: eight to twelve years. Cracked or ground corn: eighteen to thirty-six months.

Whole wheat: thirty or more years. Flour: two to three years.

If you were to bake all of your own bread each day and religiously rotate your supplies of flour and cornmeal every eighteen months, then you could get by without owning a grain mill. But if you want to store more than an eighteen-month supply of grains or have extra on hand for barter and charity, then the only viable alternative is to buy whole grains and a grain mill.

Is Grain Sold as Seed or Animal Feed Safe to Eat?

Typically "seed" grain is treated with insecticides and fungicides, but "feed "grain is not. Any whole grain (without fillers, additives, or by-products) sold as animal feed is probably fit for human consumption, but don't count on it. The FDA food-handling standards for human consumption generally don't apply. Thus, there could be excess pesticides, insect parts, insect excreta, or other contamination, including mycotoxins. This is not to say that grains packed for human food are perfect—I've found much more than just chaff in the wheat that I bought from food-storage vendors over the years, including pebbles and small dirt clods— but at least the screening is more thorough with these grains than with animal feed. The only way to be sure about safety for human consumption is to check with the feed mill/packaging company for each product.

In the southern parts of the country there are more insect problems, so much of the seed wheat is treated with pesticides. The good news is that if you can smell, you will easily recognize the pesticides on the wheat. The feed variety of wheat isn't cleaned as much as "triple-cleaned" wheat, which is normally what is sold for human consumption. Quality typically varies from one source to the next. Buy one bag to start with after telling the store owner you need nontreated wheat for animal feed. You could always winnow this out yourself if you so desired. It does offer a cheap alternative.

While animal feed at this time is not on a par with food-grade grain, these rules will be changing. The FDA is pressuring producers, storage facilities, and feed mills to bring their standards up to human-food-chain levels. We will see this transformation in the next three to five years as laws are brought forth to force the process.

A Little More on Corn

Corn is a valuable food to store, although it is not quite as versatile as wheat, nor does it store for nearly as long. Corn does store fairly well *if* its moisture content is low. Like wheat, once corn is cracked or ground, its nutritive value starts to drop rapidly. Therefore you should buy your storage corn whole, and then grind it into cornmeal in small batches as needed.

Corn stores best in whole kernels. Once it is cracked, the inner germ is exposed. This decreases its storage life and nutritive value by 80 percent. Running whole corn through a grain mill at a coarse setting to make cracked corn is quick and easy. A finer setting will yield cornmeal.

I've found that the least expensive place to buy whole-kernel corn is Walton Feed, in Montpelier, Idaho. Be careful about the moisture content—mold is the greatest bugaboo with bulk corn. Never, ever eat moldy corn. It can induce mycotoxin poisoning that is potentially deadly!

A Closer Look at Fats

An issue that is often overlooked in long-term survival/preparedness planning is the necessity of fats and oils. I believe that fats and oils are consciously ignored by food-storage vendors, because vendors love to market their "complete" three-year and five-year food-storage packages. The problem is that those food assortments do not include the requisite multiple-year supply of essential fats and oils. These vendors are doing their customers a huge disservice with this omission. Fats and oils are a nutritional necessity.

For urban or suburban preppers who don't hunt, don't fish, don't have the room to raise livestock, and don't have the room to grow peanuts, olives, or sunflowers on a large scale, there are precious few options for long-term sources of fats and oils. The first option is expensive but viable: Continuously and completely rotate your supply. Donate the unused portion of your stored stock of cooking oil and shortening/lard to your local food bank—or if it has gone rancid, set it aside for making biodiesel, candles, or soap.

The other thing that you can do is buy a case or two of canned butter once every three years. Canned butter is available from Best Prices Storable Foods and from Ready Made Resources.

Be very selective about the fats and oils that you store. Some that you buy from your local supermarket are borderline rancid and unhealthy even when "freshly made." I prefer olive oil over corn oil. I also prefer storing canned butter over Crisco-type shortening or canned lard. For those who do prefer shortening, its shelf life can be extended by repacking it in mason-type canning jars. Some brands of lard are still packed in all-metal cans, which provides a longer shelf life. Look in the ethnic-foods section of your grocery store for cans marked *Manteca*, which is Spanish for "lard."

Keep in mind, too, that a diet that has too much lean meat can lead to severe digestive problems and even malnutrition. If you plan to depend heavily on wild game or livestock that you raise, then be sure to include some bulk fiber in your diet. To provide this fiber, you must either sprout it, grow it in your garden, or store it. Don't overlook this aspect of preparing your survival larder.

Supplements and Short-Term Emergency Foods

MREs

At a fixed-site retreat, prepacked meals (such as MRE and Meal, Alternative Regionally Customized [MARC] rations) don't make much sense. But when you're operating in the field, they save time, obviate the need to carry a stove and cooking utensils, and reduce the noise, odor, and light signatures of a campsite. I recommend the retort-packaged Meals, Ready to Eat (MREs) as a supplement to a well-rounded food-storage program. Because they are fairly compact and lightweight, and require no cooking, they are ideal to pack in your G.O.O.D backpack or BOB.

My old friend who has a SurvivalBlog profile under the pseudonym Mr. Tango had a round of correspondence with the U.S. Army Soldier Systems Center, in Natick, Massachusetts, on the potential storage life of MREs. Like all other storage foods, MREs must be stored at low temperature to maximize their shelf life. The data that they sent him was surprising. Here is the gist of it:

Degrees F	Months of Storage (Years)
120	1 month
110	5 months
100	22 months (1.8 Years)
90	55 months (4.6 Years)
80	76 months (6.3 Years)
70	100 months (8.3 Years)
60	130 months (10.8 Years)

The figures above are based on date of pack, rather than inspection date.

MREs near the end of their shelf life are considered safe to eat if:

1. They are palatable to the taste.

2. They do not show any signs of spoilage (such as swelled pouches).

3. They have been stored at moderate temperatures (70F or below).

Not enough data has yet been collected on storage below 60 degrees F. However, projections are that the 130-month figure will be extended.

Time and temperature have a cumulative effect. For example: storage at 100 degrees F for 11 months and then moved to 70F, you would lose 1/2 of the 70F storage life.

Avoid fluctuating temperatures in and out of freezing level.

The above-cited figures are for palatability, not nutritive value. Most of the fat, carbohydrates, and protein will still be available in MREs, even after many years of storage, but the vitamins will not. Plan accordingly.

Because MREs and other emergency foods are relatively high in bulk and low in fiber, I highly recommend also storing a fiber supplement with each case of MREs.

Energy Bars

Commercially made "energy bars," "emergency-ration bars," and "sports bars" can provide a useful adjunct to a storage-food program. Nutritionally, energy bars alone are inadequate. But they do make a useful supplement to your food-storage program, both to provide variety and flavor in a bland diet and to serve as a very compact short-term food supply for your G.O.O.D. kit.

These bars can easily be packed in Ziploc bags (or better yet, vacuum-packed with a Tilia FoodSaver) and stored in a chest freezer. This will greatly extend their shelf life, especially in hot climates. Just don't forget to pin a prominent note on your G.O.O.D. rucksack, reminding you to retrieve them from the freezer before you head out the door.

Jerky

Nearly all of the energy bars on the market are fairly expensive. One good alternative is making traditional jerky and pemmican at home. The cost per ounce can be very low, especially if you hunt or raise livestock. But keep in mind that, just like with energy bars, if you store dried meat you will also need to store a good source of dietary fiber.

Ramen Noodles

The nutritive value of ramen is marginal, so it should not be considered a primary storage food. But there is wisdom in having some on hand as a food-storage supplement, especially in lean times, when hunger pangs will be a distinct possibility.

Cooking Facilities for Grid-Down Living

Plan ahead for cooking in grid-down circumstances and to cook over open fires if need be. Buy several cast-iron pots and frying pans, a Dutch oven, and a large kettle. You should also be prepared to cook in larger quantity. It is difficult to predict the exact circumstances, but chances are you will be cooking for far more than just your own family. At the minimum, this will require a couple of huge stew pots, two large frying pans, and lots of extra bread pans.

How to Store Food Safely

You can "do it yourself" for nearly everything required for home food storage with the notable exception of canned powdered dry milk. (It's messy to repack yourself, and because of milk's butterfat content, it stores well for long periods only with commercial nitrogen packing.) Commercially canned "year's supply" type units are needlessly expensive. Even the salt comes canned. Talk about overkill packaging. In the instance of wheat, you are paying two to five times as much for the product because of the packaging. You are better off buying your food in bulk (honey, whole grains, beans, and rice) and canning or otherwise containerizing it yourself.

Unless you have large-scale grain bins, one of the most efficient means of storing wheat and corn for small-scale animal feed or human consumption is to buy galvanized trash cans with tight-fitting lids. If they will be on a damp floor, put the cans up on two-by-four blocks to prevent rust. When galvanized trash barrels go on sale, buy a bunch. Another good storage method is five- or six-gallon food-grade plastic buckets with gasketed lids. These stack well, but be advised that they are not as vermin-proof as galvanized steel bins or barrels. Determined rats have been known to gnaw their way through plastic food buckets. So if you choose this method, be sure to set traps, and check the buckets every few weeks for signs of damage.

Crucial Equipment for Storage

Food-Grade Plastic Pails

Bulk wheat, rice, and beans are best stored in five- or six-gallon food-grade plastic pails.

If you use your own pails, make sure that they are certified food grade (most buckets made for paint are not). And if you reuse food-grade buckets, make certain that they were used only for non-smelly foods. Reusing pickle pails for rice can give you pickle-flavored rice!

Walton Feed has excellent prices and top-quality products. Pack bulk grains and legumes in plastic buckets yourself and you will save a lot of money. Note: Make sure that you use oxygen-absorbing packets (available from Walton) or the dry-ice displacement method to kill all the bugs and larvae before you seal up each bucket.

Food-grade five-gallon buckets can be found cheaply or for

free from bakeries. For any buckets you acquire that are missing lids, I recommend that you buy Gamma Seal lids. These lids are threaded, making them very convenient for accessing the storage foods that you use most frequently. Gamma Seal lids fit standard five- or six-gallon buckets, and they seem to last forever. We've been using some of our lids on a daily basis for more than twenty years. In addition to our storage-food buckets, we have them on buckets for poultry feed, wild birdseed, and dog food. They are available from Ready Made Resources, Safecastle, Nitro-Pak (nitro-pak.com), and several other vendors for around six dollars each. If you want to buy twenty or more lids, you can get them directly from the manufacturer, at gammaseals.com. Many of the above vendors also sell a "lid-lifter" tool, which is very helpful in prying open sealed buckets that are not yet equipped with Gamma Seal lids.

Keep in mind that plastic food-grade buckets are oxygen and gas permeable and will not store food for a long time by themselves. A Mylar liner will greatly slow down this process. (It will *not* stop it entirely.)

What Determines If a Storage Bucket Is Food Grade?

I've seen considerable confusion both in print and on the Internet about whether all HDPE (high-density polyethylene) plastic buckets are food grade. The number 2 (inside the "chasing arrows" recycling symbol) refers to HDPE, but not all "2"-marked plastics are food grade. The "food grade" designation is determined by plastic purity and by what mold-release compound is used—not by the plastic itself, since all virgin HDPE material is safe for food. For paint and other utility buckets, manufacturers sometimes use a less expensive (and toxic) mold-release compound for their injection-molding machines. For food grade they must use a nontoxic formulation, which is more expensive. Unless the buckets are actually marked "food grade" or NSF-, FDA-, or USDA-approved, you will have to check with the manufacturer's Web site to see if all their buckets are food grade.

Malcolm from SurvivalBlog provided some data for oxygen permeability for various materials. For long food-storage life, the lower the number, the better:

Material	ml O_2/(day-mil-sq. meter-atm)
PE (polyethylene)	6,000–15,000
HDPE	1,500–3,000
Mylar	50–100
Plastic laminate	10–400
Saran	10–350
Foil laminate	0
Steel cans	0

Grain Mills

Storing wheat and corn requires a good-quality, durable grain mill. I don't recommend electric-only mills because they will become useless ornaments once the power grid goes down. An inexpensive hand-cranked mill such as the Back to Basics or Corona might suffice for a short-term disaster, but in the event of TEOTWAWKI you will want something built to last.

We use a Country Living grain mill. It is a superior machine. With just about any mill, you will have to cycle the grain through several times to get fine flour. I recommend that you get the Power Bar handle extension for extra leverage. Country Living grain mills are available through Ready Made Resources and several other vendors. Like any other quality tool, they are expensive. But it is better to buy just one machine that you know will last you a lifetime, rather than a succession of "bargains" that turn into disappointments.

Because they have V-belt wheels, Country Living grain mills are readily adaptable to an electric motor for day-to-day use, or in the event of a grid-up scenario. For someone who has some mechanical acumen and time on their hands, it is also possible to convert a bicycle frame or perhaps a piece of exercise equipment to power a Country Living grain mill. If you have a background in welding, building such frames might make a good niche home business.

To make flour that is fine enough for bread baking, you need to run wheat through a mill twice. The best mills use stone burrs. Some of the less expansive mills use metal burrs. These are fine for making cornmeal. The metal-burr mills such as the Corona are less expensive but more labor intensive. With these you might have to grind wheat three times to make fine flour. Metal-burr grinders are available from Nitro-Pak, Lehman's, and several other vendors. Stone-burr grinders are available from Ready Made Resources, Lehman's, and many other vendors.

Home Dehydrators

Home dehydrators are very useful. Over the years, we have used ours for everything from drying venison jerky and apples to "re-animating" silica-gel rust-prevention packets. Used dehydrators are easy to find for reasonable prices, via newspaper classifieds or a localized Web service such as Craigslist. Dehydrators are a bit bulky to buy through mail order, so try to find a local source. If purchased new, they can be quite expensive. The one that we use at the Rawles Ranch is an Excalibur brand, with a variable temperature control. They are very sturdy and typically have several trays, so they can hold a lot. Ours is circa 1980 and still going strong, with no maintenance. They require AC power, so in anticipation of the grid going down, you should already have a backup solar dehydrator, or at least all of the materials that you will need to fabricate one, after TSHTF. See: snipurl.com/hoqdx, snipurl.com/hoqf4, and snipurl.com/hoqg8.

FoodSaver Vacuum-Packing Systems

One very useful tool for storage is a home vacuum-packing and heat-sealing machine, sold under the trade name FoodSaver. Yep, it's the one that you've seen on those late-night infomercials. They really do work, both for evacuating and sealing plastic bags and for evacuating mason jars. To save money, it is probably best to buy one of these used, through eBay. Just be sure that the seller guarantees against it being dead on arrival. Test it thoroughly immediately after you buy it. Be advised that FoodSavers are designed to seal only one particular thickness of plastic bag, and they have a limited maximum width. You should shop around for bags and bag material on the Internet, as prices vary dramatically.

Here at the ranch, we have a large number of No. 10 cans of freeze-dried food. The disadvantage to opening a can to eat something is that once you open it, the clock starts ticking for how long it will stay fresh. Our solution? We use widemouthed mason jars, pour the No. 10 can's contents into the jars, and use a FoodSaver V2830 to seal the lids onto the jars. This means we can take our time eating the contents, as opposed to eating the same thing day after day before it goes bad. Small quantities can also be stored in heat-sealed vacuum bags.

Freeze-dried Versus Dehydrated Foods for Storage

Because of their lower cost, here at the ranch we store nearly all bulk grains/legumes/honey and various nitrogen-canned *dehydrated* foods. We have just a few freeze-dried items, such as fruit and some peas that we got from Freeze Dry Guy (FreezeDryGuy .com). At a fixed-location retreat with copious storage space and plentiful water from a shallow well, dehydrated foods make more sense. If we were planning to G.O.O.D., then logically we would want more freeze-dried items—to take advantage of their reduced weight and volume.

Do-It-Yourself Bulk Food Storage: Buckets, Oxygen Absorbers, CO_2, and Desiccants

To save money you will probably want to buy rice, wheat, and beans in fifty-pound sacks. Sacks are problematic, since what you really want is a vermin-proof, moisture-proof container that is airtight and preferably evacuated of oxygen. Those are the keys to true long-term shelf life, and none of them are provided by a cloth, paper, or woven-plastic sack. The solution is to repack bulk foods in food-grade plastic buckets. Here is how to do it:

Bucket-Packing Method

Line a bucket with a large food-grade Mylar bag and pour in the wheat, rice, or beans, shaking the bucket and tapping it on the floor several times to get the bag completely full. You don't want any air gaps. Fill the bag so that the bucket is filled to within one inch of the top. Then toss two oxygen-absorbing packets (available from Nitro-Pak) into the bag.

Clear vinyl bags (often marked "V" or with recycle code "3") are almost always food grade. Low-density polyethylene (LDPE or recycle code "4") in film form—typically used in grocery bags and trash bags—is usually food grade, but some varieties have strange additives or coatings. To be sure, see the manufacturer's packaging for details. If the package is marked "FDA approved," "USDA approved," or "food safe," then the bags are food grade. Most Mylar is food grade, but, again, beware of odd coatings. Most Mylar bucket liners—such as those sold by Nitro-Pak—are food grade. The latter is my top choice for extending the longevity of stored grains and legumes.

Next, place a small chunk of dry ice on top of the grain, inside the liner bag. I usually use a piece that is about as big as my thumb. As the dry ice "melts" (sublimates) it will fill the bucket with CO_2, displacing the oxygen. (Insects can't breathe CO_2!) Keep a watchful eye on the dry ice. Once it has sublimated to the diameter of a nickel and not any thicker than one eighth of an inch, seal the bag with a wire twist tie. On top of the sealed bag, place a two-ounce bag of silica-gel desiccant (also available from from Nitro-Pak). Then immediately seal the bucket, securing the lid with firm strikes from a rubber mallet. This will seat the lid and compress the O-ring.

WARNING: If you don't wait until the dry ice has almost completely sublimated before you seal the bucket, then dangerous pressure could develop and you will have a "dry-ice bomb"

on your hands. You must wait until the dry-ice chunk has sublimated to the diameter of a nickel no thicker than one eighth of
an inch.

Once you open each bucket of storage food, you will probably
want to replace the standard "pound-on" lid with a Gamma Seal
lid. The end result: Very dry food in a sealed, oxygen-free environment, safe from mice. This method will triple or quadruple
the shelf life of rice and beans, and make whole-grain wheat last
literally for decades.

Home Canning

This is a subject that would take a book to explain in detail, but
a couple of good references will suffice: The first is *The Encyclopedia of Country Living*, by Carla Emery, published by Sasquatch
Books. Be sure to get the ninth or later edition.

The second book on canning that I recommend is *Keeping the
Harvest*, by Nancy Chioffi and Gretchen Mead, from Storey
Publishing.

Learning to Cook and Bake with Your Storage Food

One oft-overlooked aspect of food storage is how to cook and
bake with the foods that you've stored. Three books on this subject that I strongly recommend buying are: *Cookin' with Home
Storage*, by Vicki Tate, *Making the Best of Basics* by James Talmage
Stevens, and *The Encyclopedia of Country Living*.

Family Food Security Against Confiscation and Theft

I'm sometimes asked about the risk of government confiscation of storage food and supplies by executive order or under martial law. There is a slim but nonetheless real threat of storage-food confiscation in the United States. It is one of the many reasons why I emphasize operational security (OPSEC). If you are concerned about the prospect of martial law, then I recommend that you buy the majority of your storage food with cash, without generating a paper trail. You should pick it up in person. There are several food-storage vendors advertising on SurvivalBlog who are located throughout the country. Many of these are mom-and-pop operations that will make cash sales. With these small vendors, you don't even need to mention your name.

While keeping circumspect is important, don't become so preoccupied with secrecy that you cease being charitable. The two goals need not be mutually exclusive. You can maintain OPSEC if you dispense charity through your local church. My advice: Give, and give generously (both now and in turbulent times), but be prepared to give from arm's length. I recommend that you make arrangements in advance for your church elders to act as intermediaries for post-WTSHTF charity. Be sure to get their promise to maintain your anonymity.

Concealing Storage Food

Several of my consulting clients have asked me about concealing storage food from burglars, in unoccupied retreat homes. Some of them have asked if I suggest burying food. I do not recommend burying food unless you buy very heavy-duty containers with watertight seals. There is too much risk of moisture intrusion or destruction by vermin.

Here are a few alternative solutions for hiding modest quantities of food that I can recommend, only one of which requires the assistance of an amateur carpenter:

- Buy a used queen-size "hide-a-bed" couch. Remove and discard the entire bed frame internals and mattress. Build a framework of two-by-twos and cut a piece of three-quarter-inch plywood to support the seat cushions.

- Hide a single row of canned foods (small cans, such as soup and tuna cans) behind books on bookshelves.

- Buy a few used four-drawer vertical file cabinets. Burglars usually bypass these. Put innocuous-sounding labels in the label holders in bold printing, such as "2007 Tax Records" and "2005 Invoices." If you pack them efficiently, file cabinets can hold a remarkable quantity of canned goods and retort-packaged bricks. They are also mouse-proof if you place them on a smooth and level floor.

- One outdoor solution is to find a used, out-of-commission chest freezer. Cut off the power cord. Cover any internal vents with sheet metal. Paint the exterior with flat brown enamel spray paint. Cut or buy a cord of firewood and stack it around and on top of the chest freezer. The same technique can be used if you have a hay barn—use either hay or straw bales. Or you could buy a few hundred used bricks and make it look like a pile of used bricks. And you would of course paint the chest freezer in flat green, flat tan, or flat brick red, respectively.

- Another outdoor solution is to buy an older, used pop-up camping trailer. For some reason, burglars tend to ignore these, whereas they will often break in to traditional hard-wall camping trailers. Pop-up trailers have a remarkable amount of room inside, especially if you remove the seat cushions and mattress pads. If you pay very little for the trailer, you can even go whole hog and rip out the interior cabinets, sink, etc.

- If you have a basement or storage room, you can also use hide-in-plain-sight (HIPS) techniques. One of my favorites is to obtain a lot of used, sturdy cardboard boxes with slip-top lids—such as the type used to ship reams of copier paper. Label them in prominent Magic Marker with things like "Baby Clothes," "Infant Toys," "National Geographic Magazines," and so forth. Fill those boxes with your storage foods (in vermin-proof containers). Pile all of those boxes up against a wall. Then add a layer of camouflage boxes, containing actual worthless junk. If a burglar opens one of these, he will most likely not dig down to the successive layers of boxes.

    ~ Use your imagination. Craigslist (craigslist.com) and Freecycle (freecycle.org) can probably provide you all the storage containers and camouflage items that you need, for very little money. Many of the items that you'll need can be found "free for the hauling."

When planning your concealment strategies, keep in mind that a burglar is a man in a hurry. In most cases, he won't take the time to go through everything.

The Best Way to Stock Up on Food at the Eleventh Hour

Waiting until the eleventh hour to stock up on canned and bulk foods is not recommended, but if your circumstances necessitate it, then consider it a calculated risk. Don't hesitate once you see the first warning signs. You have only one day to shop before the hordes descend and strip the stores clean. However, instead of making these purchases at a supermarket, I recommend buying at a membership warehouse store (such as Costco or Sam's Club). Buy a store-membership card and scope out the store in detail, well in advance.

The case lots that big-box stores sell, combined with the large flat cargo carts that they provide, make large-volume procurement much more efficient than shopping at a typical grocery store with individual cans and small boxes piled into a standard shopping cart. One of the Costco cargo carts—piled up with case lots—can carry the equivalent of about eight full grocery carts. You can buy a lot of food in a very short period of time, and get better prices to boot, at a place like Costco. Items like jerky, batteries, and bottled water will sell out first, so make those your first stops. With proper planning, you could buy everything in less than two hours.

Old Storage Food

Some folks write me who put in supplies twenty years ago, or even inherited preparations from relatives, asking if those supplies are still any good. Some items, such as salt, will store for centuries as long as they are not contaminated by the rust or decay of their containers. If stored dry, hard red winter wheat still retains 98 percent of its nutritive value after twenty years. Ditto for sugar and honey. Most dehydrated foods, however, such as rice, beans, TVP, and the ubiquitous thirty-year shelf-life nitrogen-packed stroganoff, will have lost too much nutritive value to be useful after twenty years, even if they were nitrogen packed. They might still be palatable, but unless you are dieting, what is the use of eating them if they have lost 90 percent of their nutritive value?

If in doubt, throw it out. Ideally, you should continuously rotate your storage food to avoid such waste.

One tidbit of trivia: Some wheat was found in an Egyptian pharaoh's tomb. A small fraction of it still sprouted after 2,600 years. If you have any older canned gardening seeds, try them out. The sprouting yields will be low, but there could be some marginal utility there. Just don't expend too much effort tilling and tending those rows in your garden!

6

FUEL AND HOME POWER

The Coming Energy Crisis:
Hubbert Peak or Not—Be Prepared!

There has been a lot of ink spilled in recent years debating the Hubbert Peak ("Peak Oil") theory. I am a believer in global oil depletion, but I think those in the Peak Oil crowd are about twenty to twenty-five years too early in their predictions.

We cannot depend on the slow-moving bureaucracies of national governments to rescue us from the coming energy crisis. Even if we in the First World overcome the problem, the Second World and the Third World—with less money available for massive crash programs and probably with a more short-term perspective—will likely be plunged into a second Dark Ages. At the minimum that means famines, monumental migrations, huge economic dislocations, and world wars, all likely sometime later in this century. And even if our generation muddles through, we should make preparations on behalf of our children and grandchildren.

The Fragility of the U.S. Power Grid

The depletion of oil reserves will be a long-term problem, but we may also find ourselves facing a more immediate concern in the dissolution of the U.S. power grid.

I often refer to the national power grids (there are actually three: eastern and western, and Texas) as the linchpins of our modern societal infrastructure. Any interruption for more than a few weeks could precipitate a societal collapse. So much of what we rely on for our modern way of life depends on grid power. The telephone networks have backup generators, but those have only a limited fuel supply. Even the supply of piped natural gas is dependent on the grid, since grid electricity powers the compressor stations that pressurize the natural-gas pipelines. I am of the firm opinion that existing supervisory control and data acquisition (SCADA) software implementations represent a great vulnerability. The new-generation Web-enabled SCADA systems only compound the problem. (Terrorists don't even need to go on-site to inject a computer virus and foul up the power and water utilities' switching and valve hardware. They can do it remotely.)

In a grid-down world, you'll need fuel to heat your home. Depending on the norm for where you live, this could be stacks of cordwood, coal, or an extra-large propane tank. You'll also need electricity. You can use liquid fuels for lighting, but you'll need some way to charge batteries for your crucial electronics, such as communications equipment and night-vision gear. This chapter will describe your options for all of these, starting with batteries and battery charging.

The Importance of Stocking Up on Batteries

I have been corresponding with an infantry soldier (E-6) in Iraq named Ray whom I met through AnySoldier.com. In our e-mails, one of the things Ray mentioned that stuck with me is that one of the crucial logistics for modern armies is spare batteries. He described how they go through hundreds of them, for radios, tactical flashlights, sensors, laser target illuminators and designators, and night-vision gear/thermal sights. As I look ahead to potential hard times in this country, I think that we should learn a lesson from the Iraq experience: Never run out of batteries.

Without batteries, we would soon be back to nineteenth-century technology and tactics. Since modern tactical electronics are "force multipliers," the lack of them would reduce the effectiveness of our defensive measures. Making up for that loss would necessitate having a lot more manpower. And providing more manpower requires more retreat floor space and more food. That additional food means more land under cultivation, and more land under cultivation means a larger perimeter to defend, and so forth. You can see where this logic leads: Instead of owning a little two-family, twenty-acre, low-profile retreat, you'd need ten to twelve armed and trained adults and perhaps forty to one hundred acres, depending on rainfall and soil fertility. Being the local lord of the manor is not conducive to keeping a low profile.

I've resolved never to let my family run out of batteries, even if the "problem" lasts for a decade. For my mobile power system, I started with a small, five-watt solar photovoltaic panel from Northern Tool and Equipment (northerntool.com), which I rigged to charge batteries using an "automobile" (twelve-volt DC) charging tray. The tray looks like a regular home charger, but it has a twelve-volt input power cable with a cigarette-lighter plug. This gives me direct DC-to-DC charging, without an energy-hogging inverter in the middle of the equation.

Try to get rechargeable batteries for as many devices as possible. Compatibility with rechargeables should be a key determining factor when selecting any electrical or electronic equipment. My favorite source for batteries via mail order is All Battery.com. They have great prices and a huge selection. If space permits, you should store all of your small batteries in a sealed bag (to prevent condensation) in the back of your refrigerator. This will extend their life.

Batteries for Long-Term Storage

If stored "wet," typical automobile and deep-cycle batteries will sulfate to the point that they won't hold a charge after eight or nine years. The way to avoid this is to store batteries "dry," sans battery acid. Some of the larger battery distributors, including Interstate Batteries, will indeed provide truly dry batteries on special order. You need to be sure that you are getting batteries than have never been filled with electrolyte. And of course you will also need to procure some carboys of battery acid. Many of the "dry-charged" lead acid batteries sold have actually been filled, charged, and then drained. Though they will not degrade nearly as quickly as wet batteries, they will not store as well as the harder-to-find never-filled batteries.

If you do things right, with enough cash you could potentially buy yourself a thirty-plus-year supply of spare batteries for your vehicles and for your alternative home power system. They would also be an awesome barter item.

For Want of a Battery:
The Importance of Photovoltaic Systems

Without those battery-powered items you'll be at huge disadvantage. So with that in mind, you should invest in a small photovoltaic solar panel for battery charging, and a boatload of nickel-metal hydride (NiMH) batteries. If you can afford to, buy a triple or quadruple set for each piece of gear that takes batteries. Even if you don't use them all yourself, the extra batteries will be ideal to keep on hand for barter and charity. The NiMH low self-discharge (LSD) is currently the most reliable rechargeable battery on the market.

If you cannot afford a large battery bank of deep-cycle batteries, then at least buy a "jump pack" twelve-volt DC gel-cell unit. These are available with either 110 VAC (U.S./Canada) or 220 VAC (UK) utility power charging cords. You can then plug in a twelve-VDC "smart" battery-charging tray using a DC power cord with cigarette-lighter plug. This is far more efficient than using an AC inverter and then a DC transformer (like those in most home battery chargers). That way you are just changing one DC voltage to another DC voltage, instead of a DC-inverted-to-AC-and-transformed-back-to-DC proposition, which is *very* inefficient.

Unless a standard connector is already installed, you would have to wire a cigarette-lighter-type plug onto the lead wires from the photovoltaic panel. These are available from any electronics-supply store, such as Radio Shack. Typically with DC wiring the red or white wire is positive, and that would go to the "tip" terminal on the lighter plug. (Note: Be sure to double-check the polarity with a volt-ohm meter before plugging it in!) The cigarette-lighter plugs and jacks are ubiquitous, but if you are handy with a soldering iron, I recommend switching to Anderson Powerpole connectors. These are compact, genderless connectors that do not pop apart unexpectedly—as cigarette lighter plugs are prone to do. One nice thing about jump packs is that they have a built-in charge controller. (A charge controller is a bit of circuitry that prevents overcharging a battery.) If you upgrade to larger-capacity storage—such as a standard car battery—either add a charge controller to the circuit or be *very careful* about checking voltage regularly during charging so that you don't "cook" your battery.

I use an AccuManager 20 battery charger. It is a "smart" charger—so it will not overcharge your batteries. It comes with both a twelve-VDC cord (with cigarette-lighter plug) and a 120-volt AC (VAC) adapter. The charger has six channels, so it can simultaneously hold four AAA, AA, C, or D cells, and two nine-VDC batteries.

You can recharge at least twenty AA cells from a jump pack that is fully charged. With a five-watt photovoltaic panel it might take two or three days to charge your jump pack. A ten-watt panel (or two five-watt panels wired parallel) works much better, and a twenty-watt panel works even better still. Your ability to "make do" with a smaller panel depends on your budget, how many batteries you need to keep charged, and your time available to reposition the panel to keep it in full sunlight throughout the day. To keep your jump pack charged, I recommend the small PV panels available from Northern Tool and Equipment.

Solar Battery Chargers

Depending on your budget, battery-charging solutions can run from micro to mini to maxi. The inexpensive solar chargers sold by Ready Made Resources work fine as a micro solution, but be advised that they are not waterproof. I recommend setting these up on a windowsill *inside* a south-facing window. In my experience, it is best to buy at least two of these chargers, since they charge slowly, via "trickle charging."

Moving up to the mini solution, there are 6.5-watt flexible (amorphous) photovoltaic (PV) panels. Even modest-size PV systems with a small deep-cycle battery bank can make a huge difference in providing small-scale lighting and battery charging for crucial security measures such as radios and night-vision equipment. There are so many LED lights, battery-charging trays, and various pieces of electronic gear available that will run directly from twelve VDC or from a DC-to-DC converter that you might be able to skip the expense of a full-up system with a large AC inverter.

If you have a bigger budget, Ready Made Resources and other vendors can also supply larger prepackaged PV power systems, either with or without an AC power inverter. (Without an inverter, PV systems will provide only twelve- or twenty-four-volt DC power.) Ready Made Resources even has experience designing maxi systems—six-kilowatt or larger.

Keep in mind that grid-tied PV systems will be eligible for a 30 percent federal tax credit in the United States. Many states also offer their own tax credits (dsireusa.org). In some states, such as Florida and California, the combined federal and state tax credits may reduce your expense by as much as 70 percent when all is said and done.

Photovoltaic Power Systems

There are essentially three types of photovoltaic power systems:

1. Stand-alone
2. Grid-tied
3. Grid-connected but stand-alone-capable

Of the three, the only type that I do *not* recommend is grid-tied. These systems—typically without a battery bank—leave you vulnerable whenever the power grid goes down. If you want to sell power back to your utility yet still be self-sufficient, then I recommend that you install a grid-connected but stand-alone-capable system. The same would apply to wind-power and micro-hydro systems. For details on alternate-energy-system hardware, siting/exposure, and system sizing, contact Ready Made Resources. They graciously offer alternate-energy-system consulting free of charge. They can design a true turnkey system for you that will require no upkeep other than periodic battery maintenance. You can also design a system that will allow you to sell power back to your utility depending on your local laws and power-company policies. There is nothing like the joy of watching a power meter run *backward*—knowing that for more than half of each year the power company will be *paying you* for power. Selling power back to the utility company is possible throughout the United States. However, most pay you only the "avoided cost" rate—typically two or three cents per kilowatt hour—rather than at the same rate that you buy it from them. The latter is called "net metering" or "net billing." The utilities that presently pay at the net metering rate are in the minority, but I predict that it will be legislatively mandated within a few years.

If you do opt for a grid-tied system, it can be set up to provide "automatic failover"—meaning that there will be a very limited interruption of power to your home or retreat in the event of a power failure.

All of the major brands of monocrystalline weatherproof photovoltaic panels are essentially comparable in terms of their rated output, service life, glazing strength (impact resistance), and ability to withstand the weather. Most have similar warranties, although some are slightly better. For these reasons, PV panels should be considered a commodity, and as such, the price per watt should be the main determining factor in picking a brand.

Batteries are another commodity, at least if you buy traditional lead-acid deep-cycle ("golf-cart" type) batteries. Because of their high shipping weight, I strongly recommend that you buy the batteries for your system from a local vendor, such as your regional Interstate Batteries dealer. Be sure to do some comparison pricing before you buy. If the dealer offers a "core" credit and you are buying an entirely new system, be advised that dealers are often not particular about what you provide them for your trade-in. They are essentially just looking for a source of lead plates for recycling. If their core-refund terms are based strictly on battery weight or the combined amp-hours capacity, one trick is to ask around locally at venues such as Craigslist for free used car, truck, and tractor batteries. Part-time mechanics often have a dozen or more such batteries available, free for the taking. Depending on the size of your system, if you have a strong back and aren't afraid to get your hands dirty, this can save you several hundred dollars.

Mobile Solar Power Systems

A portable photovoltaic system such as the one produced by Mobile Solar Power (mobilesolarpower.net) is ideal for either someone for whom mobility is key or someone who wants backup power but can't have solar panels visible on a day-to-day basis because they live in a community with strict covenants, conditions, and restrictions (CC&Rs). After TSHTF, your problem will not be your development's Homeowners Association—it will be chaining the system down to keep someone from stealing it!

Inverters

An inverter is an electronic device that converts DC power into AC power. Inverter technology varies considerably, depending on maker. The Trace brand inverters are now sold under the Xantrex Technology (xantrex.com) name, and they still control a large portion of the market. Their major competitor in the United States is OutBack Power Systems (outbackpower.com), an up-and-coming company that was started by a group of former Xantrex engineers. The OutBack brand holds a slight margin in inverter technology.

Charge-controller technology is still advancing, but all of the major brands are roughly comparable. Just be sure to get a controller that can handle your anticipated needs, even if you eventually add a few panels. Also keep in mind that more bells and whistles on a charge controller equals greater vulnerability to electromagnetic pulse (EMP). They are fairly inexpensive, so it is wise to keep a spare, stored in a faraday-cage enclosure, such as a steel ammo can.

Running a Laptop from a Jump Pack in a Short-Term Emergency

An inverter of proper size can run a laptop computer. A laptop can be powered by a jump pack with a twelve-VDC power port. The jump box can be recharged by a hand-crank twelve-VDC generator. In a short-term disaster, during which phone or wireless service is still up, this can allow you to stay connected for business and Internet access. In my experience, running a laptop (and/or charging a cell phone) from a twelve-VDC car adapter (DC-to-DC) plugged into your jump pack is far more efficient than using an AC inverter and then a DC power-cube transformer. That way you are just changing one DC voltage to another DC voltage— instead of a DC-to-AC-and-transformed-back-to-DC proposition, which is *very* inefficient.

To keep your jump pack charged, a hand-crank generator does, indeed, work—even one MacGyvered from an electric-drill motor. But I've found that is labor intensive and time consuming. I'm more a fan of photovoltaic power panels, such as the small panels available from Northern Tool and Equipment. Jump-pack variants are available with either 110 VAC (U.S./Canada) or 220 VAC (UK) utility power charging cords.

Natural Sources of Power

You should consider buying a retreat property with its own source of fuel: A natural gas well or a surface coal seam on the property would be fantastic (although of course quite rare), but at the very least consider buying land with a good stand of hardwood timber. To supplement your PV system, you might start shopping for a large yet easy-to-maintain steam engine with a power takeoff to run a generator and to handle other stationary-engine tasks. Another option is buying is a steep parcel of land with a fairly large creek running through it, for a penstock-fed Pelton-wheel micro-hydro generator. These are offered by several makers.

Wind-Power Generators

Because of their high maintenance and the risks associated with tower climbing, I generally don't recommend wind turbines. But if you live in a very windy area with lots of cloud cover, a wind generator might be a viable option.

Small wind generators are generally more trouble than they are worth. They tend to fail in high winds, usually in the dead of winter. If a wind generator's automatic prop-feathering mechanism or its tail-vane-flipping mechanism fail, a generator can run over speed during high wind gusts and tear itself apart. This happens with alarming frequency. Who wants to climb a tower and work with hand tools to swap brushes or other parts at a time like that? For the past twenty-five years, the cost per watt for PV panels has come down steadily, but meanwhile both the cost per watt and the reliability of wind generators have remained about the same. Also consider the safety factor: Raising or lowering any large wind generator from a tower is a tricky operation. In the present day, I would recommend hiring a crane company to do so. In the event of TEOTWAWKI, when no mechanized help would be available, you would have to do it yourself, and that could be a real risk. And of course there is the OPSEC factor if there are any public roads with line of sight to your property, which could be an issue if you are trying to lie low.

If you do decide to buy a wind generator, I recommend the Hornet series, from a company called Hydrogen Appliances (www.hydrogenappliances.com/Hornet1000.html). Essentially, the company took a standard wind generator and beefed it up. They just built everything another 20 to 50 percent thicker, wider, etc., than they had to. These generators are little beasts. For any maintenance issues that might come up (which is rare), the best bet is to install them on a tip-up tower. These can be lowered and raised if necessary.

Most alternative power systems use large deep-cycle batteries. Rather than using jumper-cable clamps for connecting your deep-cycle batteries, for safety it is best to attach heavy-gauge battery-cable and terminal lugs. Use a detachable high-amperage-rated twelve-VDC polarity-protected pigtail block connector, in parallel with your vehicle battery cables. That way you can quickly disconnect and still be able to drive your vehicle without a time-consuming cable-unbolting procedure. Ideally, your battery bank will be the heart of an alternative power system that will also—as your budget eventually allows—include some photovoltaic panels. (This online primer is a good starting point: snipurl.com/hrhfm.)

Having a generator that can provide you with power during a grid-down situation will be valuable albeit not as reliable in the long term as photovoltaics. I prefer propane or diesel-engine gensets, due to the longer storage life of their fuels. Low-RPM diesels last the longest, by far (roughly twenty thousand hours for a diesel versus only three thousand hours for a gas genset). Looking at things from a big-picture perspective, you pay a lot more for gas engines in the long run, because you'll be buying one every four or five years. In contrast, a diesel may last you twenty or more years. And, in fact, if you shop around, diesels don't cost any more than a gas genset with the same output. You might also consider getting one with an extra coaxial twelve- or twenty-four-VDC winding, so that you can charge a battery bank more efficiently. Plan ahead for the future, when you might have a PV power system.

The right size for a home backup generator is 4,500 watts continuous and 5,500 watts peak, unless you have both a refrigerator/freezer *and* a chest freezer. You can always alternate between the two, with a little cord shuffling. However, if you live in a typical suburban housing development, I'd recommend that you get a ten-kilowatt unit, if you can afford it. Why? Odds are that the next time you have a lengthy power failure there will be neighbors tapping on your door—with extension cords slung over their shoulders. Believe me, they will hear your generator running.

A genset that is over six or eight horsepower and on wheels tends to "walk" when operating, but you can overcome that either by strapping it down or by temporarily removing the wheels and bolting the frame to something solid. For a midsize genset at a fixed site, you might just skip getting a wheel kit if you have a strong back and a sturdy wheelbarrow.

Because of shipping costs, you are probably better off buying locally, unless you live in a state with high sales tax, as the savings on tax would offset the freight charges.

In my experience, recoil starters are generally the weak link with most low-priced midsize (eight to twelve horsepower) gensets. Be prepared to pay a bit more for one with an electric starter (and manual backup).

Be advised that diesel has a problem with fuel gelling at low temperature. Typically, this clogs fuel filters when the temperature reaches the so-called cold-filter plugging point (CFPP). Fuel gelling can be avoided at temperatures as low as forty degrees below zero, with a diesel-fuel additive called Diesel Fuel Supplement, made by the same company that makes a popular diesel antibacterial additive. This additive also reportedly prevents gelling in biodiesel blends up to B20, which is 20 percent biodiesel and 80 percent "dinodiesel" (diesel derived from petroleum, rather than plants). There is also a product made in Germany, called Diesel-Therm, that preheats diesel fuel before it enters the fuel filter.

Other than installations in arctic climates, where diesel-fuel gelling can be a problem, diesel gets my vote.

Low-RPM Diesel Generator Availability

Low-speed diesels such as the Lister and its listeroid clones are sadly no longer being imported to the United States. But listeroid engines do pop up on the secondary market here in the U.S. Watch for them vigilantly at Craigslist and in newspaper and "nickel" classified ads. Note that not all sellers will use the correct terms *Lister* or *listeroid* in their ad titles, so also do searches for "low-RPM diesel" and "one-cylinder diesel."

The tolerances and quality control seem to be better on the listeroids that are made in India. The Chinese engines, in contrast, were reverse-engineered, and some of the parts appear to be from the "file-to-fit" school of assembly.

Secure Your Generator

Anyone who has a portable (i.e., skid- or cart-mounted) generator that is not bolted down or locked in a generator shed with a sturdy door should consider securing it with a chain and padlock. You should preferably use a hardened bolt-cutter-resistant bike-and-motorcycle security chain and a large, stout padlock that is warded to offer little room for bolt cutters to be used. Short lengths of specially hardened chain are available from Nashbar.com. Longer chains are available from JCWhitney.com.

Backup Power for a Well Pump

One of the common questions that I get is how to configure a well pump to run from generator power. You will need to make a couple of inquiries: First, ask your well/pump man if your pump is 120 VAC or 220 VAC. If it is a 220-volt model, then you will need a special generator, or you will have to retrofit with a 120-VAC pump. Next, you will need to call several local electricians and get them to put in competitive bids for installing a proper bypass breaker panel and cabling it to your generator. I've seen people describe jerry-rigged male-to-male extension-cord generator hookups, but these do not meet electrical code and are potentially hazardous—for both you and the hapless power-company linemen attempting to restore power to your community.

Can You Burn Home-Heating Oil or Kerosene in a Diesel Engine?

Virtually all diesel generators will run equally well on off-road (dyed) diesel, road-taxed diesel, biodiesel (including waste vegetable oil and freshly pressed oils), and home-heating oil. In fact, up until the recent introduction of ultra-low sulfur diesel (ULSD) all three typically came from the same production runs at refineries. In essence, they are simply marketed differently.

Home-heating oil burns fine in any diesel engine, but in many countries it is not legal to do so in a vehicle that is driven on public roads. This is a "road-tax" issue. Aside from a red dye additive, the formulation of home-heating oil is almost identical to the diesel that was made before the recent advent of ULSD. The only significant difference between the two is the federal standard on ash content. In the United States, Canada, the UK, and several other countries it is not legal to use dyed (untaxed) fuel in a vehicle that is driven on public roads. Of course if you are using the fuel in a generator set or in an off-road vehicle such as a tractor, you can't be accused of cheating on the "road tax" levied on fuels for use in vehicles on public roads. (Fuels for use in stationary engines such as generators and irrigation water pumps, or for use in off-road vehicles, are exempt from this tax.) Enforcement of these statutes varies widely, but the fines can be *substantial*, so stay legal.

Kerosene is a different matter. This fuel has insufficient lubricity to be used just by itself in a diesel engine. I have also read that it burns hotter than diesel, so it might harm injectors. However, this is largely a nonissue in all but exceptional circumstances, since kerosene typically sells for as much as one dollar more per gallon than diesel. But in an emergency, it is presumably safe to mix as much as 20 percent kerosene with your diesel and not cause excessive engine wear. The aforementioned road tax is also an issue for kerosene.

It is even possible to burn a mixture containing used crankcase oil in your diesel engines, but keep in mind that used crankcase oil has been documented to be carcinogenic, because it contains polycyclic aromatic hydrocarbons (PAH). So use great care not to let any of it touch your skin when transporting, handling, filtering, and dispensing it.

Start Buying Diesel or Flex Fuel Vehicles Now

What will transportation be like in an era when gasoline is very scarce and precious and when ethanol and biodiesel are sporadically available but nearly as expensive as gas? To prevent yourself from being stranded, make sure every vehicle that you purchase from now runs on either diesel or a fuel blend that is an 85 percent ethanol and 15 percent gasoline "flex-fuel" variant. The latter are capable of running on 85 percent ethanol. It takes a bit of extra looking to find them, but someday you will be glad that you did. Enter "flex fuel" or "E85" as search variables. Here at the Rawles Ranch, our primary "goin' into town" rig is an E85 fleet variant of the 2003 Ford Explorer 4WD. And when our little thirty-two-mpg run-about finally dies, it will be replaced by a flex-fuel compact of some sort. For maximum versatility, at least one vehicle at your retreat should be a diesel—perhaps your next crew-cab 4WD pickup, your next tractor, or your next quad ATV. See Chapter 12 for more vehicle details.

Compact Solar-Powered Refrigerators for Insulin

In most climates outside of the permafrost zone, a refrigerator is a must for insulin storage. The simplest solution is to buy a large propane tank and a propane-powered refrigerator. If you'd rather opt for photovoltaics, then I recommend the Engel brand twelve-VDC refrigerators sold by Safecastle. A modest-size photovoltaic power system, such as the 520-watt, four-panel packaged "cabin" system produced by Ready Made Resources, would provide plenty of power to run a compact Engel DC refrigerator plus a flashlight-battery-charging tray and a couple of small lights.

Lighting

It is important to think through your family's lighting requirements for an extended period without grid power. What chores will you need to accomplish? How many family members (and others) will be staying with you? Will they be old enough to safely use candles and lanterns? How many batteries will you need to keep charged? Will you need to use night-vision gear? How will you handle blackout conditions?

Candles and Lanterns

The low-tech solution to lighting is to use candles or kerosene lanterns. You will of course need to take the usual safety precautions, especially with liquid fuels. When buying candles, be sure to stock up on ones that are specifically designed for long burning. These use a special paraffin formulation that is high in stearic acid. They are sold via mail order by companies such as Nitro-Pak. You can also often find inexpensive long-burning candles at discount stores: Catholic devotional candles in tall glass jars. Soak the jars in water for an hour and the paper labels will slip off easily.

If you buy a kerosene lantern, store plenty of clean-burning grade K-1 ("water clear") kerosene. Avoid commercial lamp oil (aka liquid paraffin), since it is grossly overpriced. You will of course need plenty of extra wick of the correct width, and a few spare glass chimneys. A good rule of thumb: The younger your children, the more spare chimneys you will need.

Burning Alcohol in Kerosene Lamps and Engines?

I've been asked about the possibility of burning fuels other than standard lamp oil or kerosene in lanterns and burning alcohol in gas or diesel engines. Given the flash point of alcohol, I see no reason why it could not be substituted for kerosene in a wick-type kerosene lantern. I suspect that due to the fear of lawsuits Dietz and the other wick-lantern makers disallow the use of anything except kerosene or lamp oil. For liability reasons, manufacturers make these strong disclaimers in anticipation that someone without common sense might inadvertently fill a lantern with gasoline, which could of course have tragic consequences. However, because of the disparities between alcohol and kerosene, alcohol should not be used in a mantle-type kerosene lantern, such as an Aladdin. Alcohol cannot be expected to "generate" and cause the mantle to properly incandesce.

In regard to engines, converting an engine to run on alcohol is not a simple task. One difficultly is converting the fuel tank, lines, and filter assemblies. In most cases, stainless steel must be used for the fuel tank, and any rubber fuel lines must be replaced. I recommend sticking with diesel engines.

Flashlights and Battery-Powered Lamps

The advent of white light emitting diodes (LEDs) in the 1990s revolutionized flashlight technology. Up until a couple of years ago, I would not have recommended buying an electric camping lantern, since they were such battery hogs. But now, a new generation of white LED lanterns use remarkably little current, allowing batteries to last a surprisingly long time. For example, a Tuff Brite rechargeable LED lantern can operate for up to seventy hours on one charge. These are available from Northern Tool and Equipment and several other Internet vendors.

7

GARDENS AND LIVESTOCK

While your larder will help you to get through the tough times, there is no substitute for fresh food and meat raised on your own land. This will be a large investment of time, money, and other resources, but it will pay off when you are able to pair a fresh salad, eggs, and a glass of milk with your cornmeal made from stored grain. This chapter will address basic techniques for starting a garden and raising livestock. My wife is the real expert here, so I've relied heavily upon her for the advice on these pages.

Gardening

Sizing a New Garden

As a scant minimum, I'd recommend a twenty-five-foot-by-thirty-foot garden plot for a family of four. By using French Intensive (double-dug; snipurl.com/hrmgo) or biointensive Square Foot Gardening (snipurl.com/hrn4c) techniques, you can get a huge yield out of a small garden space, but if you have the acreage available and can afford the extra fencing material, then by all means make your fenced garden plot two or three times that size. This has several advantages. First, you will have room to maneuver a tractor. Using a tractor disk will save you a tremendous amount of labor, especially the first year that you develop the garden soil. Second, the additional garden space can be used to grow extra crops for barter and charity. You never know how many relatives will show up on your doorstep on TEOTWAWKI+1.

Even if you don't have the time or the inclination to build and fence now, at least buy the materials for fencing a big garden in the future—when such supplies may be difficult to obtain.

Small-Scale Grain Growing, Harvesting, and Processing

You will want to grow seasonal vegetables in your garden to keep your diet varied and delicious. Some of the hardiest, most nutritious, and easiest to grow are radishes, carrots, turnips, tomatoes, potatoes, green beans, summer squash, and Swiss chard. For detailed advice on how to grow these, I recommend the book *Gardening When It Counts: Growing Food in Hard Times,* by Steve Solomon. Since what you will grow will vary greatly by region and according to personal taste, we will focus on how to grow the most important part of your harvest: grain.

SurvivalBlog reader Adam in Ohio provided a link to Cornell University's Core Historical Literature of Agriculture (chla .library.cornell.edu), which includes thousands of antique farm references that could prove very useful. Keep in mind, however, that nineteenth-century safety standards were considerably more relaxed than today's, so old formularies and farm-knowledge books often do not include any safety warnings. Use common sense around chemicals, flammables, unwarded gears and cutting blades, heavy objects, and so forth. Stay safe.

The book *Small-Scale Grain Raising,* by Gene Logsdon, is an invaluable reference that every prepared family should have on their bookshelf. Used copies can often be found at bargain prices on eBay or Amazon.

When growing grain, you need non-hybrid (heirloom) varieties of seed stock, so that the seed you save from each harvest will breed true and continue to produce year after year. Hybrid varieties won't. Heirloom seed is available from the Seed Savers Exchange, Seed for Security, Everlasting Seeds, and Ready Made Resources. Bulk quantities of grain seed should be stored in the proverbial cool, dark, dry place. They must be kept very, very dry to prevent mold or unintended sprouting. They must also be kept in sturdy, vermin-proof containers. Think steel, not plastic.

One of our preferred grains for growing on small acreage is barley. As a general rule, you should plant winter barley in regions where winter wheat is grown, and spring barley where spring wheat is grown. If you live in deer country, you will probably find their depredations on your grain fields unacceptable, so you will need to erect some substantial fences. If you can't afford to install tall fences around your grain fields, one alternative is to plant bearded varieties of barley. Deer generally won't eat the awns of bearded barley.

If you have any ground that is swampy from spring to fall on your property, consider planting domesticated wild rice in those areas. Technically, wild rice isn't really rice at all, since it is in the grass genus (*Zizania*) rather than the rice genus (*Oryza*). As with other grain growing, planting wild rice will attract waterfowl and other birds, which can be a mixed blessing. So consider a shotgun and beaucoup shotgun shells to be part of your assortment grain-growing essential tools.

TOOLS AND EQUIPMENT

Raising grain takes not only seed stock but also the proper tools and equipment. Buy the best quality equipment that you can find. Concentrate on nineteenth-century technology. This is low-tech and easy to maintain. It is amazing what you can find on eBay if you check the site consistently. Unfortunately, however, some practical items such as scythes and hand mills are now sold as "decorator" antiques. Yuppies and retirees who merely want to adorn their homes have driven up prices—but keep searching, since these tools are worth owning.

PLANTING

A seed broadcaster is a must. Get an adjustable hand-crank seed broadcaster that you can strap around your waist. For really big fields, you might need a wheeled (push) row seeder. Even on a small scale, a one-wheel "dial-a-seed" planter is a huge labor-saver. These are all available through Lehmans.com. On a large scale, horse-drawn or tractor-pulled equipment is called for. (That goes beyond the scope of what I'm writing here, but it is described fairly well in Logsdon's book.) When to plant varies depending on the last frost-free day in your region. Look at standard references for planting depths, frequency, and crop rotation.

HARVESTING AND PROCESSING

For corn, you will need a couple of corn knives and some husking pegs (to strap to your palm). For wheat and other small grains, you will need at least a hand scythe for reaping, but for any decent scale of production, you will need a large, cradle-type scythe. There are plans for building a small grain-threshing machine in Logsdon's book. In a pinch, you can thresh grain by hand on a large, clean, concrete barn floor.

There are a variety of hand-cranked machines made specifically for hulling ("pearling") rice and barley, pressing oil, and shelling corn, peas, and so forth. If you grow sorghum or cane sugar, you will need yet another type of hand-crank press. Finding these machines may take some searching, because small hand-cranked machines are now essentially obsolete outside of the Third World, but they are eminently practical for folks like us, who are preparing for TEOTWAWKI. Used machines that are still in good working order can sometimes be found on the Internet, but if you don't mind paying a premium price for brand-new machines, I recommend Lehmans.com. See Chapter 5 for more details on mills.

STORAGE

Whether for human consumption or for livestock feed, your harvested grain will need to be properly stored for protection from spoilage and vermin. If the moisture content is low enough to prevent mold, then plain galvanized trash barrels (bought brand-new) will suffice for small-scale grain storage. On a larger scale, a prefabricated storage shed, such as those made by Butler, is ideal. Corn still on the cob should be stored in a traditional slatted wooden corn crib or a well-ventilated Butler building. See Chapter 5 for more details on how to store grain.

HANDLING

Buy a large, aluminum-scoop grain shovel—the lighter, the better, so that it will be less tiring to use. For moving corn that is still on ears, you will want to have a corn drag (a rake with just three or four very long tines).

"BERRY" SOAKING

Whole-grain wheat can be soaked for twenty-four hours to make wheat berries. This makes a quite palatable and nutritious breakfast food when warmed and served with milk or cream and a dash of honey or molasses.

SPROUTING

To get the maximum nutrition from the grain that you raise, you should plan to sprout the majority of it. Lay in supplies and practice the art of sprouting *before* the balloon goes up!

PRACTICE, PRACTICE, PRACTICE!

As with any other newly acquired skill, grain raising, harvesting, storage, milling, and sprouting will take practice. Develop your expertise now, when any mistakes will be merely humorous blunders rather than potentially life-threatening disasters.

Hand Tools

In recent years, the U.S. consumer market has been flooded with low-quality, flimsy products. Sadly, this includes hand tools. These have become so ubiquitous that you have to search actively for quality gardening tools. The few American-made tools still available have had significant price increases, attributable to the recent spike in steel prices and substantially increased shipping costs.

I have found that it is now better to shop for used, American-made hand tools. Ironically, many tools being sold as "antiques" are more sturdy and a have longer potential service life than the "factory-new" tools that originate in China. For used tools, watch Craigslist and even eBay. If you can't find a particular *used* tool, then one of the best mail-order sources for new American, Canadian, and European tools is Lehman's.

Proper sharpening, oiling, and storage are crucial for giving your tools multigenerational longevity. This is particularly important in damp climates. Keep tools well oiled. Depending on your climate, you might need tool chests with tight-fitting lids and plenty of silica gel. If you have any tools that are rusty, evaluate their condition. Minor rust can be removed with a wire wheel. But if any tools are badly rusted, consider either paying to get them bead blasted or replacing them completely if need be. Why? Because leaving one rusty tool in contact with your other tools that are in good condition will encourage "sympathetic" rusting and eventually ruin many more. Bead blasting is potentially a good part-time home business, if you have a side yard available to dedicate to it. (It is a bit messy.) You could even carry on this business post-Schumer if you have a generator and/or a large alternative power system.

Varmints in the Garden

Garden pests are typically just a nuisance in good times, but post-TEOTWAWKI they can mean the difference between eating well and starvation. There is no single magic bullet that will eliminate all garden pests. Be prepared to take several approaches simultaneously:

- A sturdy fence that is tall enough to protect against deer and with a fine-mesh lower section that is tight enough to repel rabbits and ground squirrels
- A couple of cats who have been trained by their parents as effective mousers. Good mousers are usually also death on gophers. Or how about terrier dogs? Before the advent of modern poisons, small dogs were used to dispatch mice, moles, and gophers.
- Plenty of traps, including buried mole/gopher traps, as well as surface mouse and rat traps (victorpest.com)
- Lots of .22 rimfire ammo and patience. More than just protection from birds and squirrels, a scoped .22 can also be used to nail tunneling gophers when they come up to push out dirt. If you live inside city limits, you will also want a high-powered air rifle.
- Natural pest killers, such as ladybugs (for aphids), lacewings, and praying mantises. These are available seasonally from Buglogical Control Systems (buglogical.com) and Home Harvest (snipurl.com/hrm2a).
- Depending on your personal beliefs, pesticides to control insects. Unfortunately, these will also kill beneficial insects.
- To repel birds, get a couple of big plastic owls to perch on your fence posts, lots of reflective (Mylar) strips (cut up used Mylar party balloons), and throwaway compact disks

(strung on monofilament fishing line and positioned so that they will spin in the wind). Anti-bird netting is also available from the larger mail-order gardening suppliers.

- As a last resort for large numbers of moles or pocket gophers, you can use a probe-bait strychnine dispenser (such as an RCO probe), along with a large supply of RCO Omega bait (snipurl.com/hrm2t) or Gopher Getter bait (snipurl.com/hrm3b). (Typically, this is strychnine .5 percent.) In some states, such as California, these supplies are difficult to obtain locally unless you are a commercial grower, so consult your state, county, and local ordinances before mail-ordering this bait. Beware that this poison could lead to the untimely demise of your pets if they actually eat their prey, because they will also indirectly ingest the poison. There is a trick to using these dispensers: As you insert the probe, when you feel a sudden lack of soil resistance, that means you have penetrated a "runway" tunnel. That is when you press the trigger to dispense the grain bait. You will have a valuable post-TEOTWAWKI barterable skill if you have the ability (and supplies) to poison moles and gophers.

Growing Indoors

DWARF FRUIT TREES

You can grow dwarf fruit trees indoors, but it can be labor intensive, as each flower must be hand-pollinated (unless you have a house full of bees, butterflies, and/or flies). That means for each piece of fruit that you hope to produce, you must transfer pollen from one flower to another. Fruit will not develop unless the male pollen enters the female ovum. This can be done with the tip of a feather. If you have room for only one tree, be sure it is self-pollinating, which means that your tree will bear both male and female flowers. In nature trees are not self-pollinating, and you would need two trees of each variety you planned to grow. The crop-yield-versus-labor ratio is fairly small for most dwarf varieties. They seem susceptible to insect and fungus infestations. Also, dwarf varieties are grafted onto rootstock, not propagated from seeds, so you cannot grow new dwarf trees from the seeds. You can grow dwarf trees in a greenhouse in a big pot (such as a wine half-barrel, or possibly a bit larger). When the danger of frost has passed, you can place the pot on a low four-wheeled furniture dolly and wheel the trees outside, and then bring them back into the greenhouse in early fall. Lemons would be a treat in long-term TEOTWAWKI, when they would no longer be available at the grocery. My great-grandma said that lemonade was a much-anticipated, once-a-year, Fourth of July treat when she homesteaded in North Dakota. And an orange for Christmas was considered a special splurge. Who knows? Perhaps someday oranges and lemons will be a fantastic barter item.

SPROUTING

Sprouting is a great way to provide essential vitamins. Ounce for ounce, sprouting seeds are the most nutritious and space- and weight-efficient form of storage food. Sprouting seeds and sprouting kits (with trays) are available from a variety of Internet vendors, such as Ready Made Resources, Nitro-Pak, and Lehman's, but anyone can produce fresh, healthy, and extremely nutritious sprouts on a kitchen counter with nothing more than a couple of plastic ice-cream containers. (Although containers with screen tops are handier for frequent rinsing.) They can provide a real respite from canned veggies while you're waiting for the crops to mature, as well as year-round fresh greens. Some great sprouting options are: mung beans, lentils, various peas and beans, radish, alfalfa, and clover. You can also make a respectable salad in your kitchen with a tray of mesclun seeds grown to a few inches high. You can get a lot of information and supplies from Sproutpeople (sproutpeople.com) or you can just buy regular seeds and beans from the supermarket or seed-supply store.

Because they are full of vitamin B_{12}, other B vitamins, and vitamins A, K, and C, as well as minerals, amino acids, and other nutrients essential to human health, sprouts should be an important component of your survival diet. Dried seeds, grains, and legumes are rich in protein and complex carbohydrates, but during the simple sprouting process, their vitamin and nutrient content ramps up significantly. As an added bonus, they are also much easier to digest—and tastier—than in their pre-sprouted state.

For successful sprouting you need only seeds and a mason jar with a mesh lid or, alternatively, a cheesecloth kept in place by a rubber band. Most health-food stores will carry seeds for sprouting and precut stainless steel or plastic tops. If you use a cloth, make sure that it doesn't become entirely wet, or it will stop air and moisture from nourishing your seeds.

After removing broken or damaged seeds (they can rot during sprouting), soak the rest (about four tablespoons per quart-size container) for six to eight hours. Rinse well before placing the seeds in the jar. Lean the jar at an angle, top down, so that water can drain out. Continue rinsing the seeds delicately in the morning and the evening. The key is to keep them moist but not totally immersed in water. No light is required for the first few days, but can be introduced later. Sprouting times vary, but you should have edible sprouts in three to five days. They can be eaten, raw or cooked, after soaking and rinsing. They are a great source of energy and fuel, and with multiple jars sprouting at different stages, you can have an endless supply.

Some beans, such as kidney, can be toxic when sprouted, so make sure to do your research and check with your supplier before sprouting.

Livestock

Dual- and Triple-Purpose Livestock

In this day and age of specialization, modern livestock have been selectively bred to be superefficient for one purpose. For example, merino sheep are bred to produce wool in abundance, and Suffolk sheep are bred to grow to market weight quickly (for meat). Many breeds of chickens no longer will sit on their eggs. They have been selectively bred to produce eggs and nothing more! They have lost their instinctive broodiness. Most of our modern farm livestock fall into this specialization category, and in the process they have lost some of their other valuable traits such as mothering ability, ability to forage, and disease and parasite resistance. Thus, these modern breeds are not suitable for survival purposes. In TEOTWAWKI we will need breeds that can survive without the vet, pharmacy, and feed store.

The survivalist would be best served by "heirloom" livestock breeds that are considered to be dual purpose. Most of the dual-purpose breeds are raised on small family farms. They are fairly rare. Dual-purpose sheep are known for producing lamb with high-quality carcasses as well as high-quality fleece. (Though usually the fleece has specialty qualities that make it much more valuable to the hand-spinner niche market than to commercial producers.) Dual-purpose cattle are those that are good milkers and excellent mothers, and their calves grow rapidly. Do a Web search of "dual-purpose sheep" or "dual-purpose cattle" to see the wide variety of animals available. An excellent Web site to learn about endangered dual-purpose breeds is the American Livestock Breeds Conservancy (albc-usa.org).

Survivalists would be best served to select heritage breeds that match the climate and terrain of their retreat. The Rawles Ranch is well watered and most of the pastures can be downright swampy. The American mustang, although an extremely hardy and disease-resistant breed of horse, is not suitable for our soggy soil. The mustang developed in the southwest and is much more suitable for survivalists in drier areas. A better breed for us is the horse breed developed in the wet Welsh mountains, such as the Welsh cob. Likewise our sheep breed needs to be suited to wetter pastures. The Navajo churro won't do, but the Welsh mountain sheep do fine here.

The survivalist might also consider triple-purpose breeds. These are breeds that produce meat, milk, and fiber. They may also be used for transportation. Nomadic tribes have built their culture around certain of these animals. Some of the more unusual are the reindeer, the camel, and the yak. The reindeer, though it does not produce fiber, is used for milk, meat, transportation, and hides. The camel not only provides transportation, milk, meat, and hides, but it also grows a wooly coat each winter, which it sheds. The fiber can then readily be felted. Or the itchy guard hairs can be removed to produce a luxurious yarn. Of the aforementioned animals, the Tibetan yak is the easiest to acquire and the easiest to handle and fence. They can be raised exactly as cattle are, with the added benefit of producing milk extremely high in butterfat, calves with low-fat carcasses, and incredibly soft under-down that sheds every spring.

A triple-purpose breed of horse is the "Bashkir," or Bashkirshy, of the Volga and the Ural mountains. They have been known to produce three to six gallons of milk a day. Some of the Bashkir have a curly coat, which can grow four to six inches long. It is shed each spring and can be spun, woven, or felted. (American Bashkir Curly breed, though it took the name Bashkir, seems to be an unrelated breed, from a distinct coat mutation. American Bashkir Curly breed does have a curly coat, but not the milk production.)

Icelandic sheep are the quintessential triple-purpose breed. They are valued in Iceland for their milk production, their fiber, and their ability to raise twins lambs to market weight in four to five months on grass alone.

Because of prolonged drought in some parts of the United States causing high hay costs, livestock prices are at an all-time low in certain parts of the country. If you can afford the hay, now might be the time to purchase livestock. Heirloom varieties are normally extremely expensive, and the best breeders will still be holding out for top dollar and butchering, rather than lowering their prices. But many small hobby farmers love their heirloom livestock like pets. They tend to keep far too many lambs/calves each year because they are all so cute. These hobby farmers would rather sell their animals to you way under value than send them to market. If you are not prepared to purchase animals now, keep in mind for next year that fall is always a good time for buyers to get lower prices.

Survivalists who love animals, like I do, and marvel at mankind's ability to selectively breed so many varieties, will enjoy visiting the Oklahoma State University animal breeds Web page (snipurl.com/hrm3r).

Buyer Beware When Purchasing Livestock

While most of my livestock purchases over the years have been satisfactory, buying livestock can be full of pitfalls. I will share some of my mistakes in hopes you can learn from them. Livestock sellers may not outright lie to buyers but they often do not volunteer important information, so it is very important that you get a detailed book for each type of livestock you plan to purchase, and do some research, so you'll know exactly what questions to ask. Make certain the book has a chapter about choosing healthy stock. It ought to give you signs of unhealthy or poorly conforming animals as well as questions to ask the sellers about the health of the animals. Some books that I recommend are: *Small-Scale Pig Raising,* by Dirk Van Loon, *Raising Rabbits the Modern Way,* by Bob Bennett, *Raising Sheep the Modern Way,* by Paula Simmons, *Ducks & Geese in Your Backyard: A Beginner's Guide,* by Rick and Gail Luttmann, *The Family Cow,* by Dirk Van Loon, and *Raising a Calf for Beef,* by Phyllis Hobson.

The first time I bought sheep, I did not know to ask if the yearling lambs I was buying had been wormed. Unfortunately the five lambs I bought had not been. Because of the parasite load they were carrying, they were not able to withstand the stress of the transport, feed change, and new environment. They quickly developed pneumonia, and despite all I did to try to keep them alive, two out of the five died, and the seller would not refund any of my money.

I paid a premium price for the first dairy cow I bought because supposedly she was due to calve in less than two months. I did not ask the seller to have a veterinarian certify she was bred. She never calved and the seller would not refund the extra that I paid for a "due-to-calve" cow. We drank store-bought milk for an extra year because of this mistake.

Then there was the pair of Angora rabbits I purchased. I assumed wrongly that buying a "breeding pair" meant they would breed. I did not think to ask the breeder to demonstrate that the male had all his necessary parts. He didn't. Again, no refund.

Temperament is another important component of purchasing livestock. Animals with bad temperaments can be difficult to work with, or downright dangerous. Don't take the seller's word for the temperament of the animals; insist on seeing a demonstration. Even better, arrive early, to see the animals before the seller has a chance to get the animal "ready."

I told the seller of my second cow that I intended to show her at the fair as well as milk her. He kept expressing on the phone to me how wonderful that would be. I neglected to ask for a demonstration of her being haltered, led, or milked. He neglected to tell me she was more feral than the March Hare. The only time I was able to milk her was when she was immobilized in a squeeze chute.

As you can see, it's important to do your homework. Find out all the questions you should ask, what parts you should inspect, and what to look out for. Insist on seeing the animals handled, haltered, led, ridden, and milked, as applicable. If the seller is able to manage the animals only with well-trained stock dogs, then how are *you* going to manage them? Do not let the seller's position as president of the breed association cause you to believe he or she would not mislead you or omit information in order to make a sale. Sadly, I have found this out the hard way; "Buyer beware" should be your watch words as you purchase livestock.

The Importance of Fat

As discussed in Chapter 5, one commonly overlooked component of a survival diet is the importance of consuming fat for nutritional and digestive balance. Raising livestock is a great way to provide not only protein but also fats for your diet. Hunting game as a source of fats isn't much of an option unless you live in bear, beaver, wild pig, or emu country. Most other wild game lacks sufficient fat. Rabbit meat is particularly low in fat.

Venison by itself has quite a low fat content. Here are some of the best livestock for fats:

PIGS

A few home-raised pigs will provide your family with both meat and a source of fat. In fact, you will probably have so much that you'll have extra available for charity or barter.

EMUS

For those readers who avoid pork, I'd recommend raising sheep or emus. Emu oil is amazing stuff. Anyone who has ever butchered an emu can tell you that there is a tremendous amount of oil stored in an adult bird.

FISH

Fish raised in ponds are another possibility. Anyone thinking of taking up aquaculture should consider raising at least one particularly oily species, such as shad, just as a source of fish oil.

COWS

If you have the room to keep one or more cow, you will have a huge source of butterfat (again, so much that you'll have extra available for charity or barter).

GOATS

If cattle are too large for you to handle, or if you live in an area with CC&Rs that restrict them, then you might be able to raise dairy goats. They are quite easy to handle (but sometimes a challenge to fence), and they do a great job of clearing brush. While goat meat itself doesn't have a lot of fat, it is possible, though difficult, to make butter from most goat milk. American Nubians have some of the highest-butterfat milk of all the goat breeds. Even so, the milk must be run through a separator before you can make butter.

CHICKENS

Egg yolks are another important source of fat.

Waste Not, Want Not

Survivalists need to seriously rethink the way they process the wild game they harvest. Odds are that you currently throw away fat, kidneys, tongues, and intestines. Some hunters even discard hearts and livers. Wasting valuable sources of fat would be foolish in a survival situation.

American Indians were famous for hoarding fat. Bear grease and fat from beaver tails were both particularly sought after. They have multiple uses, including lubrication and medicinal, and are even used as a source of fuel for lighting.

One important proviso about bears for anyone living up in polar-bear country: Avoid eating more than a quarter of an ounce of polar-bear liver per month. Because of the bear's diet out on the ocean-pack ice, like many other polar-region predators their livers contain so much concentrated vitamins A and D that it causes vitamin poisoning when eaten. A quarter of a pound of polar-bear liver contains about 2,250,000 IUs of vitamin A. That is roughly 450 times the recommended daily dose for an adult weighing 175 pounds. From what I have read, this is thankfully *not* an issue with bears in lower latitudes.

Versatile Pasture Fencing

Just as it's important to keep vermin out of your garden, it's crucial to keep livestock on your property. You'll need good, solid fencing. My favorite type of versatile livestock fencing is forty-seven-inch-tall variable-mesh woven field fencing, tensioned on six-foot heavy-duty studded T-posts that are spaced ten to twelve feet apart. This will give you a fence that will hold sheep, most breeds of goats, most cattle, llamas, alpacas, donkeys, horses, mules, and more.

Tensioning a woven-wire fence can best be accomplished with a forty-eight-inch "toothed" bar to hold the wire. These can be bought factory made or custom-fabricated in your home welding shop. But for those without welding equipment, here is a simple expedient that can be made with wood, carriage bolts, and chain: Cut a pair of two-by-fours fifty-two inches long, and install a row of protruding screws down the length of one of the wide sides. Drill a row of shallow holes in the other board, to accept the screw heads from the first board. (Like the teeth on a commercially made bar, these screws will *evenly distribute* the stress on the full height of the woven wire.) Drill through holes and position six-inch-long, three-eighths-inch carriage bolts through both boards at both ends. Sandwich the woven wire between the two boards. Attach chains to the carriage bolts, and then connect the chains to a "come-along." If no large trees are available as an anchor for the tensioning, then the towing-hitch receiver on a parked large pickup truck will suffice. **Proviso:** All of the usual safety rules when working with come-alongs apply!

In my experience, used, creosote-soaked railroad ties work fine for H-braces, anchor braces, and corner braces. To tension the diagonal wires for the H-braces, I prefer to use ratchet tensioners, rather than the traditional "twisting-stick" windlass arrangement. Be sure to wear gloves to avoid skin contact with the creosote, which is toxic.

When you're building a fence in rocky soil, a seven-foot-long, plain digging bar with hardened tips will be indispensable. If you get into an extremely rocky portion of ground along the intended fence line, you can construct aboveground "rock boxes"—the type that you might have seen in Eastern Oregon. These are cylinders of woven wire between thirty and forty inches in diameter and four feet tall that you will fill with rocks anywhere from fist-size to bowling-ball-size. Because the fence will have to be tensioned, make sure the side of the rock box that will contact the main fence wire has no rock tips projecting through the wire mesh that might hang up the main fence wire as it slides by during tensioning.

Horses, in particular, tend to be hard on woven-wire fences. Especially in small pastures, they'll often lean their necks over them, reaching for grass on the other side. You can add a "hot" wire at the top of the fence that is energized with a DC charger, such as those made by Parmak (parmakusa.com)—which is what we use here at the Rawles Ranch. In anticipation of grid-down situations, a solar-powered fence charger is best.

I do like steel-tube gates. If you strap on (or weld/braze on) some woven wire or a hog panel, the gate will become "sheep tight."

For the best security, you should mount the hinge pins with at least one pointing upward and one pointing downward. Otherwise, an intruder can simply lift a locked gate off of its hinge pins. You can also tack-weld the nuts onto both the bolt threads and the gate's hinge-sleeve assemblies to prevent them from being disassembled.

8

MEDICAL SUPPLIES AND TRAINING

Medical training and extensive medical supplies are de rigueur for prepared families.

This chapter is to help keep you alive and healthy by reviewing some common medical preparations and practices. Because the chapter will include many topics that go beyond my own expertise, I will rely heavily on articles that have been submitted to SurvivalBlog by medical professionals. Please keep in mind that this advice is in no way meant as a substitute for professional care. You should always check with a medical professional whenever possible in a crisis—and it would be wise to consult one for your personal preparedness plan as well.

Get Training

Regardless of whether your group includes a medical professional, I recommend that all adult group members get as much medical training as time allows. Start out by taking the Red Cross basic and advanced courses and their CPR course. I also recommend that at least one group member get EMT training. This is best accomplished by volunteering with your local emergency medical service. These are usually paid positions, which offsets the training expenses. Then take the field-medic course offered by Medical Corps. Several SurvivalBlog readers have taken this course, and they have all commented about how impressed they are with their training. This modestly priced training, led by an emergency-room doctor with thirty-five years of experience, will teach you many things that the Red Cross doesn't. For example, their classes place an emphasis on treating gunshot wounds.

Fitness and Body Weight

The best medicine is prevention, so what every well-prepared individual should do is stay in shape. Good muscle tone prevents back injuries and other muscle strains, and leaves you ready for the rigors of an independent, self-sufficient lifestyle. There surely will be plenty of nineteenth-century muscle work involved after TEOTWAWKI. Maintaining a healthy diet and an appropriate body weight is also very important. It will leave you ready for physical challenges, and it falls into the prepper's "one less stress to worry about" mind-set.

The rigors of a post-collapse world may be too much for some folks, unless they demonstrate the determination to control their weight and get plenty of exercise. For those of you who are overweight and out of shape, start making some changes today. Eliminate junk food from your diet. Eat healthy, catabolic snacks. If you are stuck behind a desk at your job, then at least get out on your lunch hour for a walk. Make that walk part of your routine. Park your car at the far end of the company parking lot. Use the stairs instead of escalators and elevators. Join a fitness club. Buy smaller dinner plates. It is little things like these, collectively, that will gradually make you trim and fit. It just takes some discipline.

Get fit—this includes strength, cardio, and flexibility. Of particular importance will be your hand and forearm strength (hauling five-gallon buckets is no easy task), lower-back strength, and a good, strong heart.

The Prepared Family's Medical Kit: What Do We Really Need?

Not only should you have an elaborate first-aid kit; you will also need additional supplies "in depth," at least for those items that have a lengthy shelf life. Things like gauze, sutures, most bandages, and splints have a shelf life that can be measured in decades. While some items contain adhesives that will eventually dry out, you can make up for this by purchasing several fresh rolls of bandage tape once every two or three years. You also need to plan ahead for such mundane items as drinking straws, hot-water bottles, bedpans, and baby wipes. I also recommend looking for an older-style used adjustable hand-crank hospital bed.

You will want to assemble a medical kit for your retreat. The following article was kindly provided by EMT J.N.:

The Kit, Part I

What we're most interested in is being able to carry out a few basic interventions that can treat the small problems and buy us time to get to a real doctor for the big ones.

The basic things needed for a person to live are the ABCs: **Airway, Breathing, and Circulation.**

Any major interruption to the aforementioned and you're basically done for without immediate intervention. There are also other common problems that can threaten your survival: shock, hypothermia, dehydration, fever, infection, and major injury. And there are a number of minor problems that can become major ones if we ignore them. A sprained ankle may keep you from being able to evacuate. A minor cut can lead to sepsis when you're in a dirty environment. Diarrhea is annoying, but it can kill you if it goes on for longer than a couple of days.

For the kit to be worthwhile, every item should be able to help you solve these problems and preferably have multiple uses. After substantial research, the kit listed below was settled on as a good compromise in terms of usefulness and cost. The supplies are grouped by category.

Personal Protection
  (1) 2 oz bottle hand sanitizer
  (4) Pairs exam gloves
  (1) CPR (cardiopulmonary resuscitation) shield

Instruments
  (1) Pair splinter forceps
  (1) Pair EMT shears
  (2) Disposable thermometers
  (1) Razor blade

Bandaging
(20) 1-inch Band-Aids, cloth

(2) Rolls 4.5-inch Kling gauze

(1) Small roll medical tape

(4) Gauze bandages, 4 inches square

(1) Triangular bandage

(1) ACE elastic bandage, 3 inches

(10) Steri-Strips, ¼ inch by 1½ inches

(2) Tincture-of-benzoin swabs

(2) Instant cold packs

Medications
(6) Packets triple-antibiotic ointment

(20) Benadryl tablets

(20) Ibuprofen tablets

(18) Imodium tablets

(15) Aspirin

Other
(4) Plastic vials

(1) Bag, 1-gallon Ziploc freezer-type

Here is a brief explanation of each group of items and what they might one day do for you.

PERSONAL PROTECTION

These items are there to help keep you, the rescuer, from getting a disease from someone you are trying to help.

Hand sanitizer is always useful. Ask any nurse about the importance of washing up. The alcohol-based gel is not as good, but it's the best you can get when the hot, soapy stuff is unavailable.

Gloves are a good precaution whenever bodily fluids (blood, vomit, etc.) must be handled. The more expensive nitrile gloves are better, as some people are allergic to latex. They are also sturdier.

A CPR shield is a must-have—it could mean the difference between helping someone without hesitation and not being willing to risk it.

INSTRUMENTS

Being able to dig out a splinter, cut away clothes, or take vital signs is one heck of a lot easier with some basic tools. EMT shears are inexpensive, heavy-duty scissors that can even cut through a penny. These along with the other items listed will find many uses.

BANDAGING

Bandages are used to stop bleeding and protect wounds. An assortment of cloth Band-Aids can help you deal with minor injuries, while the larger gauze pads and rolls can help with bigger cuts and abrasions. An ACE bandage can be used to treat a sprain, hold a makeshift splint onto a leg, or wrap up a severely bleeding wound that requires pressure. An additional item that might be added is one or more sanitary napkins. Aside from their feminine-hygiene use, they are excellent for soaking up blood on large injuries.

For major cuts, Steri-Strips are a way of closing up the skin without needing special equipment and training. Think of these as Band-Aids on steroids. They are thin tape strips, one quarter of an inch or so wide and three to four inches long, coated with a super-aggressive adhesive and reinforced with cloth fibers. After thoroughly cleaning a wound (a hole poked in a Ziploc bag can allow you to squirt clean water deep inside), Steri-Strips are applied much like sutures across the wound to close up the edges.

Tincture of benzoin (a sticky disinfectant swabbed on wounds) will make the Steri-Strips stick better. Properly applied, the strips will stay on for up to two weeks, even when you shower. Don't waste your money on butterfly bandages; Steri-Strips are far superior.

MEDICATIONS

These are inexpensive drugs that can be bought (at least in the U.S.) without a prescription.

Antibiotic ointment (e.g., Neosporin) should be applied to cuts to reduce the chance of infection, particularly in dirty environments.

Benadryl (diphenhydramine) is an antihistamine (anti-allergy) medication that can help treat cold and flu symptoms such as runny nose and congestion, make allergies less severe, and aid sleep. (Many over-the-counter sleeping pills contain diphenhydramine.) In addition, taking Benadryl early *could* help save your life if you suffer anaphylactic shock (a severe allergic reaction, such as from a bee sting).

Ibuprofen is a pain reliever, anti-inflammatory, and fever reducer. In a survival situation, being able to carry out important tasks without the pain of a headache or sports injury could be critical, as could reducing a dangerous fever.

Aspirin is also a pain reliever and has fever-reducing effects, although it should never be administered to children with fevers, due to the possibility of a life-threatening complication known as Reye's syndrome. Aspirin is also often given at the first signs of a heart attack in many emergency medical services (EMS) protocols.

Imodium (loperamide) is used to control diarrhea. Diarrhea can be deadly if it causes severe dehydration. A two- to-three-day course of Imodium could be lifesaving in an emergency.

With any medication, it is important that the full instructions be included in your kit. Make photocopies of the drug labels and warnings. Be sure to write down the drugs' expiration dates as well. All of these meds should be good for at least one year after purchase, but check first.

Plastic dram vials are good for packaging drugs purchased in bulk. Add a small amount of cotton if you need to protect the pills from being crushed by vibration and shaking. Don't forget to print labels for each bottle.

And remember, the best survival kit is the one you keep inside your head, in the form of training. Go sign up for Red Cross first-aid/CPR training, or take a first-responder, wilderness first responder (WFR), or EMT class. Read books or take online lessons. There are several excellent, free resources on the Internet.

OPTIONAL ITEMS

Rehydration Mix

If you should come down with severe diarrhea, you could die from dehydration and loss of electrolytes. Stocking some Pedialyte, Gatorade (dilute to 50 percent with water), or a homemade equivalent could be a lifesaver. The basic recipe is one teaspoon (five milliliters) of salt, eight teaspoons of sugar, and one liter of water.

SAM Splint (or Imitation)

This is a very versatile splint device, which consists of thin aluminum on a foam backing. You can bend and use as is to splint arms, wrists, legs, etc., or cut up with your EMT shears to make finger splints.

N95 HEPA (High Efficiency Particulate Air Filter) Masks

If you're worried about airborne pathogens, this is a good thing to have. Most hardware stores sell masks with an N95 or higher rating, and small, collapsible masks are available from medical outlets.

Upgraded CPR Mask

The one-dollar disposable shield will serve, but a better shield, with a one-way valve, will make things easier. The CPR Microshield, from MDI, is good compromise, as it is superior to the thin plastic shield, has a one-way valve, and comes on a keychain.

Suction

Keeping the airway clear is critical when someone has experienced trauma or is severely ill. Commercial suction devices are available, but a cheap, improvised solution is a standard turkey baster. For less than two dollars, this is a useful addition to a medical kit.

Thin Sharpie Marker and Paper

Useful for recording vital signs. With a Sharpie marker, you can also write the numbers on the patient's hand, in case the paper is lost during transport/evacuation.

Contact Lenses

Make sure to have at least two pairs of backup glasses in your current prescription. If you feel more comfortable wearing contacts, then I see no reason why you shouldn't stock up on spare disposable soft contacts and extra bottles of saline and cleaning solutions. Just one proviso: Do not try to stretch your supply by going longer between discarding sets of contacts. Getting an eye infection would be tragic, especially in the midst of a disaster. Once you've used up your contact-lens supplies, just switch to wearing your eyeglasses.

One excellent source for very inexpensive contact lenses and supplies is 1800Contacts.com.

Sanitation During a Grid-Down Collapse

We take sanitation for granted so often that we might lose sight of its importance. There are several areas in the sanitation arena that need to be considered:

Food

The most obvious area to consider is that of our food preparation. We are all aware of the importance of washing our hands and avoiding cross-contaminating foods like meats and vegetables. All counters where foods may be prepared should be kept spotlessly clean. This includes areas where butchering is being done. The areas should be hosed and bleached and the meat meticulously washed, making certain the contents of the animals' intestines do not come into contact with the meat. The animals should be covered with a breathable fabric bag to protect the meat from flies and dirt while the meat is hanging. All utensils, including those being used for dehydrating and canning, should be sterilized by boiling or baking. (Do not bake canning lids; place them in very hot water prior to processing.)

Daily Living

Remaining organized and clutter-free gives us access to items that may be of immediate necessity, as well as less chance of an accident—even something as minor as tripping over clutter could become life threatening. Keeping organized causes us less stress, relieving our minds so they can be put to better use. It also provides activities for the group, giving tasks to those who may not be able to do other things, or just an extra way to get involved.

Clothes that are kept clean are warmer and last longer. (Dryers are hard on fabric.) And shoes should be worn at all times outside. Personal hygiene is important not only for our physical health, but for our mental health as well. It helps us maintain some semblance of normalcy and civility in our lives not only for ourselves but also for the group. When we are clean and groomed it is also easier to spot someone who is not well.

Feminine-hygiene products that are disposable should be burned. Cloth diapers should be either boiled or bleached and hung in the sun. The ultraviolet rays kill lots of bacteria.

Your animals will also benefit from your diligent attention to their well-being. Keeping their pens, bedding, and feeders clean could mean the difference between animals used to fulfill our needs and sickly or dead critters. Most domesticated-animal waste can be safely used as fertilizer after composting with the exception of that of dogs, cats, and pigs. These should never be used around areas that will have vegetables, and pregnant women should never handle cat waste.

Waste Disposal

Waste disposal pertains not only to manure, but to garbage as well. Most containers used for foods will probably be kept for some other need down the road. However, that means time and effort to make sure they are very well cleaned and stowed properly so as not to attract rodents or flies and bacteria. That which isn't needed should be burned, composted, or deeply buried away from your area. Food scraps (not from meat) can be fed to animals, composted, or put into a worm bin (a little bit of meat is OK here), which provides great fertilizer for the garden, as well as worms for your fowl.

Human Waste

Human waste is much more of a problem. We are no longer accustomed to dealing with our own waste. The average person produces two to three pints of urine and one pound of feces per day. Multiply that by the number of people in your group for a day, a week, or longer and you begin to see the problem. If the sewer system is working you can still use your toilet by pouring water directly into the bowl to flush the waste. Otherwise, a five-gallon bucket with a toilet seat can be used as a porta-potty. Layering lime, wood ash, and good ol' dirt can reduce the odor. Buckets will have to be cleaned daily and set up in an area away from any possible contamination sites so that the contents can be used for composting, keeping the compost covered to deter flies, etc. You should not use this compost in food gardening.

A trench toilet is also an option. Dig a trench two feet wide and a minimum of one foot deep and four feet long or more. After use, cover with the dirt from the hole, filling in from one end as you go. Bad bacteria can travel three hundred feet from the original site. Pay attention to drainage, and make sure the manure is covered with lime, ashes, or dirt. The area could attract rodents, dogs, and, worse, flies. The most important things to remember are reducing the fly/rodent problem and washing your hands thoroughly when you've finished. Stock up on hand sanitizer as well as soap. Do not attempt to use the trench method for manure that will be used for vegetable or grain growing.

For those of you planning on hunkering down in place if the grid were to go down and the sewer were to quit functioning, pay attention to where the access lids to the sewer are in your area. If you are anywhere downhill, sewage may back up through these portals and even into your drains and toilets. Give this some thought.

Medical

In a TEOTWAWKI situation, people may show up late or be accepted into the group that weren't there in the beginning. We need to consider that these folks, whether loved ones or strangers, may be bringing something unwanted with them. If possible, a quarantine area should be set up, where these people could spend two weeks away from the group, to make sure they aren't sick. It may sound cruel, but these people should remain without direct contact with the group. Radio contact or distant voice communication, if acceptable, would help them significantly. Their meals could be dropped off on paper plates that they could burn after they've eaten. Anything that is needed should be brought and dropped off so as not to expose the other members of the group. The newcomers would need to remain in the quarantine area at all times and not interact with people, animals, areas, or equipment. If after two weeks they are well, the chances are greatly reduced that they have a communicable disease.

There should also be a separate area for medical procedures—a bedroom or bathroom. This area should be kept spotless at all times. All items being used would need to be boiled or steamed (a steam canner or pressure canner as an autoclave) and all fabrics baked (two hundred degrees for one hour) prior to use. Tables, trays, and equipment should be washed and bleached. Alcohol is a great bacteria killer. New garbage bags could be used to cover tables, chairs, etc., prior to use and after cleaning, and to protect between activities. They are fairly sanitary. Disposable rubber gloves and masks should be worn when treating patients, and if blood is present goggles should be worn (swim goggles, or ski goggles over glasses would work). Used dressings and the like should be burned or buried deeply, away from the area.

Rodents and flies that carry disease will probably be a major concern. In a grid-down situation they would flourish. Rodent control would be a regular requirement, but handling them could be an issue in itself—probably best done with a mask and gloves. Keep flies away from any foods and food areas.

Death

The most difficult area of sanitation we may have to deal with is death. Although many organisms in the body of the deceased are not likely to infect a healthy person, handling the blood, bodily fluids, and tissues of those who have been infected increases that risk. Many fluids leak from a dead body, including contents of the stomach and intestines. The level of decomposition depends on how long the person has been deceased, the temperature of the environment, the damage to the body, and the bacteria present. There are some basic precautions to take in handling the deceased:

- Wear disposable gloves when handling anything associated with the body, and cover all cuts or abrasions with water-proof bandages or tape.
- Wear a mask or face shield, goggles, or some other kind of protection for the mouth, nose, and eyes. Decomposing bodies can sometimes burst and spray fluids and tissues due to the buildup of gases.
- Wear aprons or gowns that can be destroyed.
- Wrap the body in a body bag or several layers of garbage sacks or plastic sheeting. The more quickly this takes place after death, the less chance of leaking bodily fluids.

Cremation requires large amounts of fuel and may not be feasible. Graves should be dug at least one hundred feet away from all open water sources and deep enough that animals won't dig them up. Thoroughly wash yourself afterward and dip your hands in a bleach solution even if no apparent contact was made. Disinfect all equipment, surfaces, floors, and so forth with a bleach solution. Don't forget to make notes on the deceased and the circumstances surrounding the death and burial. Take pictures if you can. Consider anything that you think is of importance, in case the authorities come back and question it sometime. This may be the most difficult part of a societal collapse. But the quicker it is dealt with, the better for everyone involved.

Wound Care: An Emergency Room Doctor's Perspective

As you are cutting wood and swinging gardening tools, you are at risk for wounds. Even a minor wound can be a major problem if not treated effectively. E.C.W., M.D., provided the following essay:

Arguably the most important factor in wound healing is the potential for infection.

Bleeding is nature's way of cleaning a wound, but a little goes a long way. Remember that as long as the wound is "downstream" from the heart, bleeding will be under pressure, so don't forget to elevate a bleeding extremity above the level of the heart to get control of bleeding. Scalp wounds especially bleed profusely and may be frightening to the uninitiated. Use multiple layers of absorbent material—sterile gauze or a clean towel (or the cleanest cloth you have available)—and maintain direct pressure until bleeding ceases or is at least reduced to a slow ooze. A patient who is taking aspirin will have a prolonged bleeding time, so you will have to maintain pressure for a longer period of time.

Plain soap and tap water have been shown to be just as good for washing the wound as an antiseptic soap and sterile water. I would recommend a liquid soap to avoid the bacterial culture waiting to launch itself from the bar on the counter, but would avoid the widely available antibacterial soap (which contains triclosan); it has been shown to increase bacterial resistance. In a perfect world I would prefer Hibiclens, but would certainly use a "no-tears" baby shampoo (neutral solution), or even diluted Dawn dishwashing liquid in a pinch. Apply soap to a clean washcloth wet from the tap and use it to gently scrub the wound.

The sterile water solutions that are available bottled are fine, as long as they have not been opened previously (they are contaminated once opened), but nonsterile bottled water is *not* preferable to tap water. Tap water is sufficient for cleansing of most wounds. I would not use this for an open fracture. Of course, freshly boiled water would be more reliable than nonsterile bottled water or water that you have previously drawn up in a clean milk jug, but it is better to wash a soiled wound immediately if you have clean water available than to take the time to boil and then cool water, leaving a heavily contaminated wound in its dirty state. You could always re-rinse the wound with sterilized water. The length of time that the cleanser is in contact with the wound and the degree of flushing that takes place will determine the number of bacterial contaminants remaining and thus have a significant effect on wound infection rates, so spend several minutes on this step. Of course the examiner/caregiver should scrupulously wash his hands and any instruments used to probe the wound beforehand. Thoroughly cleaning the wound will usually result in resumption of bleeding. When cleaning is finished, pressure can again be applied.

A foreign body remaining in the wound can be a focus of infection and prevent healing, so it is imperative that care is taken to rid the wound of any particles that may be present. A large syringe or squirt bottle can be used to administer a stream of water into the wound under a little pressure in order to thoroughly clean it and dislodge particulate matter. Chain-saw wounds may require debridement (cleaning and removal) of the margins with a scalpel to remove seared tissue as well as particles and clothing fibers, as searing prevents the wound edges from closing together in healing.

Boil or sterilize equipment such as a scrub brush or tweezers before removing all foreign material from the wound. (Cleaning instruments with alcohol and/or soap and water would be better than nothing.) Blood clotted in the wound must also be removed by scrubbing, as dried blood serves as a foreign body in this setting. After thorough cleansing with soap and water, if a wound is to be sutured, Betadine (if available) could be swabbed on the skin in pinwheel fashion, from the skin at the wound edges out to two or three inches away from the wound.

Anesthesia is certainly desirable prior to any painful manipulation or procedure, and if possible should be mercifully administered prior to any vigorous cleaning. Even the most stoic among us can appreciate pain relief, even if it is only temporary. So a vial of lidocaine (1 percent or 2 percent) and a syringe to administer it may be part of your wilderness medical kit. If the lidocaine has epinephrine mixed in, it will help a lot to keep the wound from bleeding as you try to suture it, but you must not use epinephrine in a wound on an extremity such as a finger or toe, as it could result in necrosis (tissue death). On the face or scalp epinephrine is a welcome additive, since these wounds tend to bleed so freely that you can scarcely see what you are sewing without it.

In addition to elevating the wound above the level of the heart, you may use limited tourniquet banding with a wide strip. (In the ER I might use a blood-pressure cuff pumped up to the point at which it stops the bleeding). This should be temporary, to maintain a bloodless field for closure only. Carefully and slowly infiltrating the margins of a wound with a few milliliters of an anesthetic solution, a learned technique, will result in control of bleeding and pain (for closure). Then you must give the anesthetic a few minutes to be absorbed before commencing your repair. Whether you use anesthetic or not it would be wise to administer pain medicine of some kind, either orally or by injection, since the wound will throb even after the repair is done.

Wound closure is a key factor in healing and infection rate as well. Wounds left open will be infected to some extent. The six-hour rule for closure is followed for minor wounds; that is, if care is sought within those limits the wound can be cleaned and sutured with impunity.

Closure may involve suturing (sewing) or may be as simple as using Dermabond (superglue), Steri-Strips, or staples made for this purpose. In the ER I tailor the method to suit the patient and the situation, but you might not have that option in the wilderness or a homebound setting. If you do, or if you can reach qualified medical help within a suitable time frame, I wholeheartedly advise you to do so. But if that is not possible, even duct tape may be preferable to nonclosure.

You must be careful to hold the wound margins together tightly to apply Dermabond, as any solution that makes its way into the wound may itself prevent healing, and with Dermabond the trick is to keep your fingers from being glued to the wound while waiting the few seconds for it to dry. I do not advise using Dermabond for a wound that has a tendency to continue bleeding the minute pressure is removed, nor in a wound that is deep or under stress. It works well on some facial lacerations, but I trust Steri-Strips to do the job, and they could easily be part of a medical kit.

Wound margins should be closely approximated prior to the application of any binding material, including Steri-Strips or tape. If you are reduced to using duct tape, first tear several inches off the roll so that what you use on the wound has not been in contact with a dirty surface. Then tear or cut three or four inches off and cut that into one-eighth-inch to one-quarter-inch strips, taking care to keep your hands from touching the part of the tape that will be over the wound. Pressing the wound edges together with one hand, or having a helper hold them together by pushing from each side, apply the strips of tape, starting on one side and pulling firmly to apply some tension before allowing the tape to adhere to the other side of the wound. Space these strips one eighth to one quarter of an inch apart to allow the wound to breathe, and then cover with sterile gauze secured by tape or an ACE wrap (or cotton bandage) to keep it from being recontaminated.

I would not worry about small defects or ragged edges. Individuals who are sensitive to adhesives may develop blisters where the Steri-Strip or tape is located, but this is usually just a local reaction and does not cause systemic allergic symptoms. In someone who is unable to tolerate adhesives, sutures or staples should be used for larger wounds requiring closure.

Suturing is a technique that is learned and should be practiced prior to use, which is not to say that any accomplished seamstress couldn't master it. Many wounds will greatly benefit from needle and thread. However, to reinforce the importance of asepsis in wound care, I should again point out that a wound should not be sutured by an untrained individual in a nonsterile environment if there is an alternative. If there is not, then any asepsis that can be accomplished by boiling or autoclaving (pressure-cooking) would be of benefit, and extreme care should be taken not to further contaminate the wound while attempting to close it in the best possible way. What is obvious to medically trained personnel—microbial contamination and how to avoid it—is the major impediment for the layperson. Sterile drapes and sterile gloves are a bonus. But most medical staff would agree that primary closure is better than a large wound left open in most cases. In our current political-legal climate one could be prosecuted for "practicing medicine" without a license if it appeared that extraordinary measures were undertaken by the layman who had other options, so be sure that you are doing so out of necessity. In a TEOTWAWKI setting, you will probably wish that you had at least studied the technique (and had obtained the proper equipment and practiced on some animal skin).

Some wounds are by definition contaminated or infected and are better left unclosed. These include puncture wounds, stab wounds (deeper than they are wide) that are not bleeding profusely, and animal or human bites. These should be cleaned and scrubbed as above, taking even more care to flush them out if possible, with bleeding controlled with pressure only. If that's not possible, then one or two sutures or Steri-Strips can be strategically placed. Be careful to draw the wound edges together only enough to control the bleeding and not to closely approximate them, as you want the wound to be able to drain easily. These are the wounds for which an ER doctor would probably give antibiotic prophylaxis, with an older drug such as doxycycline or trimethoprim-sulfa, or a cephalosporin such as cephalexin (Keflex). Crush wounds of the extremities also should not be sutured, even if they look awful, but should be cleaned as much as possible given the level of contamination and then bandaged. Because "crush wounds" can be expected to swell so much, primary closure could be detrimental.

In a situation in which it could be days before a medical professional would be consulted, you should know that sutures of the face and scalp should be removed in four to five days, lest the sutures themselves cause scarring. An uninfected facial wound should be healed in that time. Steri-Strips can be removed from the face at that time. For wounds of the upper extremities, leaving sutures in for seven to ten days is advisable, depending on the extent of the wound, and for the lower extremities up to two weeks. If Steri-Strips or tape have been used, they may need to be reapplied during that time period. Keeping the wound clean and dry is the goal, but if sutures are used to close the wound, it can be washed daily with soap and water after the first twenty-four hours. If a wound becomes obviously infected, with purulent (yellow or green) discharge, swelling, and redness, it will have to be opened up at least partially and allowed to drain to prevent septicemia.

Tetanus prophylaxis should also be addressed. Puncture wounds and deep, heavily contaminated wounds are considered tetanus-prone. The vaccine for tetanus has been used for several decades and is considered very safe if one is not allergic to any of the components, so keep your vaccination status for tetanus up-to-date.

The best way to avoid wound infection is to avoid the wound in the first place. Be careful. Make your children wear their shoes outside of the house. Lacerations from stepping on broken glass and puncture wounds from thorns or tacks in the feet are fairly common in the ER and are usually preventable. Accidents will happen to even the most cautious, but they will be proportionately less than to the heedless or reckless.

Extended Care of the Chronically Ill in TEOTWAWKI

When thinking through your plans for TEOTWAWKI, it is important to consider caring for chronically ill family members. Some of these issues can probably be foreseen, such as the need for photovoltaically powered CPAP (constant positive airway pressure) machines for sleep-apnea patients, and refrigeration of insulin. But other chronic conditions might arise *after* the onset of a crisis and are hence more difficult to anticipate and plan for.

Chronic Care

It may be difficult for us to confront the issue of care for the chronically ill, because it can seem so overwhelming. These issues demand our attention, our concerted planning, and considerable financial commitment. There is such a wide range of chronic illnesses and disabilities, and it is impossible to address them all, but I will mention a few of the most common disorders that will require advance planning:

Kidney Disease

In a grid-down situation, dialysis patients will be in trouble once the hospital backup generators run out of fuel. To see a loved one slowly dying because their blood is turning toxic would be absolutely heartbreaking. The best solution might seem extreme, but it might be your only option: Move to the Big Island of Hawaii, or to a natural-gas-producing region, or near a refinery in an oil-producing state. There are any number of different circumstances, including an EMP attack, wherein the continental-U.S. power grids will go down, but the lights will stay on in Hawaii. In Hawaii, each island has its own independent power-generation infrastructure.

Moving to a natural-gas-producing region (such as parts of Oklahoma, Arkansas, Texas, New Mexico, and several other states) would require considerable research. You would have to find a community adjacent to natural-gas fields with a kidney dialysis center that has a natural-gas-fired backup generator *and* that is in an area with sufficient wellhead pressure to pressurize local lines.

Another option might be to find a dialysis center with a diesel-powered backup generator that is within twenty-five miles of a refinery that is also in oil country. The keyword to watch for in your Web searches is *cogeneration*. A plant that has cogeneration capability is likely one that could operate without the power grid.

Diabetes

Relatively small and inexpensive (less than $3,000) packaged photovoltaic power systems with inverters (such as those sold by Ready Made Resources) can be used to operate a compact refrigerator such as the Engel compact refrigerator/freezers sold by Safecastle. A system of this size could also be used to run a CPAP machine or other AC-powered medical equipment with similar amperage demands.

I strongly suggest that any readers who are diabetic or who have diabetic relatives look into the Weimar Institute's NEWSTART nutritional and behavioral program. There are also some herbal alternatives for diabetics who are not fully insulin dependent.

For those who are indeed insulin dependent regardless of dietary changes, I recommend that you stock up on enough inject-able insulin for its full potential shelf life.

Postsurgical

Another category of chronic illness to consider is the care of postsurgical ostomy patients—folks who have had a colostomy, ileostomy, urostomy, or similar procedure. These often require keeping on hand a large supply of medical appliances, bags, catheters, and so forth. Thankfully, most of these items have fairly long shelf lives and are not too expensive to stock up on.

Lung Ailments

There are some lung ailments that can be relieved (at least to an extent) by relocating. Getting to a more suitable elevation, moving to avoid pollen or fungi, and so on can make a considerable difference. If this is your situation, then I suggest that you make the move soon.

If you are asthmatic, you can get a prescription for a handheld nebulizer that has both AC and DC car-adapter capabilities as well as a rechargeable, gel-cell battery. Thankfully, most nebulizers have fairly modest current requirements.

Buying a woodstove—a key preparedness measure—is not good for someone who has an asthmatic in their family. If that is your case, then consider moving to the southwest, where passive-solar heating is an option, or moving to an area where you can use geothermal heating.

For the many folks who now depend on medical oxygen cylinders, stock up on extras. One alternative suitable for long-term scenarios is to buy a medical oxygen concentrator. High-volume units are fairly expensive, but owning your own would be an incredible resource for charity or barter as well as for your own family's use.

Medication

The high cost of some medicines makes storing a two-year supply difficult. And the policies of most insurance companies—often refusing to pay for more than a month's worth of medication in advance—only exacerbates the problem. In these cases, I suggest 1) reprioritizing your budget to provide the funds needed to stock up, and 2) if possible, looking at alternative treatments, including herbs that you can grow in your own garden or greenhouse.

If you decide to stockpile—all the way to their expiration dates—this will require not only lots of cash but also very conscientious FIFO rotation of your supplies. To buy your medications safely and legally from a pharmacy, have your doctor write you a prescription for the generic version of your medications. If you pay for the prescriptions yourself, without relying on insurance, it will be more expensive, but you will be able to stockpile without a hassle.

As for using meds beyond their expiration dates, this requires some careful study. Some medications have listed expiries that are overly conservative. A few drugs, however, are downright dangerous to use past their expiration dates. Consult your local pharmacist with questions about any particular drug. (I lack an "R.Ph." or a "Pharm.D." after my name, so I am not qualified to give such advice.)

In my opinion, it would be better to err on the side of caution. To be absolutely safe, I recommend that you avoid both overdosing *and* out-of-date or otherwise deteriorated antibiotics. As a prepper who anticipates the possibility of infrastructure breakdown and widespread power failures, the last thing that I want is to see anyone become dependent on scheduled kidney dialysis because they saved money on antibiotics.

Alternative treatment, such as using herbs or acupuncture, is a touchy subject. Again, it is something that will take considerable research and qualified consultation, and in effect making yourself your own guinea pig. If you decide to use this approach, I recommend that you make any transition gradually, with plenty of qualified supervision. If it takes a lot of extra visits to your doctor for tests, then so be it. Just do your best to make the transition, *before* everything hits the fan.

I have seen some folks in preparedness circles on the Internet recommend stockpiling low-cost veterinary medications, but I advise using such medications only in extremis (when your only other option is certain death).

Elective Surgery

If you have an existing problem that could be cured with elective surgery, then I strongly recommend that you go do so if you have the means. If your condition worsens after medical facilities become unavailable, it could turn a simple inconvenience into something life threatening.

I've heard of several wealthy preppers who have had their nearsightedness cured by LASIK or PRK, just for the sake of being better prepared for a foreseen new era that will not have the benefit of ophthalmologists and a handy shopping mall "eyeglasses in about an hour" shop. Living free of eyeglasses or contact lenses also makes wearing night-vision goggles and protective masks much easier, and makes shooting—particularly at long range—more accurate.

Buy a Food Grinder

Many injuries and illnesses cause difficulty chewing and digesting solid foods, because of the patients' weakness, dental problems, or jaw/palate/throat trauma. It is important to have a hand-cranked food grinder available so that you can accommodate the needs of these patients. Old-fashioned grinders (the type that clamp onto the edge of a kitchen table) can often be found used for just a few dollars at yard sales. If you want to buy a new one, they are available from both Ready Made Resources and Lehmans.

Survival Dentistry

The most important dental resource that I can recommend is the book *Where There Is No Dentist,* available for free download from the Hesperian Foundation (snipurl.com/hrpdg). (But I recommend getting a **bound hard copy.** Ditto for their book *Where There Is No Doctor.* Used copies can be found on Amazon.com for little more than the cost of shipping.)

Dental instruments may be bought through online auctions. It would also be wise to stock up on other dentistry supplies such as gauze, oil of cloves, and so forth. Unless you are stranded in the backcountry, I do not recommend that you put in temporary fillings under present-day circumstances. If a filling leaks, it could cause an infection. However, in a genuine TEOTWAWKI situation, temporary fillings may be your only alternative to suffice for weeks or even months until you can get to a qualified dentist. For this reason, you should stock up on temporary-filling material such as Cimpat, Tempanol, or Cavit. There are also temporary-filling materials packaged for the consumer market that contain very small quantities (under brand names such as DenTek and Temparin), but the per-unit cost is relatively high. With those, you are mostly paying for the packaging.

I do not recommend do-it-yourself tooth extraction, except, again, in extremis. Without the support of a crown or bridge, the gap left by an extraction can cause a chain reaction, as other teeth shift to compensate for the missing tooth. This can lead to a series of complications, which are best avoided.

SurvivalBlog contributor The Army Dentist wrote the following piece:

> Dentistry may be one of the least exciting topics under preparedness. But a dental emergency can quickly complicate or even bring to a standstill daily living and tasks. In a WT-SHTF scenario this is not something you want to deal with.
>
> I would like to present a summary of the caries process and the best way to prevent dental pathology in the first place, a simple way to recognize and/or loosely categorize dental symptoms, and some simple treatment alternatives until definitive care can be obtained.
>
> Start by going to your dentist and having everything taken care of immediately. After all existing problems have been addressed, begin and maintain a preventive dental program—make it a habit. It is not a very difficult thing to do, and you can save thousands of dollars and a lot of pain by doing it.
>
> Brush your teeth and limit your sugar intake. It really does work. If you can remove the bacteria, which predominantly resides in plaque, from your mouth, you will limit its ability to create acid. The sugar-intake frequency is

more important than the amount of sugar. Every time you put sugar in your mouth, the bacteria will create acid for thirty minutes. If you drink one soda in ten minutes, and then consume no more sugar the rest of the day, then you will have acid in your mouth for only about 40 minutes. If you take the same soda and sip on it all day long, then you will have acid in your mouth all day long. Certainly limit the amount of sugar you ingest, but more important, limit the frequency with which you ingest it. Also, use a fluoride rinse every night. You should brush your teeth, rinse your mouth, drink water if you want, and then rinse with the fluoride. Then don't put anything else in your mouth, and go to bed. The fluoride will sit on your teeth and make the enamel less soluble.

Toothpaste is good but not necessary in this regimen. Toothpaste is nothing more than a mild abrasive, flavoring, and fluoride. If you want to make your own, you can use fluoride rinse and baking soda, although baking soda is much more abrasive than commercially made toothpaste and can irritate your tissues.

If you do develop a carious lesion (a cavity), do not leave your tooth untreated. You will eventually end up with an abscess and the tooth will be extremely painful to the touch. You may begin to run a fever and experience swelling. Some people say it feels like the tooth has "raised up." It has. The infection is pushing it up. If the infection, however, travels toward the tongue, neck, or sinuses, to name a few places, it can become very dangerous, very quickly. Possible complications include septicemia, airway obstruction, and pericardial infections. These are not common but are dangerous and need to be treated by a medical professional. Some of the symptoms of these serious infections include increased temperature, swelling under your jaw, under your tongue and around your chin, swelling extending toward your neck, swelling in your throat that may begin to push your uvula aside, and difficulty swallowing and/or breathing. Do not ignore these! Seek medical care immediately.

Eye Protection and Flushing

Eye protection is crucial. When anyone in my family shoots, we always wear eye and ear protection. Ditto whenever we use a chain saw. I use a Stihl brand "forestry" helmet with built-in earmuffs and a full-face mesh screen, although I've read that the Peltor brand may be superior. We now store our workshop face goggles right on top of our bench grinder, where we can't forget to use them. This is a good practice for all safety gear. Store it alongside your tools—otherwise it will be "out of sight, out of mind."

We don't drink alcohol at the Rawles Ranch but we keep a shot glass handy, since they make an ideal eyecup for irrigating foreign matter out of an eye. I plan to add a mini-eye-wash station to our workshop. That is cheap insurance.

It is important to have safety goggles with side protection for everyone in your home. Also, lay in a supply of ophthalmic saline solution that can be used as an emergency eyewash.

Stabilizing an Injured Person

As always, the best treatment for an injury is not to be injured in the first place, but if someone in your group suffers a fall and twists an ankle or fractures a forearm, you will need to stabilize them to prevent further injury. Michelle, an EMT, submitted this piece:

> You should always consult qualified medical advice on an injury that requires splinting, crutches, or any kind of assistance. In a post-TEOTWAWKI situation, that may be the medical person in your group, or *Where There Is No Doctor*, but unless you have a serious fracture that is apparent (i.e., bone sticking out of flesh, deformity, or immediate inability to move the extremity), you should make every effort to get help from a medical professional. Splinting in order to get to a facility is fine, but you really should have an injury looked at by a medical professional.

SPLINTING

We splint to immobilize an extremity. This is achieved by keeping the joints above and below the injury from moving. If it's a knee, splint the injury so the ankle can't move and the hip can move only in a forward-and-backward motion—so you can move the entire leg without bending the knee. For wrist or elbow sprains, bend the elbow ninety degrees and hold it to the chest. Apply the splint "in place"—before moving the patient. A critical assessment to make prior to and after splinting is to see if you can feel a pulse and whether the victim can feel sensation, as well as their degree of mobility. This allows you to loosen, tighten, or change the splint as needed if any of those three factors change during or after splinting.

Splinting is more about technique than the materials on hand. Anything hard and straight can be used—from tree branches and long wooden spoons to a piece of stiff plastic.

You can also buy commercial splinting supplies. There are wire-mesh types, cardboard cutouts, and, of course, the simple ACE bandage. I also highly recommend taking a basic first-aid course that will help you with splinting and immobilizing.

For treatment of sprains and twists use the RICE acronym: Rest, Ice, Compress, and Elevate.

STRETCHERS AND BACKBOARDS

While stretchers are durable and rugged, they have some serious faults. A better option for prepared families is simply to buy a backboard and put the injured person on a cart or simply carry him or her. Backboards run about one hundred dollars, and the straps (spider straps) are about fifty dollars and are easy to use.

Backboards have slots at the top and sides for handling and you can easily secure the board via hooks, ropes, or seat belts to the top and rear of a garden cart. Boards can be made out of wood but are nowadays largely made out of plastic. Backboards should be used only to move a person and not to prevent any head or neck injury (their primary design in modern medicine), unless you are trained for that level of care. Another benefit of using a backboard is that by strapping a person down you are in effect temporarily splinting the arms and legs.

Another good idea is to secure all of your first-response medical gear to the board. For about 150 to 200 dollars and a cart used for other purposes, you have a heavy-duty stretcher to get an injured person back to your retreat.

In my experience as an EMT, I have discovered that some great places to find emergency gear are SaveLives .com and Galls.com.

Transportation for the Disabled in the Event of TEOTWAWKI

As you should know by now, I strongly suggest that if it is at all practicable you make arrangements to live with your family at your retreat year-round. If you have a disabled person in your party, the habitation should be a single-story structure, on level or nearly level ground, with an easy retrofit for a wheelchair ramp to the main door. Also, if anyone in your party currently uses an electric wheelchair, get an old-fashioned wheelchair for backup in the event of a long-term power failure. And don't forget to buy crutches and canes for anyone who might end up with a sprained ankle or twisted knee down the road.

For transportation over longer distances, plan ahead for providing for your disabled family members. One great option, in my opinion, is a four-wheel-drive, full-size van conversion. Beware of buying an older 4WD conversion: Some of the 4WD van conversions that were done back in the 1970s and 1980s were plagued by reliability problems—mainly involving differential linkage and other power-train problems. But in more recent years the conversion companies seem to have gotten it down to a science. Just be sure to get a written warranty.

Vans can be "dual converted" for both 4WD *and* a wheelchair lift apparatus. See vantagemobility.com.

Preparedness for Parents with Infants

For families with infants, the Memsahib offered this advice: The most important thing is to breast-feed your baby. Your biggest practical concern will be diapers. Depending on circumstances

(availability of spring or well water and grid, generator, or photovoltaic power to run a washing machine), you will have to
decide between cloth and disposable diapers. When I nursed my
newborns, I often changed diapers more than ten times per day,
to prevent diaper rash. Untreated, diaper rash can lead to serious infections. Proper hygiene is crucial. Choose your diapering
method and then stock up.

The most useful items are:

For Childbirth:

- Sterilized cord clamp
- Betadine solution
- A bulb syringe
- Bed liners (like those made for the disabled, available at
  medical-supply houses)

For your newborn:

- Plan on breast-feeding, but as a backup consider stocking
  up on canned infant formula.
- Lanolin nursing cream
- Petroleum jelly and zinc ointment as diaper-rash preventives
- Diapers and diaper covers
- Multiple "onesies," sleepers, or sacque gowns would be a
  real blessing.

Babies spit up a lot and diapers leak. In a post-TEOTWAWKI
world, when washing and drying baby clothes won't be so easy,
having multiple changes in every size would make daily life
easier.

I also would never be without a front-pack infant carrier or armed with a good sling or baby wrap like those you can fashion yourself (wearyourbaby.com).

I highly recommend the childbirth books *Heart and Hands* and *Spiritual Midwifery*, which present childbirth as a natural process— not just as a medical condition.

Survival Labor and Delivery

Having a baby is a blessing, but home delivery is best done under the supervision of a medical professional. In a TEOTWAWKI situation, you may have to fend for yourself. John O., M.D., shares the following on childbirth:

> Home delivery is a fact that most of the survivalist community needs to face. A "normal" delivery with minor complications is the area in which preparation can make a big difference. Before we start, I believe that as a community, we need to accept the fact that the rates of death for both mother and infant are going to rise significantly if TSHTF. No amount of preparation is going to allow someone to do a C-section on their kitchen table, and even breach presentations may be more than a layman can expect to handle.
>
> The services of a good midwife would be invaluable, and the addition of a text such as *Heart and Hands* by Elizabeth Davis may be a wise supplement to your stores as a second-best choice. My goal is to help you to keep a good delivery from going bad and to prevent complications. It should go without saying that this information is for educational/ survival purposes only, and I am not suggesting a specific

course of care. Fortunately, nature really does run its course in most cases.

Labor can be divided into two phases: the first phase, when the cervix is thinning out and slowly dilating to form a canal roughly the diameter of pencil up to about ten centimeters; and the second phase, when the pushing begins and the mother actually pushes the baby out. The first phase is often divided into an early period, in which the cervix is dilated less than four centimeters and contractions are relatively mild and spaced further apart (seven to eight minutes), as well as a late phase, when the contractions are much harder and closer together. The early phase varies in length—from maybe two hours in multiparous women (having had previous pregnancies) to as much as twenty-four hours in *prima gravis* (first pregnancy). Late first phase tends to be more regular, with the average woman dilating about one centimeter per hour. Women will usually want to get up out of bed, especially in the late phase. Encourage it, as lying in a bed during labor is a bad habit that is really only necessary in hospitals due to the use of epidurals and intravenous (IV) narcotics. I have found that squatting really does help speed the progression as well as minimize labor pains. In a hospital birth a woman's cervix is checked frequently; I would urge strongly against this practice at home. In the hospital setting, a woman who is not progressing may get a dosage of the labor hormone Pitocin or may even go for a cesarean section, neither of which you will be doing at home. In addition, hospitals have a limitless supply of sterile gloves, so the risk of introducing infection into the birth canal is relatively low. In home deliveries, in which labor without Pitocin (the synthetic version of the hormone oxytocin) tends to take longer, infection prevention is crucial. You will have a pretty good idea how things are progressing just by monitoring the frequency of contractions and the look on her face.

Speaking of infection, now would be a good time to discuss an infection called Group B Strep. Group B Strep (GBS) is a bacteria that roughly 30 percent of women carry in the birth canal. While passing through the canal about 60 percent of children will be colonized if the mom has GBS. Even in modern medicine, about one in two hundred newborns will develop severe complications such as pneumonia, meningitis, or sepsis (blood poisoning). All women are currently screened for GBS at about thirty-seven weeks and treated with IV antibiotics prior to beginning labor. This has been shown pretty conclusively to reduce the amount of GBS in the canal, lowering the rates of colonization of babies. In addition, penicillin-based antibiotics readily cross the placenta and afford the baby some protection even if he or she is colonized.

Since I don't imagine people will be getting screened for GBS WTSHTF, I would recommend every woman start taking an antibiotic about ten to fourteen days prior to their due date. While IV antibiotics are currently recommended, oral were used pretty regularly until about ten years ago. Ampicillin is probably best; any -cillin or cephalosporin (medications with *ceph* or *cef* in the name, such as cephalexin [Keflex], Ceftin, Cefazolin, Rocephin, etc.) is good. You could probably use -mycin-based antibiotics in a pinch or for seriously penicillin-allergic patients. *Do not* use -cyclines or anything with *floxin* in the generic name, as these are both toxic to young children.

After getting through the first phase, the woman will

begin to feel the need to push or the sensation of needing to have a bowel movement, from the baby's head pushing on the pelvis and bowel. I generally recommend getting back into bed at this point, though some midwives keep them up. Now is the time to clean the entire pelvic area with Betadine, iodine, or high-proof alcohol, including one-half to one inch inside the vagina itself. Begin working on stretching the back wall of the vagina using KY lubricant or oil. Looking at the vagina, take the areas at about seven o'clock and five o'clock between your thumbs and forefingers and stretch sideways and outward. Start gently but work up in force. Trust me, no amount of force you apply is going to equal the stretching from the head.

As the child begins to crown, assuming that you have clean or sterile gloves, work your fingers up around the neck to make sure the cord isn't wrapped around it. If it is, you can usually pull on the stretchy cord while pushing the head slightly back in to pull the cord up over the face and head to untangle it. If you don't have very clean hands, wait a little longer, until the face is partly out, though this tends to increase the tension on the cord, making it harder to get off.

Unreduced nuchal cords (umbilical cords wrapped around the neck) are a major cause of death or brain damage in "normal" deliveries due to strangulation as they tighten. Don't forget to check for the cord around the neck! Finally the face will be out, and the child will normally stick at the shoulders, as this is the widest point on the child. Take this time to suction the baby's nose and mouth thoroughly. I would highly recommend getting several blue bulb syringes over-the-counter now for just such a situation. If you note a greenish slime (meconium) on the baby or in his mouth, this means he has had a bowel movement due to the stress of labor, or because of the above mentioned nuchal cord. It is very important to get this out of the throat and nose now, because once he comes out the rest of the way and takes his first breath, he will suck this junk down into his lungs. A small amount of previously boiled water may help to make the meconium runnier and easier to suction. The meconium itself is sterile, and is no cause for alarm, other than the risk of aspirating it.

Passing the shoulder is a little more difficult. Most of the time you can reach up and grasp the shoulders, pushing the trunk down to deliver the forward-most shoulder, then up to deliver the trailing one. Sometimes an assistant can put pressure over the mother's bladder while flexing her leg up into the air to help push the baby's shoulder down to get it to pass under the pelvic bone. You can do a Google search for "McRoberts maneuver" for a more detailed and complex explanation. Do not tug down on the head itself, as it can tear the nerves going into the arm from the neck. Also, do not push down on the top of the uterus, as this can cause some serious problems as well. In a truly desperate situation, the baby's collarbone can be broken to cause the shoulder to collapse some. While it sounds horrible, the bone heals fairly readily, and it's something I've had to do even in the hospital setting once or twice. You put one palm over the breastbone of the baby and the other behind the shoulder of the collarbone to break, then press with both thumbs in the center of the clavicle with a force slightly greater than that used to break a turkey wishbone. You will definitely feel the "pop." It is important to note that after the first shoulder delivers, the baby pretty much wants to pop right out. Try to get the mom to breathe through her nose and stop pushing while you apply pressure back in, so that the baby slides out in a controlled fashion. Letting it slide out uncontrolled will greatly increase the risk of a tear to the mom.

After the baby passes, lower him below the level of the birth canal to help his blood flow out of the placenta and back into his body. After about thirty seconds, clamp the cord with whatever you have, such as boiled clothespins. Clamp above and below where you intend to cut, which is usually about one-and-a-half inches from the baby's belly. Cut with a sterilized blade, as this is a major source of infection in the Third World. Keep the clamp on the baby for a day or two, until the vessels scarify.

Clean the baby with a dry cloth to remove all the slime, and immediately wrap him in a warm blanket, as babies have a hard time controlling their body temperatures initially. You can stimulate the baby if he isn't crying by rubbing his breastbone with your knuckle using moderate force, or by a light pinch. Try to get the baby to breast-feed right away, as it will help the mom's uterus collapse down and minimize bleeding.

Massage the mother's belly, pressing down on her uterus with moderate force (enough to be somewhat uncomfortable). After the uterus has contracted, the placenta will separate from it. After separation, apply gentle traction to the end of the placenta to get it to pass, taking care not to use too much force, which can cause the placenta to tear and leave behind a piece that can be a source for later infection. Be sure to apply traction only after the placenta has separated—doing so too early, when the placenta is still attached, can cause an internal hemorrhage and the mother to bleed to death.

Ibuprofen works well to help with postpartum soreness and residual contraction pain. Eight hundred milligrams will usually do the trick. As an aside, try to avoid aspirin products, because they thin the blood and will increase bleeding, especially if taken before the actual delivery.

I have not addressed breach births, as whole chapters can be written on the topic. One relatively simple procedure that can be tried before labor starts, if the head is felt to be up instead of down, is called external cephalic version. There are some risks, such as an early water breakage, but it is probably better to try to fix the problem early, rather than waiting until the baby has entered the birth canal. Once again, this is for informational/educational purposes, and is not a substitute for proper medical care.

Group Planning for a Flu Pandemic

There is no way to be certain to avoid exposure if an influenza outbreak is in close proximity. (See Appendix C for details.) The odds are that the first outbreaks will be in distant regions. That will be the time to act.

9

COMMUNICATIONS AND MONITORING

There's a Whole Spectrum Out There

Plunging into the world of two-way radio communications and monitoring can seem daunting for newbie preppers. It is a technical field that has more than its share of jargon and acronyms. I suggest that you team up with someone who is a licensed amateur ham operator, and have that person walk you through the basics of the frequency bands, radio-wave propagation, the various equipment, and the legalities. Yes, there are *plenty* of legalities. Stay legal!

A ham who mentors new hams is called an "Elmer." You can find an Elmer through your local ham-radio club affiliated with the American Radio Relay League (ARRL). Elmers are almost always willing to help, and quite generous with their time.

The radio-band designations can be confusing to folks who are newcomers to the shortwave-listening and amateur-radio worlds. One major source of confusion for newbies is hearing hams mention things like "on the forty-meter band" or "I was talking on two meters." For a useful chart from the ARRL that puts the band designations into an easy-to-grasp graphic format go to snipurl.com/hsu6d.

Getting Started

I highly recommend that all preppers at the very minimum buy a shortwave radio and a multiband police scanner, and become familiar with their use. WTSHTF, hardwired telephones, cellular phones, AM and FM commercial radio, the Internet, and television may be essentially unavailable or unusable. Most radio and TV stations have enough fuel to run their backup generators for only few days. Ditto for the telephone company central offices (COs). After that, there will be an acute information vacuum. You may find yourself listening to overseas shortwave broadcasters for your daily news, and to your police scanner for updates on the local situation—to keep track of the whereabouts of looter gangs. Be sure to buy a CB radio and few walkie-talkies so that you can coordinate security with your neighbors. (The CB, FRS, and MURS bands do not require any license in the U.S.)

What to Buy for Disaster Communications and Monitoring

Shortwave Receiver

Your first receiver should probably be a compact, portable general-coverage AM/FM/weather band/CB/shortwave receiver. There are several brands on the market, most notably Grundig, Sangean, and Sony. I consider the recently-discontinued Sony ICF-SW7600GR receiver among the most durable portable general-coverage receivers for the money. It is about the size of a paperback book. The secrets to making a receiver last are to buy a couple of spare hand-reel antennas (the most fragile part), show care in putting stress on the headphone jack and power-cable connections, and always carry the radio and accessories in a sturdy, well-padded, preferably waterproof case. (I find that a small Pelican brand case with "pluck-and-chuck" gray foam inserts proves ideal for my needs.) One low-cost alternative is to cut closed-cell foam inserts to fit inside a .30 caliber United States Government Issue (USGI) ammo can. GI ammo cans are a very sturdy, inexpensive (often less than ten dollars each at gun shows) alternative, and they provide very good protection from nuclear EMP effects.

At auto wrecking yards, you can sometimes find a Becker or Blaupunkt brand Europa, Mexico, or similar model AM/FM/ shortwave radio pulled from a European car such as a Mercedes-Benz, for less than fifty dollars. These are not only very reliable radios but will also give you the opportunity to get time signals from the WWV and WWVH radio stations operated by the NIST, and some international broadcasts.

Transceivers

Your first transceivers should probably be a pair of MURS band walkie-talkies.

CB Radio

Next, an SSB-capable CB radio, such as the time-proven Cobra 148GTL.

Field Telephones

You'll also want a pair of military-surplus field telephones, for coordinating retreat security. To someone who was first trained on the older-generation TA-1 and TA-312 simplex-only mode field phones, like I was, the current TA-1042 DNVT-generation phones seem very *Buck Rogers*. It is a great design. Having reliable field telephones is essential to coordinate retreat security in a post-TEOTWAWKI world. For semipermanent installation, it is best to buy cable that is rated for underground burial (UB), to conceal and protect all of your lines. For TA-1042s you will need four conductor cables (or two parallel runs of two conductor cables). Burying your lines will prevent both intentional and unintentional line cuts and breaks. Don't overlook getting a few extra field phones, so that you can run commo wire to your neighbors and coordinate with them as well. Watch eBay for a circuit switch (AN/TTC-39D). The TA-1042 DNVT field telephones themselves are currently available from Ready Made Resources. They sell these field phones in pairs, with a free civilian photovoltaic panel included.

Table Radio

Then, you may want to get a relatively EMP-proof vacuum-tube-technology table radio, preferably one with shortwave bands. Something like a Zenith TransOceanic H500 would be a good choice. Tabletop vacuum-tube radios can often be found on eBay. It is wise to purchase redundant commo gear. There is certain logic in buying three, four, or even five older, used Radio Shack receivers for around nine hundred dollars rather than spending the same amount on just *one* shiny new Drake R8B.

Two-Way Radio Communications

Amateur radio is a very do-it-yourself hobby. I would strongly recommend that you get a ham operator license no matter what. In the United States, it is illegal to transmit on the ham bands without an FCC-issued license and call sign.

I have long been an advocate of using field telephones and relatively low-power handheld transceivers for most retreat communications. Why unnecessarily blast out forty to fifty watts with a 2 meter rig when a few watts with a MURS radio will suffice? Save the higher-power transmitters for longer-range communication, and then use them only when needed.

My favorite band for walkie-talkies is the Multi-Use Radio Service (MURS) band, since most MURS radios can be programmed to operate in the 2 meter band, and they have much better range than FRS radios. But like FRS, they are unregulated in most private use. (No license required!) It is also important to note that the CB channels, FRS channels, and 2 meter band frequencies will likely be very crowded WTSHTF, particularly in the suburbs, but the less well-known and less populated MURS frequencies will probably be largely available at any given time.

Once you've mastered short-range communications and public-service band monitoring, the next step is to join your local ARRL affiliate club and study to get your amateur license. Someday you may be very glad that you did.

If you want a higher-power system, I would recommend buying used marine band radios on eBay. (Search for "marine band radio.") These do not require a license except for "vessels over sixty-five feet in length," but be advised that there are FCC restrictions on inland use. Fines by the FCC can be and usually are substantial.

Since most marine band radios draw more current than a MURS handi-talkie, you will need a more capable backup power system for battery charging. I suggest a couple of large six-volt DC deep-cycle (golf-cart-type) batteries for each radio. The beauty of the MURS band and the VHF marine band is that they are both essentially private bands in many areas. But, of course, don't consider them secure, since they can still be detected and monitored with a multiband scanner.

Some of my blog's readers have suggested establishing Bulletin Board System, or BBS–style radio networks for communication after TEOTWAWKI. Since traditional telephone services, DSL, cellular services, ISPs, and the Internet are all more or less dependent on grid power, I expect them all to go down within a few days of each other in the event of major catastrophe. There will, however, be some utility in ham-radio-based packet-radio and digipeater networks, which can operate like BBS servers and even like a quasi-Internet. These can operate over long distances in the HF ham bands. There are also some regional 2 meter band networks that are partially served by photovoltaic-powered repeaters, so parts of those networks might remain intact. Because many older hams are retiring, there are lots of used radios and packet TNCs on the market, selling for very reasonable prices.

Rather than reinventing the wheel, I recommend joining and expanding existing packet HF BBS networks. One word of warning: Do not simply bookmark the BBS pages. Like all the other World Wide Web pages, they will vanish if the power grid goes down, so be sure to print out an updated hard copy roughly twice a year. Mark your calendar.

I also recommend joining an existing topic-based, scheduled ("same time, same frequency") HF ham call-in.

Regarding "off-band" (or "out-of-band" or "freeband") transmission: Such transmissions are not legal in the United States except under emergency conditions.

Family Radio Service (FRS) Radio Capabilities

I am often asked about the range and capabilities of "bubble-packed" FRS and GMRS radios. Their effective range can vary greatly. Indoors, the key question is: *How much* reinforced concrete? Reliable communication in a cluttered urban environment is iffy for the typical FRS and GMRS handheld transceivers on the consumer market. My preference is for the MURS band handhelds. Not only will you get better range but you will also be operating in a less commonly used frequency band. This will give you marginally better communications security (but with the oft-repeated proviso: *no* radio transmission should be considered 100 percent secure). I recommend the MURS Radios company as a reputable source of transceivers. They also do custom frequency programming, and sell both accessories and MURS-compatible perimeter-intrusion detection systems.

Licensing Requirements for FRS Versus GMRS Radio Transmission

The most common FRS/GMRS radios come with several prepro-grammed channels, usually numbered 1–22. No license is required in the U.S. for transmitting on Family Radio Service (FRS) channels (channels 8–14). Channels 1–7 and 15–22 are GMRA channels. You must have a GMRS license issued by the FCC to legally transmit on those channels, except in an emergency. For licensing information and application forms, see the FCC Web site (fcc.gov) or call the FCC Forms Distribution Center at 1-800-418-3676.

Military service members: Consult your COMSEC office and/or spectrum allocation coordinator before utilizing FRS or GMRS bands for unencrypted tactical communications. These bands are some of the least secure in terms of interception risk.

Alternative News Sources When the Grid Goes Down

Many people now rely on the Internet and blogosphere for their news and information. Although the Internet is designed to be highly resilient (a carryover from its original design as a U.S. military network), it cannot be expected to survive a grid-down situation. The best that we could hope for in those circumstances is a combination voice and data packet network, via high-frequency (HF) shortwave. At the very minimum, to gather local, regional, and international intelligence, weather data, and accurate time of day, and to maintain overall situational aware-ness, you should own at least two radios, neither of which need be very expensive:

1. A general-coverage AM/FM/shortwave receiver. Most of these cover all the way from 500 kHz all the way up to 30 MHz. This includes the AM and FM broadcast bands, many of the amateur bands, the international HF broadcast bands (for stations like BBC, Radio Netherlands, HCJB, WWV, and so forth), and the citizens band (CB) channels. The inexpensive Kaito KA1102 radios are ideal for anyone on a budget. If you have a bigger budget, I would suggest the following: the Sony ICF-SW7600G, the Sony ICF-2010 (both discontinued, but used ones are available on eBay), and, if you have a "the sky is the limit" budget, get a Drake R8A.

Even if you eventually buy a more expensive receiver, I recommend that you keep a couple of the little Kaito KA1102 radios as spares, preferably stored in metal ammo cans to protect them from EMP.

2. A VHF police/marine/aircraft/weather band scanner. Try to get one of the more recent models that can demodulate trunked traffic. One relatively inexpensive "trunked" model is the Bearcat BC898T. If you have a big budget, get a digital model. Nearly all scanners cover the National Oceanic and Atmospheric Administration (NOAA) weather bands.

A Primer on Radio Transceiver Antennas

To begin, one-half-wave antennas are theoretically the most efficient. Shorter fractional-wavelength antennas (quarter-wave, one-eighth-wave, etc.) are used primarily for compactness and lower cost. To illustrate some practical aspects of wavelength: CB radio frequencies have a wavelength of around ten meters (about thirty-three feet). It is possible to use a half-wavelength

CB antenna at home or at a retreat, but not mounted on a vehicle. (On a vehicle, even a half-wavelength antenna is often too tall.) The MURS band (my favorite for short-range communications) has a wavelength of around two meters, so using a half-wavelength antenna is much more practical. The ARRL (arrl .org) has information that can give you an understanding of how both transmitting and receiving antennas work.

A ground plane is a reflective, flat surface that limits the downward radiation of an antenna. When operating a transceiver with an antenna mounted on a vehicle with typical steel body panels, the vehicle itself forms a ground plane. This is why the most efficient antenna mounting location is at the top center of a vehicle. But, unfortunately, this also places an antenna at the greatest risk of impact damage. This explains why bumper-mounted antennas are more popular, despite their distorted transmission characteristics and inefficiency.

A log periodic antenna (LPA) or yagi-type antenna can be very effective, but keep in mind that like other antennas, they need to be properly polarized. Most mobile two-way radios use vertical polarization. Hence, your LPA or yagi will *not* have the traditional horizontal TV-antenna appearance—rather, it will be flipped on its side, for vertical polarization.

Is Radio Direction Finding a Potential Threat for Survivalists?

Some people have expressed concern that radio direction finding (DF) could be used by looters to locate people with working radios (and thus power and supplies). However, the only people who have effective DF equipment *and* the requisite expertise to operate it are:

A. The National Security Agency (NSA) and a few other government agencies such as the FCC—mainly for tracking down unlicensed pirate stations.

B. Ham-radio operators themselves, who practice playing "fox and hound." Hams tend to be very law-abiding folks. I can't imagine many of them going renegade and turning into looters.

However, I *can* foresee many looter gangs showing rudimentary signals intelligence (SIGINT) skills and using portable public-service band ("police") scanners, so it is wise to use low-power and directional antennas. Never mention surnames, locations, latitude/longitude, map coordinates, or street addresses "in the clear." In my estimation, it is not likely that looter gangs would be sufficiently sophisticated to use DF gear. But never take anything for granted. If and when the Schumer hits the fan, you should construct your own brevity codes and change your call signs and frequencies often.

One further note: We now live in the age of Bluetooth. WT-SHTF, if you have a wireless network for your home computers, you should plan to turn the transmitter off and use it as a strictly "hardwired" Ethernet device. A clever looter might leave a laptop turned on in his vehicle, sensing when the vehicle passes an active wireless network. Even if you keep blackout shutters up—making your house look like all of your neighbors' homes that are without power—an active wireless network could mark your house as a lucrative target. Ditto for cell phones and cordless phones. Assuming that the phone circuits are still working during a period of lawlessness (not likely, but possible), be sure to switch to landline only for the duration.

I'll close this chapter with one big proviso: Don't make the mistake of becoming overly dependent on gadgets. Time and weather will take their toll. (As the Memsahib is fond of saying, "It's *entropy*, Jim, entropy.") Always have a Plan B and C for communications, and be ready and able to revert from high tech to *no* tech. Train for both best-case and worst-case situations when it comes to your electronics.

10

HOME SECURITY AND SELF-DEFENSE

Threat Escalation

As much as I would like to believe that order and decency will prevail in a crisis, I'm afraid the reality is that the thin veneer of humanity may crack under pressure. I hope that the worst never happens, but if it should, you need to be prepared to protect yourself, your family, and your supplies. As I see it, the biggest threat from your fellow man will be from home invasions and looting.

Modern military planners often talk in terms of "threat spirals" when a given threat escalates and inspires a defensive countermeasure. Ideally you should anticipate your opponent's next escalation and take countermeasures, insulating yourself from the future threat. Here are some potential home-invasion threat escalations WTSHTF:

1. More frequent home invasions. The worse the economy gets, the more crime we can expect. Home invasions and kidnappings are likely "growth" areas.
2. Use of dynamic-entry tools by home invaders. We can expect them to use commercial or improvised door-entry battering rams and Hallagan Tools—like those used by police. This means that standard solid-core doors by themselves will be insufficient.
3. Possible use of vehicle-mounted battering rams
4. Larger, better equipped, and better organized home-invasion gangs. Larger gangs will be able to invade a home.
5. The potential use of cell-phone jammers
6. More elaborate ruses as pretexts to get homeowners to open their doors. For example, not only will the "point man" be dressed as a UPS driver, but there will be a very convincing-looking UPS truck parked at the curb.
7. More use of pepper spray and other irritants by home invaders
8. Use of large diversions such as explosives to draw law enforcement away from the scene of a planned crime

Don't Be Caught Off Guard

Almost the entire American citizenry has been systemically off guard since the end of the U.S. Civil War. There are two fundamental weaknesses that make American homes vulnerable to home invasions: a condition-white mind-set, and appalling architectural weakness.

Condition-White Mind-set

First and foremost is an almost universal condition-white mind-set. This refers to the Cooper situational awareness color code for "unaware and unprepared." The vast majority of the urban and suburban population spends 90 percent of their daytime hours in condition white. They do a lot of idiotic things, such as failing to lock their doors and failing to keep guns handy.

Architectural Weakness

Secondly, one hundred fifty years of relative peace, stability, low crime rates, and cheap energy have worked together to push American residential architecture toward very vulnerable designs. Modern American homes are defensive disasters. They have huge expanses of glass, they lack barred windows or European-style security/storm shutters, they lack defensible space, and they often have no barriers for the approach of vehicles. Another ill-conceived innovation is the prevalence of floor plans that situate the master bedroom at the opposite end of the house from the children's bedrooms, which is a nightmare in a home invasion.

For the past twenty-five years, one of the hallmarks of "bad neighborhoods" in the United States has been the prevalence of barred windows and beefed-up doors. These are neighborhoods where the prevailing crime rates have pushed the majority of the population into condition yellow as a full-time baseline mind-set. Given the upswing in crime rates that will undoubtedly accompany the coming depression, I wish that everyone in the ostensibly "good neighborhoods" had this same outlook.

One of the most chronic defensive lapses in American suburban architecture is exterior-door design. Typically, entrance doors have windows either immediately adjacent to or set into the doors themselves. Even worse is the ubiquitous sliding glass door. Nothing more than a brick or a paving stone tossed through the glass and bingo—instant access for home invaders, with the fringe benefit of startling the occupants.

The Ultimate Solution: Designing for Security from the Ground Up

Hidden Retreats Versus Visibility

This is one of the most frequently asked questions from my consulting clients. It is the classic contradiction: concealment versus defendability. The most defendable positions are on barren hilltops, but those are also the most visible from a distance.

Ideally, you would pick a retreat parcel that can provide both open fields of fire out to fifty or sixty yards yet not have a house visible from nearby roads. But of course this isn't always possible. So you have to ask yourself: What do I expect to happen in my region in the event of a socioeconomic collapse? Will there just be an increase in burglary, or out-and-out attacks/home invasions by large, organized groups of looters?

In my estimation, light discipline will be more important than line-of-sight issues. A post-TEOTWAWKI world will be very dark at night. Just a few weeks into the problem, even the houses owned by people who have backup generators will go dark, as they begin to run out of fuel. Again, if you have an alternative power system, don't flaunt it. It is essential that you put blackout curtains backed by black sheet plastic inside all of your windows. Be sure to check for light leaks, preferably using night-vision goggles. Even heavy wool blankets and drapes tacked up inside your windows will leak light, but backing them with heavy black sheet plastic (not just black trash bags) will do the trick. Tape the sheet plastic in place over the windows, leaving no gap where the sheeting meets the window frame, using opaque duct tape. Without proper blackout precautions, your house will be a "come loot me" beacon that can be seen for miles at night. But with appropriate light discipline, at least your house will look anonymously dark—like those of your neighbors who have no power.

Consider getting infrared (IR) floodlights to light the exterior of your house. They can be motion-sensor activated. That way, unless your potential attackers have night-vision gear, your house will appear dark, but your yard will actually be well-illuminated (as seen through your night-vision goggles).

If you can afford to buy a large parcel of land, I recommend a layered defense that is adaptable to changing circumstances—all the way up to the dreaded "worst-case" societal collapse. Install your seismic intrusion-detection sensor in the outermost layer. This gives you early warning of approaching malefactors. If it would not look too out of the ordinary in your neighborhood then you might consider planting a "decorative" thorny hedge around as much of your perimeter as possible, and installing a gate across the bottom of your driveway. The gate should have a spiked top to discourage gate jumpers. Make the hedge and the gate the maximum height that you can without being branded as the poster child for paranoia. Any access roads should also have a MURS-frequency Dakota Alert (or similar) wireless IR-beam motion detector. Then, depending on your situation, you might want a screen of trees for concealment. Next, some open ground, then a tall chain-link fence. Then more open ground close to your house and outbuildings. This area should be crisscrossed with tangle-foot wire. Lastly, thorny bushes beneath each window, and beefy steel shutters.

Even well-manned retreats should supplement their guard staff with both dogs and intrusion-detection systems. Reliable night-vision gear is also a must. But please note that technology by itself is insufficient. Intrusion-detection, communications, and night-vision technologies are force multipliers, but you still need underlying *force*. It takes 24/7 manpower to defend a retreat. I describe how to set up and man LP/OPs and a CQ desk in my novel, *Patriots*.

Now, getting back to concealment: There are advantages in most situations to adding some "privacy-screen" trees to block the view of your house from any regularly traveled roads. Depending on the lay of the land, leaving thirty yards of open ground (for defense) and then another ten yards of thickness for the privacy tree screen will probably necessitate a property that is at least ten acres.

Some fast-growing screening-tree varieties include Portuguese laurel (*Prunus lusitanica*) and Leyland cypress. In cold climates, Lombardy poplars do well. A continuous hedge of all the same tree variety will be perceived as an obvious man-made planting at just a glance, so it is best to plant a mix of trees with semi-random spacing, to make your screening grove look more natural.

Regardless of what you decide to do in terms of concealment, be sure to leave at least twenty yards (sixty feet) of open ground for last-ditch ballistic defense. To impede intruders, think in terms of gates, cables, and "decorative" berms to stop vehicles. A chain-link fence will keep your dog(s) in and at least slow down the bad guys.

Keep some concertina wire or razor wire handy, but do not install it in pre-Schumer times. This wire should be installed only after it is clear that law and order have completely broken down. At that point appearances and pre-Crunch sensibilities won't be nearly as important as a ready defense. In fact, odds are that when your neighbors see you stringing concertina wire, they will ask if you have any extra that you can spare! You can install concertina wire or razor wire on the top of your fence, and if you have plenty of it available, add some staked-down horizontal rolls just beyond your fence.

Both inside and outside of your "last-ditch" fence, you can crisscross some tangle-foot wire. This type of wire is designed to slow down attackers—preventing them from charging your house. It should be strung at random heights between nine and forty inches off the ground. This is just one of the last layers of a layered defense. Every second that your various obstacles slow down attackers represents one more second available to stop them ballistically.

Chain-Link Fences for Incremental Retreat Security

Shortly after TSHTF, a chain-link fence can be quickly upgraded with a course of coiled razor wire fastened to the top, but only *if* you've bought the wire and mounting hardware in advance. It is also important to buy a couple of pairs of protective "concertina gloves" (also called staple gloves), a face visor, and some heavy-duty protection for your forearms during the installation process. The hardest to find of these are special wire-handling staple gloves that are reinforced. These are a must to protect your hands while working with military concertina wire or civilian razor wire.

Of course, only in a *worst-case*, out-and-out TEOTWAWKI would you want to erect military-concertina-wire arrays, but just in case, it would be prudent to have the materials on hand to do so.

Unless you have a big budget to buy commercially made razor wire (also called barbed tape), then think *surplus*. Used concertina wire can sometimes be found at U.S. Army Defense Reutilization Management Office (DRMO) surplus-disposal auctions—often for as low as scrap-metal prices. Keep an eye on the calendar of auctions to attend one in your region (snipurl .com/hojy7). Army camp/fort auctions are your best bet for finding concertina wire. Used, slightly rusty wire has two advantages: First, it does not have the reflective sheen of new wire, so it's not as obvious to casual observers at long distances. Second, the sight of rusty barbs might get the bad guys thinking about tetanus. Yes, I know that the tetanus risk from punctures by new wire is nearly as great as that from dirty or rusty wire, but at least here in North America the bad guys all grew up hearing about the perils of "rusty nails."

Temporary and Permanent Obstacles for Retreat Security

In heavily wooded country, dropping some trees to form an aba-tis is a viable expedient. But keep in mind that obstacles often work both ways: They will keep the bad guys out, but also keep you in. That is why my favorite roadblock is a Caterpillar ("Cat") or similar tracked tractor, parked perpendicular at a narrow spot on a road, with its blade dropped and ignition system disabled. That will stop just about any vehicle short of another Cat. The biggest advantage of this method is that a Cat can be moved quickly to allow the passage of "friendlies."

If you don't own a Cat, then parking cars or trucks perpendicular at a narrow spot works fairly well. Remember: In most foreseeable circumstances, emplacing multiple obstacles of marginal utility is as good as emplacing just one massive obstacle. One fairly inexpensive technique is to emplace multiple five-eighths-inch-diameter steel cables at twenty- to fifty-foot intervals strung eighteen inches above the ground, secured with heavy-duty padlocks. To gain entry, even someone equipped with large bolt cutters would have to repeatedly reduce each obstacle. And during that time, they could be warned off or directly engaged with rifle fire.

Advice on Sources for Sandbags and Sandbag Filler

One often-overlooked security measure is laying in a supply of sandbags. Modern American residential architecture is not designed with ballistic protection in mind. Sandbags can be quickly—albeit laboriously—filled with soil from your backyard and stacked to make fighting positions. This might sound a bit over-the-top, but here I'm talking about an absolute worst-case scenario, in which there will be no law enforcement available to call, and/or no working phone service to call them. You will be on your own. In inimical times, sandbags will be cheap insurance, providing you with a good chance to avoid getting ventilated by the local riffraff.

In the U.S. there are several good sources for sandbags, but prices do indeed vary widely (from as much as $3.75 each in small quantities to as little as thirty-eight cents each if you buy in lots of one thousand), so shop around. For example, see preparedness.com and 1st Army Supply (snipurl.com/hnfk9).

If you want to buy in quantity (perhaps a group purchase that you can split several ways), it is best to order direct from a manufacturer, such as Dayton Bag and Burlap (snipurl.com/hnfpb),

Mutual Industries (snipurl.com/hnfrv), or United Bags (snipurl
.com/hnfwj).

Be sure to buy the later-variety, synthetic (such as polypropylene) sandbags. The early burlap (or Hessian) bags tend to rot
and rip out too quickly. The latest and greatest military-
specification bags use linear low-density polyethylene (LLDPE)
or polyethylene film laminated with a third layer of molten polyethylene. These have the best UV protection and hence the longest useful life out in the elements, but they are also the most
expensive. Even the standard military polypropylene bags will
last two to three years in full sun, and much longer if painted or
kept in the shade.

As for filler material, if sand is expensive in your area, then do
some comparison pricing on "one half minus" road gravel deliv-
ered by the dump-truck load. This is gravel that has been
screened so that the largest pieces are no more than a half-inch
in diameter. I don't recommend using soil, since sand and gravel
are superior for stopping bullets. If you must use soil, then try
to get either very sandy soil or heavy clay soil. Dry loam soil is
the least effective for use in sandbags. Remember: The more
vegetable matter in the soil, the lower its ballistic protection.

The Legality and Ethics of Blocking Roads and Bridges After TEOTWAWKI

Legally and ethically, as an individual you can block roads only
on *your own* property. But if a small community makes a collec-
tive decision to block a road or bridge, then that is another matter. I would assume that every state in the Union has laws
forbidding blocking any public road. Federal law prohibits blocking interstate freeways.

By using a mobile roadblock that is under armed observation 24/7, you will minimize the risk of alienating your neighbors. Who is to say how long a crisis might last? If, however, you were to block a road with earth or rock piles, or even with wrecked cars, you would probably infuriate any neighbors who decide to return to a normal life of work and commuting, as well as any who resume hauling produce or livestock to market.

Keep in mind: Physical obstacles are just *delays*—not absolute safeguards. People will find a way through them, over them, or around them—on foot if need be.

Prowlers and Lighting

In regard to security lighting, I need to address two disparate circumstances: pre-TEOTWAWKI and post-TEOTWAWKI.

Pre-TEOTWAWKI

Under present circumstances, security lighting is a benefit. You have law enforcement available to call. Prowlers aren't likely to shoot at you. For pre-TEOTWAWKI, it is best to think in terms of active defenses, such as vapor lights, 1,000,000-candlepower twelve-volt DC handheld spotlights, full-spectrum trip flares, barking dogs, peafowl, and noisy electronic alarm systems.

Post-TEOTWAWKI

At some future date, security lighting could be a potential hazard. If and when the power grid goes down, the few families who have alternative energy will be very noticeable, especially as time goes on and stored fuel for generators begins to run out. If you still have power, you will be very conspicuous unless you are careful to prevent light leakage from your home.

For post-TEOTWAWKI, it is best to think in terms of passive defenses, such as starlight scopes, infrared chemical light-stick trip flares, quiet (but alert) dogs, tangle-foot wire, concertina wire, and silent alarm systems.

With the exception of infrared illuminators, I generally discourage mounting lights on guns intended for use post-TEOTWAWKI. If left turned on for more than just an instant before shooting, a visible light mounted on a gun can turn you into a natural target. If you feel the need to illuminate targets for post-TEOTWAWKI security, then I'd recommend that you be the armed man hidden in the shadows who remotely turns on a floodlight, as opposed to the man holding the light—or holding the gun with an attached light—who announces, "Here I am!"

Motion-activated floodlights are inexpensive and very easy to install. They are available at home-improvement and hardware stores such as Home Depot and Lowe's. If the power grid goes down and you are forced to stay, then floodlights might suffice. Under those circumstances, a pair of night-vision goggles would be a must. And if you have those, you might want to retrofit your floodlights to use infrared bulbs. Being battery powered, your Dakota Alert system will continue to operate without grid power. But of course keep plenty of spare batteries on hand for all of your flashlights and other home-security and communications electronics.

Safe at Home

I recommend that the next time you move, you buy a brick or other masonry house and upgrade its security, or better yet, start with a bare lot and custom-build a stout house with an integral safe room. Two good starting points for house designs are Mexican walled courtyards and buildings with square bastions (also known as Cooper corners). These projecting corners eliminate the blind spots that are common to typical square or rectangular houses.

For greater detail on this subject, I recommend Joel Skousen's book, *The Secure Home*. My novel, *Patriots: Surviving the Coming Collapse,* also has some detailed design description for ballistically armored window shutters and doors, as well as details on constructing neo-medieval door bars.

If you are serious about custom-building or retrofitting an existing house for increased security and/or adding a safe room, then I recommend the architectural consulting services of both Safecastle and Hardened Structures (hardenedstructures.com).

Safe Rooms and Vaults

I can think of no better way to foil the bad guys than building a dedicated safe room. Such a room could serve multiple purposes, including panic room, gun and valuables vault, storm shelter, and fallout shelter. I'm amazed when I hear some of my relatively wealthy consulting clients tell me that they don't own a home gun vault or safe room. Yes, they are expensive, but not nearly as expensive as having some of your key survival tools stolen.

Putting a lock on your bedroom door is insufficient. Since most interior doors are hollow-core, they typically use lightweight hinges, and they have insubstantial strike plates. Most of these doors can either be knocked down or kicked though, in very short order. I recommend replacing your bedroom doors with heavy-duty exterior-type doors (preferably steel) with sturdy hinges and one or more deadbolt locks. If your house has all the bedrooms isolated on one hallway, then you can add a heavy-duty door at the end of that hall and keep it locked at night, basically creating a safe wing. Then, inside that safe wing, you should have a far more secure, dedicated safe room that your entire family can retreat to.

A built-in basement walk-in safe room is ideal. In areas with high water tables, where a basement is not practical, a safe room/shelter can be built on the ground floor of a newly con-structed "slab" house, or as an addition to an existing house, with a reinforced poured-concrete floor, walls, and ceiling. Re-gardless of the design that you choose, it is important to specify a vault door that opens inward, so that it won't be jammed shut by debris in the event of tornado, hurricane, or bomb blast. The folks at Safecastle can do the engineering and source the vault door for you.

Another important thing to keep in mind for your safe room is that redundant communications are important, so that you can solicit outside help. Both the master bedroom and the safe room should have hardwired POTS telephones that are serviced by underground lines with no visible junction boxes. Be sure to test using a cell phone (as a backup) from every room. Having a CB radio in your safe room also makes sense.

I realize that most readers cannot afford an elaborate walk-in safe room, but 95 percent of you can at least afford a heavy-duty steel gun vault with a Sargent and Greenleaf dial lock with re-locker. Be sure to bolt your vault securely to the floor and, if possible, build it into a hidden compartment or hidden room. There are a lot of vault makers in the U.S. and Canada, so it is a very competitive market. Do some Internet research and comparison shopping and you can save a lot of money on your vault purchase. Vaults are quite heavy (typically around seven hundred pounds) and shipping them is expensive, so it is generally best to buy one that is made within two hundred miles of where you live. If you move frequently, I recommend the free-standing gun vault made by Zanotti Armor (www.zanottiarmor.com). Zanotti makes vaults that can be taken apart into six manageable pieces for ease of transport. They cost only about one hundred dollars more than comparable vaults that are welded together in the traditional manner. Assembly is a three-man job, since extra hands are needed to get everything lined up before the pins can be noisily driven into place. It takes only about a half hour, and disassembly takes about ten minutes.

Constructing a Hiding Place for Precious Metals in a Home

Your last line of defense will be inside your home itself. If you don't have a vault, I recommend that you construct one or more secret caches in your house. If the weight is modest, you can simply hide a bag or box of silver coins under the insulation in your attic. It will probably be resting on top of horizontal ceiling drywall, so keep the weight under fifteen pounds.

To conceal up to two hundred pounds of silver, you can make a Rawles Through the Looking Glass wall/door cache. Even someone with just rudimentary skills can make one of these between-the-studs wall caches. These are simple to construct and will go unnoticed by all but the most astute and methodical burglars. Here is how even someone inexperienced with carpentry can do so, in typical North American wood frame-houses—with modern Sheetrock walls:

Pick out a section of drywalled interior partition wall in a bedroom where a wall-mounted mirror wouldn't look out of place. Go to your local Home Depot or Lowe's and buy a vertical mirror that is at least sixteen inches wide and four feet tall. Ideally, you should get one that is the same width as your wall's stud interval, so that the mirror-mounting screws will attach through the drywall into the studs. Such mirrors typically come with a set of L-shaped mounting clips that attach to a wall or door with screws. Figure out where any wiring might be running through the wall. Typically it will run horizontally, about one foot up from the floor, between your power outlets. Do not pick a section of wall that is near a light switch, since vertical wires may be running though those wall sections. Plan to mount the mirror at least six inches above the wiring. Look for small indentations, puckers, or other signs of nails attaching the drywall. These will typically be centered either eighteen or twenty-four inches apart. If you can't spot the nails or screws you can either buy or borrow an inexpensive magnetic stud finder. A bit of judicious tapping to hear pitch changes can also be helpful. The nails will be driven into vertical studs, and you will cut your hole between two two-by-four studs. It will provide you a caching space that is about fifteen inches wide and three-and-a-half inches deep.

Once you've estimated where the studs are, drill some small exploratory holes in the drywall at a sharp angle. Probe inside each hole with a length of coat-hanger wire to confirm where the vertical studs are located and whether there are any horizontal two-by-four fire-stop blocks. Those are typically halfway up each wall. Then, with a power jigsaw or a Sawzall, cut a hole (or holes) to provide access to the wall-cache dead space. Leave at least two inches of drywall width around the hole, which will be covered by the mirror. Remove any insulation from the cache area, and vacuum out the drywall dust. Place your valuables in the cache. If there is substantial weight, do not rest it directly on top of any wiring at the bottom of the cache. You should first cut a support block out of two-by-fours and screw it in place with drywall screws. Then neatly mount the mirror over the hole, measuring carefully and/or using a level so that the mirror will be mounted straight.

Accessing the cache will just take a few minutes to remove the mirror. If you need to access the cache frequently, you'll find that if the screws are screwed only into drywall and not into studs behind, then the screw holes in the drywall will become enlarged and the screws will eventually loosen. If that happens, you can install anchor bolts behind most of the screws. This same technique can be used to create a similar—albeit more shallow—cache inside a hollow-core bedroom door. One neat trick with a door cache is to only remove the top mirror-mounting brackets when you access the cache. With those removed and the door slightly open you can simply slide the mirror up to reveal the cache opening.

Alarm and Camera Systems

No matter what sort of vault or hiding place you choose, you should supplement it with a home security system. Monitored alarm systems can be expensive—especially with monthly service contracts. But these days, webcams are dirt cheap. Buy several of them and mount them in locations where they are not likely to be spotted immediately, such as among the books on your bookshelves. Unless the motion-triggered images captured are immediately uploaded to a server that is off-site, it is essential that the computer that controls the cameras and the hard drive that stores the images be housed inside your gun vault or safe room. Otherwise the burglars will walk off with the evidence. Don't forget that any disruption of phone service or grid power will nullify the protection of a monitored alarm. Anyone living off grid or anyone who foresees a period of extended blackouts should get a battery-powered self-contained camera system, such as those sold by Ready Made Resources. Photographic evidence is crucial for both tracking down perpetrators and substantiating insurance claims. Don't skimp on this important piece of your preparedness.

Insurance

Another must is fire and theft insurance. Given enough time, determined burglars can penetrate even the most elaborate vault. Many homeowners-insurance policies have specific limits on firearms, often absurdly low dollar amounts, unless you get a separate rider to your policy at additional cost. If you aren't sure about your coverage, pull out your policy and read through it thoroughly. The National Rifle Association offers a modest-dollar-value firearms-insurance policy that is free with NRA membership.

I also recommend making a list of serial numbers and detailed descriptions of each gun, camera, and electronic gadget that you own. I have found that using three-by-five index cards is convenient for updates, since your inventory will change over time. Also take a few detailed photos of each item. Store the index cards and hard-copy pictures annotated with each item's serial number in a vault belonging to a relative or a trusted friend, and offer to do likewise for him or her.

Advice from an Expert: Firefighting Equipment for Rural Homes and Retreats

Todd S. is a former volunteer firefighter who shared his expertise on home firefighting: "Due to response time(s), everyone who can afford it should have the following setup on the property to use during those fifteen to thirty minutes until emergency services arrive. It may take that long from your call to having equipment on the scene. The farther out you are, the longer it will be, and in the winter, you may be on your own due to road impassability.

I sometimes suggest to clients that they purchase an old fire truck or water tender that is in decent shape, but only if they have the skills to service those types of units. Prices vary but most of the time you can get a nice working 1960s to 1970s vintage truck for five thousand to ten thousand dollars.

Purchase a portable pump along with a portable bladder if you do not have a pond, swimming pool, or year-round stream within 100 to 150 feet of your retreat, then add some one-and-a-half-inch hose and a nozzle or two, and you'll have a fairly economical safeguard against structure fire or a wild land fire on your property."

OPSEC: Keeping Your Preparations Low Profile

Of all of the aspects of preparing for a crisis, perhaps the most overlooked in survivalist literature are privacy and operational security (OPSEC). Your preparations must be kept secret from all but your most trusted friends. All of your expensive logistics could disappear in a few hours soon after TEOTWAWKI. Your

hidey-hole could be stripped clean by looters or overzealous government agents wielding "emergency powers." You must resist
the urge to mention your preparations to anyone who does not
have a need to know about them. I am not suggesting that you
lie to anyone, but be discreet and learn how to redirect conversa-
tions. Doing so is simply prudent.

What is legal today may be deemed illegal tomorrow under
martial law or at the whim of some bureaucrat who is handed
emergency powers. Witness the mass confiscations of privately
owned firearms following Hurricane Katrina in 2005. With the
help of the media the concepts of saving and storing may be
demonized and redefined as "hoarding" immediately after disaster strikes.

If you have been saving during times of plenty you are not a
hoarder. A hoarder is someone who removes a disproportion-
ately large chunk of logistics *after* shortages have occurred. By
saving and storing now, well in advance of a crisis, you represent
one fewer person who will rush to the grocery store after disaster strikes. You won't be part of the problem. You'll be part of
the solution, especially if you dispense your excess supplies as
charity.

If you have reason to believe that your anonymity has already
been compromised, then consider that:

1. You can't get anonymity back unless you change your name
   and completely drop out of sight (impractical for most).
2. You will have to take some countermeasures.

Perhaps the best countermeasure is to make a fresh start the
next time that you move (ideally to your retreat location). Do
not send forwarding cards for any magazine subscriptions. Consider buying your next home in someone else's name, perhaps a

sister or an aunt or uncle with a different surname and a low profile. Another option is establishing a land trust and having the trust make the purchase. Your attorney could be the trustee of a trust that owns the land. Yet another option is to set up a Nevada or Delaware corporation and have the corporation make the land purchase. See Boston T. Party's book *Bulletproof Privacy* (javelinpress.com) for further details on making a clean break.

Make all cash (no paper trail) acquisitions of guns, bulk ammo, and bulk logistics. Never use a credit card for such purposes. Unless you already have a very high profile, resist the urge to buy your ammo, reference books, and assorted gear via mail order. The only exception would be if you used an assumed name and a drop box.

It is essential to impress upon your family the importance of keeping quiet about your preparations. Maintaining a low profile involves common sense and knowing when to keep your mouth shut—and it just might prevent your safety being compromised.

The Neighborhood Watch on Steroids

If times truly get bad the crime rate will undoubtedly skyrocket. You need to be able to provide for your family's security. Since you can't stand guard 24/7, this may necessitate teaming up with your neighbors to form what I only half-jokingly dubbed a Neighborhood Watch on Steroids.

11

FIREARMS FOR SELF-SUFFICIENCY AND SELF-DEFENSE

In order to be fully self-sufficient, you will need to kill wild game and livestock. This chapter will walk you through the best guns for every situation, including the undesirable scenario in which, as a last resort, you may need to rely upon firearms to defend your home. Having the right guns and ammunition is an important part of any preparedness plan.

Selecting Your Survival Gun Battery

There are several requirements that must be considered when selecting guns for use on a farm, ranch, or survival retreat. First and foremost, they must be versatile. A single gun might be pressed into service for shooting crows or starlings at ten yards, rabbits or coyotes at one hundred yards, or rattlesnakes at five feet. While there is no single gun that can handle any task, it is important to select firearms with at least some degree of versatility. It is not realistic to believe that you can get by with just one gun, or even just one rifle, one pistol, and one shotgun. Like the tools in a carpenter's box, each type of gun has its special place and purpose.

The second major consideration for survival guns is that they be robust and reliable enough to put up with constant carry and regular use. When the nearest gunsmith is a two-hour drive away, you have to depend on your own resources. Since they are carried quite frequently and in all sorts of weather, farm/ranch/survival guns need to have durable finishes. Stainless steel is by far the best choice for most situations. Unfortunately, however, not all guns are available in stainless steel. For guns that are made only with a blued finish, there are several finishes available. My personal favorite of the exotic coatings is called META-COL (metal color), which is offered in a wide variety of finishes by Arizona Response Systems (snipurl.com/ht0fs). Exotic material finishes are quite durable and offer rust protection that is exceeded only by stainless steel.

Because trips to town to procure ammunition might be infrequent (or impossible in a severe survival scenario), and reloading will likely be the norm for those seeking self-sufficiency, you'll want to limit the number of different cartridges that you stock. Having ten different guns chambered in ten different cartridges will complicate logistics. Further, it is best to select only guns chambered for commonly available cartridges. Small country stores stock ammo like .22 long rifle, .308 Winchester, .30-06, and 12-gauge, but probably not .264 Winchester Magnum, .300 Weatherby, or 28-gauge.

Small Game

There are several categories of firearms that belong in the gun racks of nearly every farm or ranch. The first and most frequently used variety are small-game/pest-shooting guns. These guns are used to hunt small game for the pot (squirrels, rabbits, etc.), to shoot garden pests (crows, starlings, gophers, etc.), and for shooting to deter marauding predators (coyotes, foxes, weasels, ferrets, etc.). They also end up being the guns most frequently used to slaughter livestock.

Good cartridges for small game/pest shooting include .22 long rifle (.22 LR) and .223 Remington. The most common shot shells for this use are .410, 20-gauge, and 12-gauge. The .22 LR will suffice for everything up to the size of a rabbit at conservative distances. It is inexpensive to shoot and quiet, and has hardly any felt recoil. The .223 Remington is a good cartridge for shooting perched birds that would be out of range for a .22 rimfire, or for shooting feral dogs, feral cats, or coyotes.

Both handguns and long guns are needed for small-game/pest shooting. A long gun would of course be the ideal choice in most circumstances, due to its inherently higher velocity and longer sighting radius (and hence greater accuracy). There are times, however, when it is not practical to carry a long gun. When mending fences, feeding livestock, hauling wood, riding a tractor, or doing most gardening work, it is usually not practical to carry a long gun. On farms and ranches, long guns tend to be left behind inside buildings or in vehicle gun racks. They are only rarely carried when doing chores or just walking down to the mailbox at the county road. This is where handguns come in.

Rimfire Handguns

A good-quality .22 rimfire pistol may be one of the most useful handguns in your battery. These guns are used for dispatching those "uncatchable" chickens for the stewpot, for shooting small game/pests, and for inexpensively maintaining marksmanship skills for those more powerful (and more expensive to shoot) handguns. My wife and I use a stainless steel Ruger Mark II with a 5½-inch bull barrel and Pachmayr grips. The Ruger is also offered in 6⅞-inch and 10⅝-inch barrel lengths. But we find that the 5½-inch barrel is a handy length for holster carry. Another well-made stainless steel .22 autopistol is the Smith and Weson Model 622. It is available with a 4½-inch or 6-inch barrel. If you prefer a revolver, the stainless steel Smith and Wesson Model 617 is a good option. It is available in a 4-inch, 6-inch, or 8⅜-inch barrel length.

Regardless of which brand of .22 rifle you buy, you should consider mounting it with a telescopic sight. Because of its low energy, proper placement of a .22 rimfire bullet can mean the difference between crippling and cleanly killing small game. Mounting a scope will in most instances give you the ability not just to hit an animal's center of mass, but rather to hit a precise aiming point, such as its head or neck. If you do decide to mount a scope, use a full-size (one-inch-diameter) scope rather than one of the inexpensive three-quarter-inch-diameter scopes made specifically for air rifles and .22s.

Centerfire Handguns

If you are seeking a particularly versatile handgun, you might consider the Thompson/Center G2 Contender or the earlier T/C

Contender. These single-shot pistols use readily changeable barrels in a wide range of chamberings. Some of the most useful of the more than twenty chamberings are .22 LR, .223 Remington, and the .45 Colt/.410 shotgun barrel.

At the Rawles Ranch, we now carry Colt stainless steel Gold Cup (Model 1911 pattern) .45 ACPs with Pachmayr grips, extended slide releases, and Trijicon tritium-lit sights. When we moved to bear country, we sold off the Smith and Wesson 686es and standardized with the .45 automatics. We wanted to be able to put a lot of rounds into a bear in a hurry, and .45 autos are far faster to reload than revolvers—at least under stress, in our experience. Granted, the chances of surviving a bear attack are slim, but we feel that we have a better chance with the Gold Cups. At least when they find all the ejected brass around our mangled corpses, they can say that we put up a good fight.

Speaking of bears, for homesteaders living in brown-bear or grizzly-bear country, a more powerful handgun than even the .45 ACP is often recommended. A stainless steel Smith and Wesson Model 629 (6-inch) .44 Magnum, or Ruger Redhawk (5½-inch) .44 Magnum, or perhaps the Colt Anaconda (6-inch) .44 Magnum would be good choices.

Rifles

A lightweight rifle chambered in .223 Remington is particularly useful for shooting both perched birds and predators. Remington, Ruger, and Sako all make good-quality .223 bolt-actions. Selecting one is largely a matter of personal preference. We use our .223s on coyotes, which currently abound in great numbers in the western United States, and are a constant source of trouble in our area. They have a penchant for devouring ducks, chickens, pet cats, and newborn lambs. We use three different guns on the uncommon occasions when we have a chance to snipe at coyotes. These guns include a Remington Model Seven bolt-action chambered in .223 Remington, a Colt CAR-15 M4gery, and a scoped L1A1 semiauto chambered in .308 Winchester (virtually identical to and in most cases interchangeable with the 7.62mm NATO cartridge used by the military). A .308 bolt-action is used when we spot a coyote beyond three hundred yards. With the Remington Model Seven available, the CAR-15 is largely superfluous. But we like its easy handling, and the fact that we can get off a quick second shot when shooting at running rabbits or coyotes.

Combination Guns

The next category of guns is combination or "garden" guns. These range from expensive imported rifle/shotguns to inexpensive combination guns made domestically. The European three-barrel combination guns or "dreilings" (often anglicized to "drillings") can easily cost two thousand dollars or more. Guns typical of this breed are the Colt Sauer drillings, Krieghoff drillings, and the Valmet over/unders. They typically feature a high-power rifle barrel mounted beneath side-by-side 12-gauge shotgun barrels. Domestically produced two-barrel combination guns, while not as aesthetically pleasing, cost far less than European drillings. These guns offer the ability to fire either a single shotgun shell or a rifle cartridge, with the flick of a switch. They are by far the best gun to have at hand when out doing garden work. They give you the versatility to eliminate a pesky gopher or marauding birds, whether they are perching or in flight. One of the best of the inexpensive combination guns now on the market is the Savage Model 24F with a Rynite fiberglass stock. In the past, Savage Model 24-series guns were made in a wide range of chamberings, such as .22 LR over .410, .22 LR over 20-gauge, .22 Magnum over .410-gauge, and .357 Magnum over 20-gauge. All of these now-discontinued guns featured wooden stocks. They can often be found used at gun shows or in gun shops at modest prices. Due to their versatility, they are well worth looking for. Because most of the Savage 24-series guns come with a blued finish, it is recommended that they be upgraded with a more durable finish such as Teflon or Parkerizing.

Long-Range Rifles

Big-game-hunting/countersniping rifles are the next group of guns to be considered. The selection of a big-game rifle depends on the variety of game to be hunted. In the lower forty-eight states, a bolt-action rifle chambered in .308 Winchester or .30-06 will normally handle most big game. Regional differences will determine exactly what you need. No matter which chambering you select, it is important that you buy a well-made rifle with a robust action. Remington, Ruger, and Winchester, among others, make guns with these qualities. After you buy the rifle itself, you will probably want to have a more durable finish applied to its metal surfaces. You might also want to mount a telescopic sight if you will be hunting in open country. If you'll be hunting in brushy or densely wooded terrain, you could find that a scope is more of a hindrance than a help. Scopes are more prone to failure than any other part of a rifle, so it is wise to select a rifle with good-quality iron sights, whether or not you intend to mount a scope. If and when a scope should fail, you will have the recourse of removing the scope and reverting to iron sights. The need for a cartridge more powerful than .30-06 is normally a consideration only in Alaska or parts of Canada, where moose and grizzly bear are found. Several powerful cartridges are currently popular. These include the .35 Whelen, the .338 Winchester, and the .375 H&H Magnum. For our type of big-game hunting (normally deer, but nothing bigger than elk), my wife and I selected a pair of Winchester Model 70s. Because either rifle might also be used tactically, we had their muzzles threaded for flash hiders (half-inch by 28 TPI-thread—the same as that used on the M16) by Holland Shooters Supply, of Oregon, and had Holland slim-line muzzle brakes installed (hollandguns.com). We decided to get the muzzle brakes because they don't draw as much attention as a flash hider. However, if we get into some deep drama, we can quickly switch to flash hiders.

Shotguns

The next gun categories to consider are upland-game and waterfowl shotguns. If you will have the opportunity to hunt upland game or waterfowl, you will of course want to include one or more good bird-hunting shotguns in your battery. As you will likely be carrying your shotgun more often than the average city dweller, a durable finish is desirable. Remington's Special Purpose versions of their Model 870, Model 11-87, and Model 1100 fit this bill nicely. They come from the factory with a nonglare stock finish and a dull gray Parkerized finish on all their surfaces. Several makers produce (or produced) Parkerized-finish pumps and autos comparable to the Remington Special Purpose series. One such is the Winchester Model 1300 Waterfowler.

Like most other currently produced domestic shotguns, the Remington Special Purpose guns come with screw-in choke tubes as standard equipment. A twenty-six-inch barrel length is best suited to upland-game hunting, while a twenty-eight- or thirty-inch barrel is normally recommended for pass shooting at ducks and geese. Because odd-gauge shells might be difficult to obtain in rural areas (or regardless of where you live in times of turmoil), it is best to buy either a 12- or 20-gauge shotgun. Also, given the trend toward steel shot, a three-inch-length chamber is recommended. The longer chamber allows the use of Magnum loads, which are needed to give the less dense steel shot the same killing power as traditional lead-shot loadings. In addition, screw-in choke tubes are advisable. As steel shot wears out chokes quickly, replaceable choke tubes can greatly increase the usable life of a gun.

One gun that deserves special mention is the .410-gauge Snake Charmer II single-shot shotgun, made by Sport Arms of Florida. This lightweight little gun just barely meets the federal size minimums (18-inch barrel and 28½ inches overall length). It is constructed of stainless steel and has a synthetic stock with a compartment that holds spare shot shells. Because it is compact and lightweight, our Snake Charmer gets taken along on walks when heavier, bulkier long guns would usually be left behind. This gun has been used to kill several rattlesnakes and a good number of quail.

Despite popular misconceptions popularized by Hollywood, shotguns must be aimed, much like a rifle. The bead sights that are installed on most shotgun barrels are insufficient. I recommend either buying a replacement barrel with rifle sights or having these sights retrofitted.

Retreat Defense

Self-defense guns are the final category to be considered for farms, ranches, and survival retreats. Post-TEOTWAWKI, we all may be on our own—with no law enforcement to call on or any way to call them even if they are still available. Even in relatively peaceful times, a lot can happen before help arrives, so it makes sense to be prepared. If you expect bad economic times or other sources of social unrest, you should make a concerted effort to stock up on defensive guns, plenty of ammunition, lots of spare magazines, and a good selection of spare parts. At our farm, we have a variety of guns whose main job is defense but that are also used for other purposes. Our L1A1s double as long-range coyote eliminators. Our large-frame handguns are primarily self-defense guns, but are also usable for hunting and shooting pests.

If you like the ballistics of the .45 ACP but prefer the action of a revolver, you might consider purchasing a Smith and Wesson Model 625 revolver. This is a stainless steel revolver built on the "N" frame—the same heavy frame used for the Smith and Wesson .44 Magnums. The Model 625 uses "full-moon" spring steel clips to hold six rounds of .45 ACP. Unlike most speed loaders, with the full-moon clips there is no knob to twist, nor any mechanism that could potentially fail. You just drop the whole works into the cylinder. This makes them just as fast, if not faster, than any speed loader. The Model 625 is offered in three-, four-, and five-inch barrel lengths—the latter of which is just about ideal. Because the .45 ACP has the same bore diameter as the .45 Colt cartridge, a spare cylinder and crane assembly can be fabricated for the more potent .45 Colt cartridge (commonly, but inaccurately called ".45 long Colt"). This combination would make a particularly versatile handgun.

Shotguns are also well suited to defensive work. A spare short riot-gun barrel for a pump or automatic shotgun can make it double as a formidable home-defense weapon.

The "Battery"

Just how many guns will you need? If you are on a budget, you might get by with a good-quality bolt-action rifle chambered in .308 or .30-06, a 12-gauge pump shotgun with a spare riot-gun barrel, a .22 LR rifle, and a .45 automatic pistol. However, in order to have the versatility required for the many shooting tasks at most farms and ranches, you will likely need at least twice this many guns. For a more complete discussion of guns suitable for a self-sufficient and self-reliant lifestyle, the late Mel Tappan's book *Survival Guns* (The Janus Press, Rogue River, Oregon) is generally recognized as the best general reference in print. And for a more complete discussion of guns suitable for self-defense, I highly recommend the book *Boston's Gun Bible*.

Purchases should be made systematically and dispassionately. As with buying any other tool, you shouldn't skimp on quality. A well-made gun can deliver years or even generations of reliable service.

One final note: You can buy the best guns in the world, but unless you practice with them often, you are *not* prepared. Getting training at a top-notch firearms school is money well spent.

Storing Guns and Magazines

The precautions that you need to take depend a lot on where you live. If you live in a humid climate, then you need to be particularly vigilant with your guns, magazines, and other tools. The higher the humidity, the greater the degree of protection required, and the greater the frequency of inspection for rust.

Wear lightweight cotton gloves when you do your gun maintenance. This is particularly important if you have sweaty hands. My college roommate was notorious for inducing rust on guns because of this, and he has always had to take special precautions.

A light coat of gun oil such as Rem Oil will suffice in a dry climate. Although exotic lubricants such as Break-Free CLP are great for lubricating, in my experience, they leave so little residue that they are actually inferior to traditional gun oils for preventing rust. In damp climates, I recommend Birchwood Casey Barricade (formerly sold under the product name Sheath). Rem Oil and Barricade are both available from a number of Internet vendors, including Brownells (snipurl.com/hneta). And even Amazon.com now sells Barricade.

For long-term storage, all metal parts (inside and out), especially the bore, chamber, and breech face, should get a coating of grease. There is always the tried-and-true USGI "grease, rifle," but I prefer rust-inhibitive grease (RIG), which is available from Brownells, as well as from other Internet vendors. Even though you will know how the gun was treated before storage, someone else in your family might not. I therefore strongly recommend attaching a warning note: "Warning: grease coating—bore, chamber and bolt face! Remove grease before firing!"

Small quantities of magazines stored inside a humidity-controlled gun vault (with a Golden Rod or similar dehumidifier) or in sealed ammo cans with a large packet of silica-gel desiccant probably won't need more than a light coat of oil and annual inspection. Any larger quantities of magazines that are stored outside of your vault in non-airtight containers should probably be rubbed down with RIG. In most cases this requires disassembling magazines, to get at their innards. Don't forget that the spring needs rust protection.

Frequency of Firearms Practice

I recommend shooting as frequently as your time and budget allow. Once a week would be ideal to stay in top form. Dry practice (commonly called "dry firing," with an unloaded weapon) is quite useful, particularly for developing muscle strength and motor control. Note, however, that some stringent safety rules must be enforced and a safe backstop constructed, to eliminate the risk of a negligent discharge.

The Memsahib reminded me to mention that bird watching with heavy binoculars or a camera with a long lens is also great exercise for building arm muscles, acquiring targets, and practice with holding a considerable weight perfectly still.

How Much Ammunition to Store

It is important to maintain balance in your preparations. Food storage, first-aid supplies, and heirloom-seed storage should be priorities. But after those have been taken care of, it makes sense to stock up on ammunition. As long as you store your ammo in sealed military-surplus cans, there is no risk in overestimating your needs, since ammunition has a storage life of more than fifty years if protected from oil vapors and humidity. Consider any extra ammo the ideal barter item. The late Col. Jeff Cooper rightly called it "ballistic wampum."

For your barter inventory, I recommend that you stick with the most common calibers. For rifles: .22 LR, .223, .308, .30-06 (and in the British Commonwealth, .303 British). For handguns: 9mm, .40 S&W, and .45 ACP. For shotguns: 12-gauge and 20-gauge. You might also buy a small quantity of the regional favorite deer cartridge for your area (snipurl.com/hofoq), as well as your local police- or sheriff's-department standard calibers. (Ask at your local gun shop.)

I consider the following figures minimums:

2,000 per battle rifle
500 per hunting rifle
800 per primary handgun
2,000 per .22 rimfire
500 per riot gun

If you can afford it, three times those figures would meet the comfort level of most survivalists. In an age of inflation, consider that supply better than money in the bank. Ammo prices have recently been galloping, so do some price comparisons before you buy. Bring photocopies and "print-screen" printouts of prices with you when you shop, as bargaining tools.

Some Internet ammunition vendors that I recommend are:

AIM Surplus (snipurl.com/hoft7)
Cheaper Than Dirt! (snipurl.com/hofrw)
Dan's Sporting Goods (snipurl.com/hoftv)
J&G Sales (snipurl.com/hofvt)
MidwayUSA (snipurl.com/hofx9)
AmmoMan.com (snipurl.com/hofy1)
Natchez Shooters Supplies (snipurl.com/hofz6)
The Sportsman's Guide (snipurl.com/hog02)

Both to save money and to maximize your privacy—since umpteen heavy crates being unloaded from the back of a UPS truck is pretty obvious—I recommend that you be willing to drive a distance to take delivery in person from a regional vendor. Ammo is best bought by the three-quarter-ton-pickup load. Also, keep in mind that by buying in large quantities all at once from a big vendor, you will typically get ammo for each caliber from the same lots, which will result in more consistent accuracy.

Affordable Yet Reliable Night-Vision Scopes

For versatility, I prefer weapon-mounted scopes that can be detached for use as handheld monoculars. Make this your first purchase. If you have a big budget, then you can go on to buy goggles, but get your weapon sight first.

I'd recommend that you purchase a professionally remanufactured U.S. military–contract Gen 2 scope such as the AN/PVS-2B. Beware the many "kitchen-table" remanufacturers out there. Buy a full mil-spec scope from a reputable vendor such as Ready Made Resources or S.T.A.N.O. Components (snipurl.com/hoiuh) that will have a genuine, new Gen 2 image intensifier tube with a bona fide data sheet.

Late-issue Third Generation (also called or Third Gen or Gen 3) starlight scopes can cost up to three thousand dollars each. Rebuilt First Gen (early-1970s technology) scopes can often be bought for as little as five hundred dollars. Russian-made monoculars (with lousy optics) can cost less than one hundred dollars. One Russian model that uses a piezoelectric generator instead of batteries is the best of this low-cost breed. These are best used as backups—in case your expensive American-made scopes fail. They should not be purchased for use as your primary night-vision devices unless you are on a very restrictive budget, but they are better than nothing. Buy the best starlight scopes, goggles, and monoculars that you can afford. If you can afford to buy only one, make it a weapon sight such as an AN/PVS-4, with a Gen 2 (or better) tube (or the bulkier AN/PVS-2 if you are on tight budget). Make sure to specify that the tube is either new or has very low hours, that it has a high line pair count, and it that displays minimal scintillation. Again, it is important to buy your starlight gear from a reputable dealer. The market is crowded with rip-off artists and scammers.

Even passive night-vision gear casts a backlight. This is the light of the image that you are seeing being cast on your face. Through another night vision device this looks like a bright flashlight. For this reason, I discourage buying any night-vision scope that does not have a baffled ("flap") eyecup-type eye guard. The baffle opens only when you have the scope pressed up against your eye, minimizing backlighting. This fault is common with nearly all of the commercial night-vision gear on the market.

My recommended suppliers for starlight weapon sights and goggles are JRH Enterprises (jrhenterprises.com) and Ready Made Resources. For full mil-spec units as well as spare intensifier tubes, talk to S.T.A.N.O. Components.

One lower-technology alternative to starlight technology is a tritium-lit scope, such as those made by Trijicon. The half-life of tritium (a gaseous isotope of hydrogen) is 11.2 years, meaning that through radioactive decay they have one-half of their original brightness after 11.2 years, so the practical effective life of a tritium scope is 22 years, and the practical effective life of tritium iron sights is more than 33 years.

Selecting and Assembling Web Gear

There are umpteen opinions out there on web gear, so take the following as just one man's view. Although they are currently all the rage, I am not a fan of load-bearing vests. I still primarily use the old tried-and-true ALICE gear, although I have upgraded from the traditional Y-suspender harness to the more heavily padded Eagle Industries Ranger H-harness.

The new modular MOLLE vests are more versatile than the older-generation Woodland camouflage vests that have stitched-in magazine pouches, but I prefer having nearly everything handy at belt level. I've found that it is slow and cumbersome to get magazines in and out of pouches that are any higher than my solar plexus.

Adding body armor to the equation changes things considerably, since full interceptor body armor (IBA) with a modular/integrated communications helmet (MICH) weighs anywhere from nineteen to twenty-five pounds, depending on sizes and how many add-on pieces—such as upgraded small arms protective insert (SAPI) plates—are included. And keep in mind that those figures do not include the weight of ammo, magazines, a full hydration bladder, and various gadgets. When you're wearing non-concealment body armor, a load-bearing vest/carrier does make sense. Talk to the folks at BulletProofME (bulletproofme.com) for details on getting set up with body armor, pouches, and hydration systems that are practical and comfortable. Fit is crucial with body armor, so talk with an experienced dealer with a big inventory and responsive customer-service policies that can fit you properly.

For a brief overview on the older ALICE-generation U.S. military web gear, you can visit snipurl.com/hnd4h. Greater detail can be found in "Care and Use of Individual Clothing And Equipment" (FM 21-15), which can often be found at Amazon.com, MidwayUSA.com, GR8Gear.com, and LoadUp.com.

The majority of ALICE and MOLLE items are interchangeable—meaning that in most instances you can clip an ALICE magazine pouch onto a MOLLE vest, or attach a MOLLE pouch onto an ALICE belt. Don't worry about mismatched colors or camouflage patterns. Practical civilian survival "ain't a beauty contest." In real-world camouflage, randomness is a *good* thing. Anyone who tries to tell you that all your gear has to be color coordinated is a poseur.

Both ALICE and MOLLE gear are available from a variety of Internet vendors.

Holster, Sling, and Web Gear Recommendations

It is important to think through how, where, and when you will need to carry or access your guns on a day-to-day basis. How will you carry in your car, on your tractor, on your quad, or on your horse? How will you carry a pistol if you need to conceal it? How will you carry in foul weather? What will you carry when gardening or doing other chores? How and when will you carry accessories such as cleaning kits, bipods, and spotting scopes? What other items will you need to carry in the field that will also need to be kept handy, such as binoculars, flashlights, nightvision gear, and GPS receivers?

I cannot overstress the following: You must tailor a full webgear rig for *each* of your long guns. This should include a USGI LC-2 web belt, Y-harness (or H-harness) type padded suspenders, two ammo pouches, a couple of first-aid/compass pouches, and a canteen with a cover. Granted, you can carry only one long gun at a time, but odds are that you will be arming a lot of family and friends after the Schumer hits the fan. So you will need a set of web gear for each gun. To simplify things, I bought a pile of new nylon sleeping-bag stuff sacks in various earth-tone colors and placed a set of web gear and magazines in each of them. I then attached a label card to each sack's drawstring, associating it with its respective gun, for quick grab-it-and-go reference.

I do not advocate thigh-level pistol holsters. These seem to have proliferated in recent years mostly because they look snazzy in SWAT television shows and movies. They are actually quite impractical for just about all situations except rappelling. At thigh-level, a holstered pistol is quite tiring to wear when hiking. It is also slow to access. My advice is instead to buy a sturdy belt holster and leave those thigh-level holsters for the mall-ninja crowd.

For holsters, I recommend Blade-Tech brand Kydex holsters and mag pouches (blade-tech.com). The Blade-Tech holsters are inexpensive enough that I put one holster and pistol magazine pouch on each of my sets of long-gun web gear. And when carrying just a pistol by itself, we use modestly priced Uncle Mike's brand black nylon/Velcro belts. They are plain-Jane but sturdy and functional. We do have a couple of leather Summer Special concealment holsters, made by Milt Sparks Holsters (miltsparks .com). Their belts and holsters are highly recommended. I've been doing business with this company for more than twenty years. They don't skimp on quality.

Shoulder holsters are undesirable in most situations. They do make sense, however, when you are in a car for more than an hour.

For rifle slings, I recommend a traditional two-loop military sling design. They really help steady a rifle for accurate long-range shooting. Attending a weekend Western Rifle Shooters Association (snipurl.com/hn8xj) or Appleseed rifle-shooting clinic (appleseedinfo.org) is highly recommended and will show you how to properly adjust a two-loop sling for various shooting positions. Once you've identified your "summer" sling-adjustment notches (when wearing just a shirt) for prone and sitting positions, I recommend using a black Magic Marker to circle the holes and mark them with underlined "P" and "Sit," for quick reference. Draw another line or preferably a "W"—for winter—at each adjustment, and again circle the notch holes, to indicate the longer adjustment needed when wearing a winter coat, a target-shooting jacket, or a field jacket. I don't advocate using standing unsupported positions for either hunting or most defensive shooting situations. It takes just a moment to sit down, and just a bit longer to get prone.

For shotgun slings, in my experience a padded nylon extra-long sling (such as an M60 sling) works well.

Locking quick-detachable (QD) sling swivels are a must, because there are many tactical situations in which you won't want a sling at all. You need to be able to attach and detach a sling quickly.

For horse or quad (ATV) scabbards, I like the brown Cordura nylon scabbards that are now on the market. Leather is more traditional, but it takes a painfully long time to dry out, which can induce rust on a gun in short order. Brown nylon won't win any beauty contests but it works.

Dull (non-glossy) olive-drab (OD) duct tape is your friend. Buy a couple of big rolls of it. It has umpteen uses out in the field. I wrap each of my Y-harness snaps with duct tape to keep them from rattling or coming loose. It is also useful for toning down any reflective objects. The best field gear is very quiet, very secure, and very unobtrusive. Applying OD duct tape helps with all three.

Canes, Walking Sticks, and Umbrellas for Street Self-defense

Striking weapons have some utility for street self-defense. I highly recommend training to use a cane, a walking stick, or a traditional full-length umbrella. This is particularly important for readers who live in gun-unfriendly nations or in states like California, New York, and New Jersey, where it is very difficult to get a carrying concealed weapon (CCW) permit. And even if you *are* a concealed-firearms permit holder, you should learn these valuable skills. Why? You never know when circumstances might dictate that you cannot carry a pistol.

If you are well dressed and groomed, then law-enforcement officers in most jurisdictions will hardly give you a second glance if you are carrying a walking stick. But if you are shabby-looking, then expect to get plenty of grief. Canes, especially aluminum ones like those that look like true walking aids, are far less likely to attract suspicion than walking sticks. Folded umbrellas can also be used quite effectively for jabbing.

My general preference is to use a shoulder-width, two-handed grip in most situations, to maintain control and, more important, to assure retention of the stick. This is akin to what has been taught for many years by police academies in the use of long ("riot") batons. The last thing that you want is to have Mr. Bad Guy gain control of your weapon.

Do some research on your local laws. In most jurisdictions, any blow with a striking weapon to the neck or head is considered potentially lethal. So don't escalate unless you are absolutely certain that your life is threatened and you have no other choice. Essentially it is the same as firing a gun—at least in the eyes of the law. Most courts look at things in terms of equal force and a graduated response, roughly as follows: If Mr. Bad

Guy uses his fists, then you can use your fists. If he uses a weapon, then you can use a comparable weapon. If he strikes above the chest, then you can strike above the chest.

Show restraint, and never dole out punishment. Just reduce the threat with a quick jab or two, disengage, and then engage your Nike-jitsu technique. (Run!)

When carrying a striking weapon or an edged weapon of any sort for self-defense, be sure to develop the same situational awareness skills that you would for carrying a concealed firearm. Extensive training in self-defense combative techniques is worthless if you don't see an attack coming. Be alert.

If you don't live near a school that teaches cane and stick fighting, there is a forty-minute training DVD produced by the Gunsite academy titled *Defensive Techniques: Walking Stick*. It is available from Blade-Tech and directly from the Gunsite Pro Shop.

Blinding Flashlights for Self-defense?

When lasers blind, they do so permanently, by destroying the human retina. The "dazzling" effect is quite different from *blinding*. Never use a "non-eye-safe" (blinding) laser against an attacker, or you will very likely be sued.

There are indeed flashlights with a temporary dazzling effect designed for self-defense, but I have not tested them. At least one publicized prototype uses pulsating LEDs designed to induce dizziness and/or vertigo. Keep in mind that these dazzling effects might work well in controlled, low-light conditions, but they cannot be trusted to be effective in split-second real-world confrontations, which can take place in all sorts of light conditions.

Knives

I am by no means a knife expert. (Although the Memsahib claims that I am a seasoned expert at *buying* knives.) My general preference is for folding knives, because you will almost always have a folding knife in your pocket. Big sheath knives get left behind—often when they are needed the most.

I prefer low-end stainless steel folding knives with a positive lock and tanto-style blade tip. For versatility, I also tend toward knives that are serrated on the back half of the blade (commonly called "50/50" or "half-serrated"). My everyday carry knife is an extra-large (five-inch blade) Cold Steel 29 Voyager. On occasions when I need something smaller, I carry a CRKT M16 with a two-and-three-quarter-inch blade. Again, it is stainless and half serrated, and has tanto-style tip. During deer and elk season, I substitute a Case clip-point folder.

I've never spent more than fifty-five dollars for one of my pocketknives—and I've spent far less for most. A knife should be an everyday tool to use, not an object of art to admire. The Cold Steel, CRKT, and Benchmade brands are some of the best *affordable* knives on the market.

When shopping for used pocketknives, one trick I've discovered for searching eBay is to search for the desired brand name *and* "knives" *and* "TSA," searching both titles and descriptions (or alternatively, the desired brand name *and* "knives" *and* "confiscated"). These searches will show you lots of used knives that were confiscated by airport screeners. These are often name-brand knives sold in groups of two to ten, typically resulting in winning bids between 10 percent to 30 percent of the lot's normal retail value.

Regardless of your choice of knives, a top-quality knife-sharpening system is a must for your retreat. At home, I prefer the Lansky Sharpening System. When out in the field, I use a compact Cam-Nu sharpener. Be sure to get a diamond-impregnated sharpener if you have any knives that are made with the modern stainless steels such as ATS-34. These knives are usually hardened to a high Rockwell scale number, so you'll find that they are difficult to resharpen with a set of traditional stones.

A Final Note

In closing, you can own the very best guns or knives and have the very best holsters and accessories, but they will be marginal at best in *untrained hands*. Once you've invested in your first gun, you should follow through and invest in the best training available. If you are serious about preparedness, then you should get the best training available. Remember: Tools without training are almost useless.

12

G.O.O.D. VEHICLES AND THE DREADED TRIP OUTTA DODGE

A key part of your survival planning should be your vehicles; both your pre-TEOTWAWKI and post-TEOTWAWKI vehicles will be addressed in this chapter.

A Mix of Vehicles

For the best chance to G.O.O.D. successfully and survive post-TEOTWAWKI, you will ideally have several vehicles. Here are some you might want to consider:

A Fuel-Efficient Runabout

A car like a used Geo Metro or Toyota Corolla is good for day-to-day. For serious preparedness planning you may want to avoid the high cost and complexity of a hybrid. If you need four-wheel drive, consider buying a used Subaru.

The Old Station Wagon

A late-1960s to early-1970s station wagon with a big-block engine would be ideal as a collision-resilient Get Out of Dodge vehicle. They get pitifully low gas mileage, but they have lots of cargo room, as well as clearance for a roll bar behind the bench front seat. You can also add a roof rack for relatively lightweight items such as spare tires, tents, and camouflage nets.

To my mind, perfection in a gas-engine G.O.O.D. station wagon would be a flat-brown 1970 Buick Estate with a 455-cubic-inch four-barrel V-8 engine. What a ride: plenty of power, very tough in collisions, easy to maintain, EMP protection near ground zero, and even a touch of class.

Motorcycles

Consider getting a moped or motorcycle for handling some of your errands in the current pre-WTSHTF times. In a "slow-slide" situation in which the power grid stays up and law and order are maintained, a motorcycle could have great utility. With high fuel prices, a fuel-efficient motorcycle makes sense for day-to-day commuting and for other purposes. A motorcycle has great mobility advantages over most other vehicles—especially in stalled traffic, or for off-road trail riding—but keep in mind that you will also be far more vulnerable than when riding in an enclosed vehicle.

My general preference is for air-cooled medium-displacement-engine motorcycles with off-road suspension (aka dirt bikes) that are also qualified as street legal. About 350cc is ideal, but sadly that engine class is no longer available in the U.S. (There are, however, lots of *used* 350 dirt bikes on the market.) Heavier bikes with large-displacement engines (500cc or larger) have inferior fuel economy and are very difficult to get back to an upright position following a mishap in which you "drop" your bike. (The limit might be as little as 300cc for someone of small stature with limited upper-body strength.)

Perhaps the ultimate for preppers would be a Kawasaki KLR650 diesel/JP8 bike, which is a 611cc civilian equivalent of the M1030 tactical motorcycle now fielded in small numbers by the U.S. Army, USMC, and U.S. Air Force. They are a bit heavy, but they are quite sturdy.

If you plan to use a motorcycle as a last-ditch G.O.O.D. vehicle, then I recommend that you conceal any spare fuel cans inside panniers to reduce the likelihood of being targeted by looters. Auxiliary cargo racks for dirt bikes are made by Pro Moto and are available from CycleBuy.com.

Just as with buying a car, it is best to buy a used motorcycle, to get the most for your money. Just be sure to have it inspected by a qualified motorcycle mechanic before you make a purchase.

There is certainly no "one size fits all" solution when buying a motorcycle. An enduro-type design (trail and street capable) is a compromise, but it is probably best for those of us who can afford to buy only one motorcycle. There are some who argue that bigger is safer (on pavement), while others assert that dropping a big bike is a sure trip to the hospital. Regardless of what you decide on, be sure to get plenty of training, and of course wear a helmet and all the safety gear.

A Fleet Surplus Propane-Powered Pickup

Utility companies often use these. Watch for auction announce-ments. If you could get a propane-powered truck that is 4WD, that would be ideal. But even if you can't find a 4WD, one option is find-ing a gas-engine 4WD of the same year and the same make as your 2WD propane-engine truck, and then combining parts to create a "Frankentruck." Another option, albeit more expensive, is convert-ing an existing 4WD to propane. Because propane tanks are large, this is best accomplished with a 4WD pickup. I have seen pairs of forty-seven-gallon "torpedo tanks" installed above the wheel wells in a pickup box. This allows nearly full use of the pickup bed space. Since a propane conversion will likely void a warranty, it is best done with an older vehicle that is out of warranty.

E85 Vehicles

In the new fuel-price paradigm, having at least one E85-compatible vehicle is certainly wise. These flex-fuel vehicles (FFVs) have fuel tanks and lines designed to handle alcohol, as well as igni-tion systems that automatically sense the flash point of the fuel and compensate accordingly. Hence, they can run on unleaded gasoline, E85, or any mixture of the two. It is just plain common sense to buy the most versatile vehicles and generators avail-able, especially when getting that flexibility doesn't cost much more than buying standard single-fuel engines. Rather than doing a conversion, which will void most manufacturers' engine warranties and can even require a gas-tank replacement for older vehicles, I generally recommend simply waiting until the next time you replace a vehicle. Finding an FFV is getting easier with each passing year, since they are being produced in greater num-bers by nearly all of the major car and truck makers. The best way to find one is to do a used-vehicle search at Edmunds.com and include the phrase "flex fuel" or "FFV."

If the price of regular gas rises above $4.50 per gallon (and it likely will), I suspect that E85 ethanol will remain under $3.60 per gallon in the Midwest, making it quite cost effective. Although E85 has a 100 to 105 octane rating, an FFV burning E85 gets 28 percent fewer miles per gallon than when burning unleaded gasoline.

As always, regardless of the make and model you choose, there are huge cost savings in buying a vehicle with twenty thousand to thirty-five thousand miles on the odometer.

Electric ATVs

If your budget allows it, consider getting an electric vehicle. An electric ATV makes an ideal retreat utility vehicle, particularly for someone who has a large alternate power system with a battery bank.

Electric golf carts have limited range but are very quiet. You should consider that most gas-powered golf carts are much quieter than a comparable-size ATV. If you don't plan to go more than a few miles, then get an electric cart. Lift kits are available for retrofit for three popular brands of electric carts: E-Z-GO, Club Car, and Yamaha. You can even get brush guards and other ATV-esque accessories for golf carts (garage-toys.com/custom cart.html). Photovoltaic battery-charging panels and charge controllers are available for retrofitting a golf cart, from vendors like Ready Made Resources. A charge controller is a must on any system with more than just one small trickle charging panel. Otherwise you will overcharge and badly "cook" your batteries. There are also PV panels that are factory-original equipment on electric carts like the Cruise Car Sunray.

Propane Vehicles

Because propane might be hard to come by on the road, I don't recommend it for Bugout vehicles, unless your retreat is within range of one tank of fuel. But propane is ideal for trucks and tractors that will not often leave your retreat property. I prefer converting pickups rather than SUVs, since propane fuel tanks are relatively large.

There are some issues involving payment of road taxes in some states when converting to propane. If it were not for that, I believe that propane conversions would be much more popular. Consult your state and local laws before doing a conversion.

For the sake of versatility and flexibility, I highly recommend that one of the vehicles at your retreat can run on propane.

Diesel Vehicles

I recommend having at least one diesel tractor and one diesel car at every retreat. Although they are fairly scarce, in my experience, a pre-1986 Mercedes diesel 300D-series station wagon (on the W123 chassis) is worth looking for. These share a drivetrain with the much more common 300D-series four-door sedans, so parts are readily available.

Ready Made Resources offers an affordable small-scale biodiesel-making system. The recent spike in diesel prices will give you a big advantage in bargaining for a price when buying any diesel vehicle.

For short-term low-amperage power requirements, a vehicle with a diesel engine can act as an impromptu power generator. As long as the engine is left running at low to moderate RPMs, then using a vehicle's alternator as a power source—for DC loads and/or to run a small 120-volt AC inverter—will not cause excessive wear and tear on your battery or alternator. You may have to rig a manually controlled set throttle. Just keep in mind the usual safety precautions, such as carbon-monoxide venting and making sure that the transmission lever does not get bumped into Drive. To conserve your precious fuel, it is best to buy a bank of deep-cycle (golf-cart-type) batteries that you can charge whenever you run the engine.

Rather than using jumper-cable clamps, for safety it is best to attached heavy-gauge battery cable and terminal lugs. Use a detachable high-amperage-rated twelve-volt DC polarity-protected pigtail block connector, in parallel with your vehicle battery cables. That way you can quickly disconnect and still be able to drive your vehicle without a time-consuming cable-unbolting procedure. Ideally, your battery bank will be the heart of an alternative power system that will also—as your budget eventually allows—include some photovoltaic panels.

For twelve-VDC devices "downstream" from your battery bank that draw thirty amps or less, I recommend standardizing with Anderson Powerpole connectors rather than flimsy cigarette-lighter plugs and jacks.

Run-Flat Tires

Run-flat tires are available on BMW 3-series cars, as well as the Toyota Sienna. Many tire manufacturers now produce them for after-market installation for a variety of cars and light trucks. These include: Bridgestone RFT (run-flat tire), Dunlop's DSST (Dunlop self-supporting technology), Firestone RFT (run-flat tire), Goodyear EMT (extended-mobility technology), Michelin ZP (zero pressure), Pirelli RFT (run-flat technology), and Yokohama. These are all "self-supporting" designs, meaning that they are supported by special sidewall designs rather than a rim-mounted insert. The latter would be preferable. I suspect that run-flat tires will become commonplace in the next few years, since car manufacturers would surely prefer to save on the space and weight of carrying a spare tire.

For maximum mobility, the best of all possible worlds would probably be a vehicle with a central tire-inflation system (CTIS)—such as that used on the military High Mobility Multipurpose Wheeled Vehicle (HMMWV) and its commercial Hummer H1 counterpart—used in conjunction with a Michelin PAX-type auxiliary supported tire system.

EMP

If you are concerned about electromagnetic pulse (EMP) disabling your vehicle, then buy either a diesel or a pre-1975 gasoline-engine vehicle. Some later vehicles can be retrofitted with traditional ignition systems that don't have microcircuits. (Ask your local car mechanic.) With diesels, the main EMP issue is that the newer vehicles use microcircuits in their glow-plug circuitry. You should have an experienced diesel mechanic show you how to bypass the glow-plug switch with a clip lead from your battery's positive terminal. Keep that clip lead in your glove box at all times.

The major U.S. (Detroit) car and truck manufacturers started using electronic ("computer") ignition systems in or around 1975. Chrysler was the first of the Big Three manufacturers to abandon the traditional "points and condenser" for an electronic ignition. That was in about 1974. Ford and GM followed with most of their product lines around 1975. The conversion in ignition systems usually took place in automobile product lines before trucks. By 1976 or 1977, virtually all gas-engine cars coming out of Detroit had electronic ignitions. Trucks all transitioned to electronic ignitions by 1978.

Camouflage Painting?

My general advice is to camouflage vehicles only after you have made it to your retreat, and *only* if it is a truly Schumeresque situation. In the present day, a camouflage-painted vehicle will attract unwanted interest—either from malefactors or from law enforcement. A flat paint job in one earth-tone color will not attract suspicion. You should also keep the materials handy to spray-paint, Bowflage-brand paint, or camo-tape over any chrome parts, if and when things get really bad. (Bowflage paint seems to be best for reducing infrared signature.) But in most parts of the country a camouflage paint job simply screams "Prepared guy!" Be sure to weigh the costs and benefits.

When parked, vehicles can be made far less visible with military camouflage nets (supported by spreaders to break up any expected vehicular outline), and burlap sacks to cover high-albedo windows and headlights.

Horse Power

For the really long term, learn as much as you can about horses, and change your purchasing plans if this approach matches your needs and the pasture-carrying capacity of your retreat. There is a lot to this: horsemanship, hay cutting (preferably horse-powered), hay storage, pasture fencing, a barn, tack, veterinary supplies, and so forth. Here at the Rawles Ranch, our saddle-horse money pit may soon have some new friends in the pasture.

Hay and grain prices have been sky high for a full year now, so this has pushed the price of horses down tremendously. As this book goes to press, in much of the western United States good saddle horses are literally being given away. Just ask around. If you are not yet an experienced rider, then limit your search to older, gentle, "bomb-proof" mares or geldings. If you have plenty of pasture and hay ground, take advantage of the current low prices for horses. Buy them while they're cheap. Watch your newspaper classified ads and Craigslist for horses as well as tack, hay mowers, and a horse trailer. In addition to saddle horses, think in terms of working horses. While you are searching for saddles, also look for wagons, buckboards, horse collars, long reins, log chains, and other workhorse tack.

Fuel in a Grid-Down Collapse

You will need to access gasoline in underground gas-station storage tanks if electrical pumps become inoperable. Typical retail gas-station fuel tanks are less than fourteen feet deep, including the height of the filler necks, so a fifteen-foot draw hose is more than long enough.

Every well-equipped retreat should have at least one "field-expedient" twelve-VDC fuel-transfer pump. These pump rigs are popular with dirt-bike, ATV, and snowmobile enthusiasts. They are very simple to construct. Here are the materials that you will need:

(1) Automobile or truck electric fuel pump (The least expensive pumps come from automobile wrecking yards.)
(2) 15-foot lengths of heavy rubber hose—approved for use as fuel line—of the proper diameter for the fittings on the fuel pump
(2) Stainless steel fuel-line clamps (such as Breeze Aero-Seal brand, or similar, which are tightened with a screwdriver)

(15 to 20 feet) 16 AWG (or heavier) gauge insulated two conductor wire (This will be the power cord for the pump.)

(1) Cigarette-lighter-type male plug, available from any Radio
Shack store (for the power cord for the pump)

(1) Roll of black plastic electrician's tape or, better yet, some
thermoplastic "heat-shrink" tubing

(1) Scrap of ⅜-inch-thick (or greater) plywood, measuring
roughly 16 by 16 inches (to mount the fuel pump)

If you'd like, you can add an electrical switch to the power
cord for convenience, but make sure that you get a high-amperage
switch that is rated for DC, and that you position the switch
within a couple of feet of the dashboard plug so that the switch
is inside the cab of your vehicle. That way there is far less chance
of generating a spark inside a gas-vapor cloud.

If your vehicle uses an electric fuel pump, then I suggest that
you use a pump identical to that used in your vehicle as the basis
for your transfer-pump project. That way you will have spares on
hand in the event that your vehicle's fuel pump or any portions
of your fuel system's flexible-fuel lines ever fail.

You can also add an in-line fuel filter to your fuel-transfer
pump rig. Again, it is best to use a filter cartridge that is identical to that used in your vehicle. (Always think: "Spares and redundancy, spares and redundancy.")

One other optional nicety is a one-foot-square scrap of plywood to bolt the pump onto. This will keep the transfer pump
out of the mud or snow. It also provides a handy place to mount
some large hooks, so that you will have a neat way to coil up the
power cord and the fuel-transfer hoses for storage. A fifteen-foot
length of hose should be able to reach any vehicle fuel tank, or
even down into an underground tank.

There are commercially made equivalents of this fuel-pump rig, but they cost more, and they won't provide you with a spare compatible fuel pump—in the event that your vehicle's original pump goes Tango Uniform.

Important Provisos:

1. All of the usual commonsense precautions for handing gasoline and gas cans apply: Use only DOT-approved fuel containers; no sparks; no open flames; don't turn on any radio transmitters; beware of static electricity buildup, etc.
2. Some later-model vehicles have anti-siphoning filler necks on their gas tanks. Check for this before you head for the boonies with an ATV trailer.
3. Cover any exposed electrical connections with tape or heat-shrink tubing, to avoid sparks or shorting.
4. Keep one eye on your vehicle's gas gauge and your other eye on the can that you are filling (or pumping from). It is not just an expensive waste to spill gas on the ground. It is also toxic and a fire hazard!

Odds are that you *will* be able to find the station owner to make payment, at least while there is still fuel in the station tanks. If you build two or more such pumps in advance, then you could probably use the extras in barter—most likely to trade to gas-station owners for some of their fuel.

E85

I predict that within a few years the price of E85 in the U.S. will be about half the price of unleaded gasoline. But the bad news is that by the time this happens, standard gasoline will be probably be up to six dollars per gallon. I am hopeful that within a few years E100 ethanol vehicles will become available. These will run on pure ethanol (grain alcohol) or methanol (wood alcohol). That would be ideal for a survival retreat, where you could presumably build your own still. But for now, E85 vehicles are highly recommended. They are still fairly scarce. To find one for sale near you, do a search for "Flex Fuel" on the Edmunds.com vehicle-search page.

The E85 ethanol blend has a longer storage life than standard gasoline, but it is essential that it is stored in tightly sealed containers. Otherwise, the alcohol will absorb moisture. If enough water is absorbed, the alcohol will separate from the gasoline and go into solution with the water (read: ruined fuel, and an engine that won't start). So keep your containers full and tightly sealed. The higher the humidity, the faster this will occur.

Pri-G (available from Nitro-Pak) or Sta-Bil (available at your local auto-parts store) brand additives can and should be added to E85 that is stored for more than a couple of months, to protect the 15 percent of the blend that is gasoline. But of course you need only about 15 percent of the additive per gallon that you would normally use to treat standard gasoline. The alcohol component of the blend needs no special stabilization. As with storing standard gasoline, it is best to buy E85 for storage during winter months, when you will presumably be buying a winter blend that has extra butane added for cold-weather starting. This also extends its useful storage life.

If you are concerned that your stored E85 has been contaminated with water, you can pour some of the fuel into a clear glass tube and wait thirty minutes before inspecting the sample. If there is water contamination you will be able to see a separation of ethanol water from gasoline, with the colored gasoline floating above the clear ethanol-water mixture.

Keep all fuel tanks as full as possible for long-term storage, to prevent the empty space above the fuel from passing water into the fuel.

Fuel Storage

Storing extra fuel for your vehicles is a priority for family preparedness. If you use propane, consider buying a larger tank. The bigger, the better. That fuel will be like money in the bank. Ditto for gasoline and diesel fuel. That way you can buy during occasional dips in the market as well as have a reserve that will help you ride through any spot shortages. Consult your local fire code for any limits where you live. I generally prefer underground tanks, for both OPSEC and fire safety.

I predict that there will be a long lag time while the price of propane catches up to the price of other fuels. The cost of electricity will also lag behind, especially in regions that have predominantly hydroelectric power. In the long run, however, these prices will also undoubtedly catch up. Exploit this lag time to build up the alternative-energy potential of your retreat. Think through your options, do some comparison pricing, and then get busy. Consider the merits and drawbacks of photovoltaics, wind, micro-hydro biogas, biodiesel, geothermal, wood-fired steam/co-generation, and so forth. For more on this, see Chapter 6.

13

INVESTING, BARTER, AND HOME-BASED BUSINESSES

We are entering perilous economic times. I expect continued massive layoffs and chronic unemployment in this nascent depression. As the fictional Sarah Connor puts it so succinctly: "No one is ever safe." Anyone can get laid off. You can be an outstanding worker, in a presumably "safe" industry, yet in a depression you can still lose your job.

This chapter will present strategies for ensuring your financial security. I'll provide advice on savvy investments to make now to protect your money, suggestions for sources of income, and effective bartering techniques you can use WTSHTF.

Inflation Is Insidious and Inexorable

I recently helped some elderly cousins move from their two-story home of many years into a smaller one-story apartment in a retirement community. During the move, we cleaned out a storage space that hadn't been touched in more than forty years. Many of the boxes had newspapers used as padding in the top. Pulling out these papers, which were mostly from 1958, was a real eye-opener for our kids. Here are some examples of the advertisement prices that our kids read aloud with much laughter:

Beauty Salon: Ladies' styled haircut $1; Revlon manicure 75 cents; shampoo and set $1

Flooring Store: Rubber tiles 12 cents each; inlaid linoleum tile 5½ cents; vinyl tile 7½ cents

Grocery Store: Leg of lamb 65 cents/lb; breast of lamb 15 cents/lb; picnic hams 29 cents/lb; a fifth of Johnnie Walker scotch $6.38; Hills Bros. coffee 49 cents/lb

Car Dealerships: Current-model-year Cadillac convertible $4,395; 1957 Chevy (one year old) $2,195; 1950 Buick sedan, "real nice," $165; 1954 Ford Crown Victoria V-8 $875

The prices in these ads illustrate the slow but relentless debasement of our currency. Before 1965, our coinage was 90 percent silver, and paper money was still redeemable in silver. Granted, wages were proportionately less, but since that time, any savings held in dollars has been inexorably eaten away by inflation, year after year. It is no wonder that the savings rate in the U.S. recently went *below zero*. Americans presently spend $1.06 for each dollar that they earn, piling up debt instead of savings. The inflation of the money supply is gradual enough that it insidiously goes without raising public alarm. Because inflation is so relentless, I recommend investing in tangibles— things like productive farmland, gold, silver, guns, and common-caliber ammunition. The dollar will surely continue to plummet in value, but for the most part tangibles will hold their value.

The debt merry-go-round cannot go on forever. When the average consumer runs out of credit, when the U.S. Treasury itself is no longer considered creditworthy, and when the U.S. dollar is recognized for what it really is (nicely printed toilet paper), then things will get ugly. If you stop making the payments on your car, the banks send a repo man to tow your car away. And when entire nations go into default, it usually signals cataclysmic events. Be prepared.

Inflation and Property Taxes

Creeping tax increases is one of the reasons that it is now nearly impossible for someone to "live off the land" on small acreage. Even if you own your house and land free and clear, property taxes are inescapable. Thus, in self-sufficient mode, although you can feed yourself, you still need a cash-earning job, just to pay the taxes. I pray that at the far end of the coming depression, our debt money system—which is the root of inflation—will be replaced by a system of sound currency that is redeemable in specie. That is the only sure, long-term solution to creeping inflation, and corresponding creeping taxation.

Although the chances of a long-lasting deflationary depression are fairly small (since I suspect Ben Bernanke will try to inflate his way out of this mess), it is prudent to do your best to maintain a cash income as a supplement even if you are able to live off the land.

Residential Real Estate

With the recent collapse of the mortgage market, my advice to you is if you have a second home, sell it *muy* pronto. And if you anticipate moving within the next two or three years, sell your house and rent. The hassle of moving to a rental is nothing compared to the mental anguish of being "upside down" in a mortgage in a plummeting market. The next five years will be a great time to be a renter.

One unusual approach that might be prudent: Sell your house to a property-management company, and then rent it back from them. Let them watch the value of the house go down. Meanwhile, you'll sleep well.

Depression-Proof Jobs

In these economic times, which are marked by increasing corporate layoffs, many people have asked me about recession-proof jobs. If you get laid off and can't find work in your chosen field, then you ought to consider taking a cut in pay to take a far less glamorous job. In Japan, these jobs are called the "Three-K" jobs: *kitsui* ("hard"), *kitanai* ("dirty"), and *kiken* ("dangerous"). If you are willing to take on any of the Three Ks, and you do cheerful, ardent work and have exemplary attendance, then you will likely have a job that will carry you all the way through a deep recession or even a depression. Some of these are low-level city and county payroll jobs. Sanitation workers, animal-control officers, sewer technicians, and highway-maintenance workers are a vital part of any society. Don't let your family starve or end up homeless. There is no shame in accepting hard work. If you take a job that brings in only one half of your old income, consider that you'll actually come out ahead of your contemporaries who are laid off for more than half of each year. Further, you will have uninterrupted benefits, such as health insurance.

A Home-Based Business: Your Ticket to the Boonies

The majority of preppers tell me that they live in cities or suburbs but would like to live full-time at a retreat in a rural area. Their complaint is almost always the same: "But I'm not self-employed. I can't afford to live in the country because I can't find work there, and the nature of my work doesn't allow telecommuting." They feel stuck.

Over the years I've seen lots of people "pull the plug" and move to the boonies with the hope that they'll find local work once they get there. That usually doesn't work. Folks find that the most rural jobs typically pay little more than minimum wage and are often informally reserved for folks who were born and raised in the area. Newcomers from the big city certainly don't have hiring priority.

I often encourage folks who are preparedness-minded to develop a second income stream with a home-based business. Once you have that business started, then start another one. There are numerous advantages to this approach, namely:

- You can get out of debt.
- You can generally build the businesses up gradually, so that you don't need to quit your current occupation immediately.
- By working at home you will have the time to educate your children, and they will learn about operating a business.

- You can live at your retreat full-time. This will contribute to your self-sufficiency, since you will be there to tend to your garden, fruit/nut trees, and livestock.
- If one of your home-based businesses fails, then you can fall back on the other.

Ask yourself: What are you good at? What knowledge or skills do you have that you can utilize? Next, consider which businesses will flourish during bad times. Successful home-based businesses usually center around unfilled needs. If you live in a rural area, ask your neighbors: Is there anything that you buy or rent, or a service that you hire on a regular basis that currently requires a forty-mile drive to town? Those are your potential niches.

A successful recession-proof home-based business is likely to be one in which the demand for your goods and services is consistent—even in a weak economy. These include septic-tank pumping, home security/locksmithing, care for the very young and the very old, and escapist diversions such as DVD rentals. It is noteworthy that the movie industry was one of the few sectors of the economy that prospered in the 1930s.

Another category of business that prospered in the 1930s was repair work. Obviously, in hard economic times, people try to make do with what they have. So repair businesses are a natural. Perhaps there is some small appliance that you could repair that could be mailed from and back to the customer. This might include: DVD-player repair, laptop-computer repair, and so forth.

Another category is secondhand stores. People on tight budgets will be actively looking for secondhand goods rather than buying new items. A secondhand store in a medium-size town might do just fine in a depression.

Yet another approach, for those with mechanical aptitude

who don't mind strenuous outdoor work: Own one or more pieces of fairly expensive machinery that a lot of people need to rent (or hire the services of) on a semi-regular basis but that are expensive enough that they cannot justify buying one. Typically, this is machinery that sells for two thousand to twenty thousand dollars that you can hire out in a relatively unregulated business (not requiring any special licenses, guild membership, or a union card). Examples include Ditch Witch trenching machines (ditch witch.com), vehicle-mounted posthole augers, vehicle-mounted well-drilling rigs, portable sawmills, cherry-picker bucket hoists, Bobcat tractors, small tracked excavators, and so forth. Once you've identified a clear unfilled need, and after you've confirmed that nobody else in your local area already has a machine that they presently rent out, then start looking to buy one. Ideally, you'll want one that is a few years old (since brand-new machinery is usually too expensive), in reliable running condition, and reasonably priced. As necessary, get a trailer to transport it. Practice with it at your own property, so that you'll be competent and confident that you can do a good job. Practice loading, hauling, and unloading your machinery (if needed) a few times, so that you won't look like an idiot when doing so. Be sure to get liability insurance started before you officially launch your business. Then it is simple enough to advertise your services on the Internet and through your local chamber of commerce, and post flyers at the local feed store and supermarket. You can "scale" the size of your second business (read: how busy you'll be) by setting your prices. If you want a lot of hours, then price it low. If you are getting too much work, then just start raising your rates to slow down your business. Then, if and when you ever lose your primary income stream, you can drop your rates on your secondary business substantially, so that it can take up the slack for your lost income. If necessary, add a second or third piece of equipment that you can rent out, to diversify your business.

Some other good examples of home-based businesses might include:

- Mail order/Internet sales/eBay auctioning of preparedness-related products
- Locksmithing
- Gunsmithing
- Medical transcription
- Accounting
- Repair/refurbishment
- Freelance writing
- Blogging (with paid advertising). If you have knowledge about a niche industry and there is currently no blog on the subject, then start your own. (It worked for me!)
- Mail order/Internet sales of entertainment items. (When times get bad, people still set aside a sizable percentage of their income to "escape" from their troubles. For example, movie-rental shops have done remarkably well during recessions.)
- Burglar-alarm installation
- Tinsmithing
- Broom- and basketmaking
- Wheel- and barrel-making
- Pewter casting
- Weaving and spinning
- Candle- and soapmaking
- Leatherworking

Keep in mind that if you choose publishing or another mail-order venture selling something compact and lightweight, then you can take advantage of a national or even global market. But if you are selling a service or a relatively bulky or heavy hand-crafted item, then your market will be essentially local, so choose your venture wisely.

Tangibles

If after you have expanded your food-storage program and developed a home-based business you still have some remaining cash, then it should be used either to pay down your mortgage or to invest in tangibles. If you expect chronic deflation, then apply it to your mortgage. But if you expect Uncle Sugar to inflate his way out of the current economic morass (as I do), then put it in tangibles. I recommend that you put your money in productive farmland in lightly populated dryland farming regions, precious metals, and guns. Unlike dollar-denominated investments, these can't be inflated away to nothing.

Precious Metals as a Hedge—Not an Investment

Looking at the past fifty to a hundred years, the current bull market in precious metals is a bit of an anomaly. The precious metals, in general, are not an investment per se. Rather, they are more like a form of protection against the destruction of the U.S. dollar. With the exception of the present day—which, again, is anomalous—people can expect to buy precious metals with no firm hope of a return. Rather, they can be expected to keep up with the rate of inflation. I recommend that every family have a core (nonspeculative) holding of 5 to 10 percent of their net worth in precious metals.

As of this writing (2009) we are just in the opening stage of a bull market, so you haven't missed the boat. I strongly recommend that if you own any metals you hold on until the market goes into the final phases of the bull cycle. In the nascent run-up, that probably means tops of around ninety dollars per ounce for silver and twenty-five hundred dollars for gold. That equates to a gain of nine times current spot prices for silver and 4.4 times for gold. In this bull, I think that silver will outperform gold considerably.

In a major disaster that creates an economic collapse, precious metals will have their greatest utility as a recognized store of value to facilitate barter in the latter stages of a post-collapse economy, as regular commerce starts to resume. Before that, you can expect only canned foods and common-caliber ammunition to be accepted in barter. The free market will determine their value, as it always has. If the dollar is completely wiped out, the old dollars will probably be declared worthless, and a new currency unit will be established, most likely pegged to gold.

In the short term, the metals markets—particularly for silver and platinum—are indeed quite volatile. But it is important to step back and look at the big picture. Forget the daily fluctuations. Instead, look at the 120-day moving averages (DMAs) and the five- and ten-year charts at Kitco.com. The federal government's profligate spending and both government and consumer debt point to a long-term bear market in the dollar, and a corresponding long-term bull market in precious metals. I don't expect Uncle Sam to change his spendthrift ways anytime soon, so take advantage of the long-term trend.

I recommend buying silver rather than gold coins. Gold is too compact a store of wealth for most barter transactions. If you want to buy a gallon of kerosene, a box of ammunition, or a can of beans, then gold will be awkward. How would someone make "change" for a transaction that is priced at one hundredth of the value of a one-ounce American Eagle or Krugerrand gold coin? With a cold chisel?

I recommend that you use two methodologies to purchase and maintain two distinct hoards of silver, and that you do not commingle them:

1. Your designated barter silver stockpile. The barter portion of your silver stockpile should be in small, divisible units, ideally pre-1965, 90 percent silver U.S. dimes. Those coins could presumably be used for day-to-day purchases in a recovery-stage (post-collapse) economy. Your barter silver should be considered a core holding, never sold for the sake of profit. If you don't ever have to use it for barter, then count your blessings and just pass it along to your children or grandchildren so that they will have something to use for the same purpose. If you can afford it, I recommend buying one bag with a face value of one thousand dollars for each member of your family.

I'm often asked about one-ounce silver "Trade Dollars." I don't recommend buying the one-ounce rounds. They often carry a higher premium per ounce than circulated ("junk") pre-1965 coins, and they will probably be suspect as counterfeit in a barter situation.

Typically, dealers run most pre-1965 silver-coin orders through a mechanical coin counter. This is true for any orders large enough to be sold loose or bagged. (By bagged, I mean clanking together in a bag, rather than in rolls.) A quick visual inspection will show you that all of the coins are pre-1965. Scan for any rims that show a copper streak—which would indicate that post-1964 clad-copper coins got mixed in. There is certainly no need for you to count ten thousand dimes. As long as the bag weighs at least fifty-two pounds, then you got your full 715 troy ounces of silver. (That troy-ounce figure also applies to circulated silver quarters and half-dollars. But because of the different composition specifications of silver dollars, $1,000 bags of these coins contain around 765 ounces of silver.)

The quick way to gauge the value of a $1,000 bag versus the spot price of silver on any given day is simply to multiply the spot price by 715. Thus, at a spot silver price of $13.85 per ounce, a $1,000 bag of dimes is worth $9,902.75 (or just think of it as 9.9 times face value).

2. Your second portion of silver should be your designated investment-silver stockpile. The best way to buy this—with the lowest dealer premium per ounce—is serial-number-stamped one-hundred-ounce bars from a well-known maker such as Engelhard, A-Mark, or Johnson Matthey. The big, one-thousand-ounce industrial bars almost always require assay for resale, which is expensive and time-consuming—not to mention that they are a pain to transport.

This stockpile is designed as a time machine to protect your wealth from one side of a currency crisis to the other. You buy it in current-day dollars. After a currency collapse has come and gone, when a new, stable currency (hopefully backed by something other than hot air) is issued, then you can convert part or all of your investment-silver stockpile into the new currency. Odds are that most if not all of your original purchasing power will be preserved by this method. Leaving your money in dollar-denominated investments—and I mean *any* dollar-denominated investments—for the next thirty years will be disastrous. This is because the currency unit itself represents the biggest risk. In the long run, as with all other unbacked fiat currencies, the U.S. dollar will end up like the Zimbabwean dollar—inflated away to nothing.

Silver dollars—even those in poor condition—sell for about 20 to 30 percent more than the equivalent in silver dimes or quarters, both because of their slightly higher silver content (per dollar) and because even cruddy-looking silver dollars still have some numismatic value. So for barter you are probably better off with dimes and quarters. However, it is noteworthy that U.S. silver dollars will be even more recognizable and trusted than the smaller-denomination coins, so if you presently own any silver dollars, save those for transactions with your most reluctant barter customers.

Firearms Magazines

Other than silver and productive rural land that could be used as a survival retreat, my personal favorite tangible investment is full-capacity magazines. I'm talking about the kind that hold cartridges for firearms—not *Architectural Digest* magazine. Not only will these shelter you from further declines in the dollar, but they are also likely to zoom up in price if and when another federal magazine ban is enacted. During the last federal ban, which ran for ten years before thankfully expiring (due to a "sunset clause" in 2004), the price of a Glock pistol magazine jumped from fifteen dollars to seventy-five dollars. Even relative "commodity" magazines like U.S. Government Issue alloy M16 magazines doubled or tripled in value. Magazines would also, of course, be very desirable barter items WTSHTF. I expect that if and when a new federal ban is enacted it will have no sunset clause. Thus, it will have the same effect as the civilian transferable machine-gun freeze enacted in 1986. With no end to that ban in sight, prices have skyrocketed.

Keep in mind that several states and localities have enacted high-capacity-magazine bans, so research your laws before purchasing.

My guidance on full-capacity-magazine purchasing is:

1. Buy only magazines that are either original military contract or from original factory makers (no aftermarket junk). Beware of marketing terms such as "GI Type" and "top quality." If it isn't original, then don't buy it, or you will be buying grief. Not only will it have poor feeding reliability, but it will also have only marginal resale value.
2. Initially, buy extra magazines for the guns that you already own.
3. Next, buy extra magazines for the guns that you definitely plan to buy. If a ban is enacted, then all semiautos may end up like Valmet rifles are today: The guns are easier to find than their spare magazines. The law of supply and demand is inescapable.
4. Next, buy extra magazines for the guns that you hope to buy, or that you expect that your children might need someday.
5. Next, buy extra magazines for the pistols and rifles that your local police and sheriff's departments issue. If they don't carry their long guns in visible racks, then ask them what model they carry in the trunks of their cruisers.
6. Next, buy a fairly large quantity of ubiquitous magazines that will serve well as barter items (mostly M14, M16, Mini-14, M1 Carbine, Glock, and Beretta M92).
7. Buy a smaller but carefully selected supply of scarce European magazines (Steyr AUG, HK, SIG, Valmet, etc.). The day may come when not even large wads of cash will buy you any full-capacity magazines, but some owners will be willing to trade for magazines that they want or need.
8. Once you have your supply of magazines in hand, divide them into three coequal piles and store them in three separate loca-

tions, to protect yourself against burglary or other unpleasant future circumstances.

Ballistic Wampum: Common-Caliber and Regional Favorites

Common-caliber ammunition is preferable to precious metals for barter. In the U.S., I recommend stocking up on extra .308, .223, 9mm, .40 S&W, .45 ACP, 12-gauge (2¾-inch only), and .22 long rifle rimfire. You might also lay in a smaller supply of the two or three most popular big-game-hunting calibers in your region. They do vary quite a bit. Ask at your local sporting-goods store which are the most popular. Where I live, it is .30-06, but in other parts of the country it might be .30-30 or .243 Winchester.

Horse Tack

Horses will be very important post-Crunch. So buying horse tack is a great idea. You can also consider those purchases part of your just-in-case Peak Oil insurance and just one more tangible investment. But be sure to keep that leather well oiled, inspected often, and away from moisture and vermin.

One alternative to leather is purchasing the Biothane nylon tack that is now favored by some endurance riders. Regardless of what tack you select, think ahead in terms of maintaining it. Buy extra hardware, rolls of different widths of nylon webbing (in olive green and brown, of course), sheet leather, leatherworking tools, a sewing awl, spools of heavy nylon thread, Barge Cement, Shoo Goo, etc. These are all available from Tandy Leather Factory (tandyleatherfactory.com). I have found that slightly used tools can often be bought at garage sales and flea markets, and via eBay, from people who flirted with the hobby but gave it up when they discovered that it was too much like work.

Those tools and supplies could form the basis for a second post-Crunch source of income or barter. Post-TEOTWAWKI there will suddenly be lots of people who want to carry hand-guns daily but are short on holsters.

Strategies for Bartering, Dickering, and Survival

Since there is effectively only one currency in our country, it is the only way to do business. It may prove difficult, but you need to discard your traditional mind-set about the currency and real-ize that we are riding a down escalator. An inflationary environ-ment stands traditional logic on its head, since saving becomes losing, and investing is almost like throwing coins into a pond if the rate of return of any investment is lower that the real-world inflation rate. The only noteworthy exception, as already dis-cussed, is investing in tangibles.

Here are some suggestions for protecting yourself from infla-tion by mastering the art of bartering:

Buy in Bulk

Buy most of your staple foods and groceries at a discount or warehouse store such as Costco or Sam's Club. Don't overlook the "closeout" and "dented-can" stores. (But avoid buying any bulging cans or those with dented rims.) Stock up on nonperish-able items whenever they are on sale: things like lightbulbs, paper products, bar soap, cleaning supplies, laundry detergent, lubricants, and so forth. As long as you protect these supplies from theft, moisture, and vermin, they are better than money in the bank. These are tangibles bought at today's prices, which you can use for many years to come.

If your local zoning and fire regulations allow it, buy your own gas and diesel fuel tanks. Also consider installing oversize propane or home-heating-oil tanks. When getting competitive bids from tank suppliers, be sure to ask them to lock in the price per gallon for the initial fill for each new tank. To win your business, the tank salesman might be willing to commit to a price that is a few pennies per gallon below current market. See Chapter 6 for more on fuel.

Learn to Barter

Barter, by its very nature, shields you from inflation. Instead of using depreciating paper tokens as a means of exchange, you are *directly* exchanging a tangible for another tangible, or a service for a tangible, or a service for a service. I strongly advocate stocking up on extra items for barter. However, it is with the proviso that you do not embark on buying goods dedicated for barter until after you have your family's essential beans, bullets, and Band-Aids squared away, following a well-balanced logistics plan.

To be useful in barter, choose items that have most or all of the following seven attributes:

1. Appeal/usefulness to the majority of the citizenry. Nearly every family uses soap, but just a few need #7 Singer sewing-machine needles.
2. Immediate recognizability. Name brands need no introduction. All others are suspect.
3. Longevity. Keep shelf life in mind. If you cannot barter it all away before it goes bad, then you are buying too much. Even coal has a shelf life.

4. Easy divisibility. Boxes of matches, boxes of cartridges, coils of rope, balls of twine, and cans of kerosene are perfect examples. If you plan on dividing a commodity in barter transactions, then be sure to have the containers needed for parceling it out.

5. Relative compactness and transportability at reasonable cost. Toilet paper has great appeal, but just five hundred dollars' worth would nearly fill my garage.

6. Consistent quality. For example, precious metals, coins of known purity, or ammunition from a major manufacturer such as Winchester, Remington, or Federal.

7. Limited availability. In North America, jars of freeze-dried instant coffee would be ideal, but in Central America, they would probably be worthless.

Learn Several Valuable (Barterable) Skills

As discussed previously, every family should have at least one home-based business that they can fall back on in the event of an economic recession or depression. Concentrate on skills rather than goods for barter. The beauty of having skills to barter is that most of them don't require much raw material, so unlike with barter goods, you will never run out. A profession or skill that also requires a specialized tool set is fine; however, if the skill also requires delivering a factory-made device to complete each transaction, then you might consider doing something else. For example, installing burglar alarms might be profitable as long as you have a source of resupply, and as long as the power and telephone networks are functioning. But in a grid-down TEOTWAWKI, how long could you continue running such a business?

Avoid developing a skill that appeals only to wealthy customers for discretionary spending. Those are the purchases that will be delayed or skipped altogether in an economic depression. Hence, shotgun checkering and engraving are poor choices, but septic-tank pumping is a good one.

Concentrate on a business that can be operated without the need for grid power. It is notable that most of the businesses in this category existed in the nineteenth century. Who knows? Maybe buggy whip makers will make a comeback in the Second Great Depression.

Bartering

Being ready to barter is *not* just a matter of having a pile of "stuff" to trade. While barter and charity logistics are important, what is even more important is what is between your ears. Bartering takes practice. Dickering is an acquired skill. I suggest that you start attending gun shows, garage sales, and flea markets and learn how to haggle.

Practice bartering on a very small scale at first to sharpen your eye for value and your ability to dicker in a manner that will result in a fair trade that is mutually agreeable and mutually beneficial. The occasional transaction in which you end up slighted is hardly cause for concern, but unless you develop the proper bartering skills, you'll end up on the weaker side of bargains again and again, and you'll fritter away your tangible working capital. The attributes that will put you in a superior bartering position include specific knowledge about what is being traded, knowledge about who's sitting on the other side of the table, and good old-fashioned horse sense.

Barter Knowledge and References

The more you know about the goods being exchanged, the better you'll be able to dicker. Armed with this knowledge, you'll be able to honestly yet persuasively talk up the virtues of your own goods, while politely talking down the defects of your trading partner's goods. Hence, the greater your technical knowledge of the goods, the better. Take the time to study and develop an appraiser's eye for the condition of used merchandise, the relative value of goods from one maker versus another, and knowledge of the overall market. With that knowledge you can articulate the scarcity of any particular item in your barter stock. After all, as with any other free-market transaction, the key factor in determining value is the supply/demand ratio. If you are trading for a collectible item, then knowing how scarce it is can put you at a tremendous advantage in negotiation. You need to authoritatively know which maker, model, variation, grade, year of production, etc., to look for.

Similarly, knowing exactly how to gauge properly the condition of a used item is quite important. For example, with firearms, the percentage of original bluing remaining, cracks or wear to a gun's stock, bore condition, chamber condition, bolt-face erosion, action tightness, headspace, and so forth all make a huge difference in the value of a used gun.

Detailed knowledge is also crucial when determining the value of a rare coin. For most of us, that knowledge is too specialized to be of much use. It can take many years to develop coin-grading skills, so a novice can get in over his or her head very easily. The difference between an MS-66 coin and an MS-68 is very subtle, yet that difference can mean thousands of dollars' difference in a coin's price. I therefore recommend that novices trade *only* professionally graded coins that have been graded and sealed (or "slabbed") by either Professional Coin Grading Service or Numismatic Guaranty Corporation. A coin dealer Bluesheet (snipurl.com/hn5a4) is a crucial reference for measuring the current value of coins with particular mint marks and dates in any given grade on the Sheldon scale. Even having an out-of-date Bluesheet is better than nothing, since it will show relative values of coins, which change fairly gradually. Again, this is not for a novice or a part-time dabbler.

Tools

To be ready to barter with bullion gold coins or scrap gold it is important to have a touchstone, an acid-test kit, test needles, a very accurate scale, and a set of Fisch coin-authenticity dimensional gauges.

When bartering for canned goods you should have a Julian calendar (since some packers use Julian dates) and a hard copy of the mealtime.org chart showing how to decipher date-of-pack codes from various canners and packers.

For liquid fuel, it's important to know if the fuel has been contaminated or adulterated. UR-2B-Prepared.com sells water test strips.

For batteries, you'll need a voltmeter. For the greatest versatility, buy a volt-ohm meter with test probes on leads, rather than a typical tray-type home battery tester.

For examining the fine details of just about anything—such as reading hallmarks—a jeweler's loupe (magnifying glass) is a must.

For evaluating firearms, at minimum buy a six-foot tape measure and a fiber-optic bore-inspection light.

Dickering Tactics

Above and beyond getting technical knowledge is the hard-to-quantify people skill of dickering. Dickering skills can take years to develop. Part of this is learning how to read the face and body language of the gent on the other side of the table. How anxious is he to unload something that he has, or to acquire something that you have? How quick they are to make or accept an offer is a key indicator. And if there is a savvy trader sizing *you* up, you have to learn to keep a poker face, not revealing how excited you are to see a particular item being offered.

Take your time in carefully examining any item offered to you. This gives you the opportunity to spot any flaws, defects, or signs of wear on the item being offered, and if you spend more time examining an item, it will lead the seller to doubt the value of what he is offering. If you make an offer for an item and it is rejected, or the counteroffer made is ridiculously high, then the very best thing you can do is put the item back on the table. This psychologically distances you from the item, and, again, makes the seller begin to doubt its value. In the dickering process one of the most valuable phrases that you can use is "Is that the best you can do?" If the seller won't budge and you are close to an acceptable price, the next-best thing to do is offer to sweeten the deal with additional goods offered on your side of the bargain. If you still can't reach an agreement, it probably wouldn't hurt to subtly talk down the value of what's being offered to you, and talk up the value of what you are offering. "This is a mighty fine widget. It's too bad about this crack and this wear . . . If it weren't for that, I think your asking price would be fair."

The next most valuable thing you can learn is how to say nothing. After making an offer and receiving a counteroffer, silently start counting to twenty. There is something about a long pause that causes all but the most stalwart dickerer to want to fill that silence. And nine times out of ten, he will fill that silence with another offer, usually one that is more agreeable.

As a last resort, thank the seller and start to walk away from the table. This will be your final gauge of just how anxious the seller is to move his merchandise. If you hear "Wait, wait, wait, come back here . . . ," then you know that the seller still has room to negotiate on price or quantity. Keep in mind, however, that this is a risky tactic. Once you walk away without the seller voicing objection, if you return later, you have boxed yourself into the previously offered price. If you come back later for the same item, the seller will know that you are anxious to purchase it and did not find a better deal for a comparable item elsewhere, so he'll probably hold to the same price.

When selling, keep in mind that you can negotiate down, but not up. Always make your initial asking price somewhat higher than what you really want for it. Some people will not agree even to a good deal unless they can extract at least one price concession from you. So set a fairly high price, and then negotiate down.

If your counterpart brings an item to offer you, but that item is of no interest to you, always thank him for his time: "Thanks, but I'm not interested in that right now. Do you have any X available?" describing what you are looking for in trade. Remember, a sales venue is an opportunity to gather information about other items a seller may have available but may not have with him. It might not hurt to make arrangements to see him at the next event, reminding him to bring those items so you can make a deal next time.

Image

When going to attend a flea market, gun show, or horse-trading session, it is important to dress down. If you wear a fancy watch or designer clothes, consciously or unconsciously your counterpart will size you up as being made of money. So dress very casually, including your shoes. Leave your jewelry, pens, and nice watch at home. Wear your cheap plastic digital watch for these excursions.

You also need to learn to be observant about your counterpart. Is he a collector who happens to sell on the side, or is he a journeyman salesman whose livelihood is this business? Is he retiring and selling off inventory? Is he selling merchandise on behalf of a friend or relative? The bottom line is: Just how anxious is your counterpart to make a deal?

Timing and Rapport

When approaching a vendor for the first time it is important to first wait until the vendor has finished dealing with any previous customers. Don't interrupt a man when he's making a deal! Smile and make eye contact, and if appropriate for the venue, introduce yourself and shake hands. If you are a fellow vendor, wear your badge or otherwise make it known that you also have a table or booth. This lets the seller know that he is talking to a wholesale rather than retail customer. This can make a tremendous difference when negotiating price. Even if the vendor appears to have a pile of worthless junk on his table (with perhaps a few nice items of interest), make a point of expressing your admiration for his merchandise. Say something like, "You've got a real nice inventory here," or "I can see that you have good taste in widgets." While it doesn't hurt to point out a defect on an individual item while negotiating for it, do not "run down" the quality or condition of everything that you see. Doing so could skunk the entire deal-making process. Don't be shy about pointing out defects in your own merchandise. "Oh, in case you didn't notice, there is one dent here . . ." In a subtle way, that lets your customer know that you are reputable.

Another key aspect of buying-and-selling psychology is the stage of the game. At the beginning of a show or sale most journeymen sellers arrive inventory rich and cash poor. Near the end of the show, they will likely have more cash (or precious metals) on hand and then will be in a better position to make offers. Although some of the best items may have already been sold, one of the most advantageous times to make a purchase or trade is near the end of a show, when some sellers have had a slow show. At flea markets and gun shows, wait until just before the vendor's tear-down-and-pack-up time begins. Depending on his situation, he might be desperate to make a good sale or a couple of good swaps so that he can feel he's made the show worthwhile. So if you saw an item earlier in the show and could not negotiate an agreeable price, wait for the end of the sales event. This is a particularly valuable tactic if the item in question is especially bulky or heavy. It is the unspoken goal of every seller to go home light.

If you encounter a seller who has the sort of merchandise that you think would be of future interest, then get his particulars so that you can contact him later. Take copious notes. The same applies when you encounter a seller who has a particularly valuable area of expertise or a rare stock of items—especially spare parts. These are people well worth networking with.

Never Trade Hard for Soft

When negotiating a trade, keep in mind the absolutely fundamental rule: "Never trade hard for soft." This means if what you are offering in a trade is a compact, valuable, durable, tangible item that is in short supply or highly valued, don't make the mistake of trading it away for items that are less durable or desirable. Otherwise, at the end of the day your counterpart will be going home with the better goods. The only exception to this rule is if your counterpart is willing to trade a much greater quantity of his items and you know that you have a ready market for them. It is better to trade your bulky for his compact.

Barter takes time to learn. Invest that time. Also invest in the proper references. Lastly, invest in a stock of top-quality barter goods that you predict will be sought after in a post-collapse world. With the right goods and the requisite knowledge, you and your family will never starve.

14

IT COMES DOWN TO YOU

The "Come as You Are" Collapse:
Have the Right Tools and Skills

I have repeatedly and strongly emphasized the importance of living at your intended retreat year-round, but I realize that because of personal finances, family obligations, and the constraints of making a living at an hourly or salaried job, this is not always realistic—except for a few of us, mainly retirees. If you are stuck in the big city and plan to Get Out of Dodge at the eleventh hour, then pre-position the vast majority of your gear and supplies at your retreat. You will most likely only have one—I repeat, *one*—G.O.O.D. trip. If there is a major crisis there will probably be no chance to go back for a second load. So WT-SHTF, it will truly be a come-as-you-are affair.

We must recognize that in these days of rapid news dissemination, it may take as little as ten hours for supermarket shelves to be cleaned out. It make take just a few hours for queues that are literally blocks long to form at gas stations—or at bank branches in the event of bank runs. Worse yet, it may be just a few hours before the highways and freeways leading out of urban and suburban areas are clogged with traffic.

The come-as-you-are concept also applies to your personal training. If you haven't learned how to do things before the balloon goes up, don't expect to get anything but marginal to mediocre on-the-spot training after the fact. You have the opportunity to take top-quality training from the best instructors now, but you certainly won't once the Schumer hits the fan. Train with the best—with organizations like Medical Corps, Wilderness Emergency Medical Services Institute, Front Sight (frontsight.com), Gunsite (gunsite.com), the RWVA/Appleseed Project, the WRSA, and the ARRL. Someday, you'll be very glad that you did.

As for provisions and equipment, the come-as-you-are concept definitely applies. The demand for them during a societal collapse will be tremendous. How could you compete in such a scant market? Anyone who conceivably has spares will probably want to keep them for a member of their own family or group. Use the advice and lists in this book and take precautions.

Stock your retreat well. If there isn't someone living there year-round, then hide what is there from burglars. Maintain balance in your preparations. In a situation in which you are truly hunkered down at your retreat in the midst of a societal collapse, there might not be any opportunity to barter for items that you overlooked. What you have is what you got. You will have to make do, so be sure to develop your lists of lists meticulously (see Chapter 2). If you have the funds available, construct a combination storm shelter/fallout shelter/walk-in vault. It would be virtually impossible to build something that elaborate in the aftermath of a societal collapse.

Don't overlook the "you" part of the "as you are" premise. Are you physically fit? Are you up-to-date on your dental work? Do you have two pairs of sturdy eyeglasses with your current prescription? Do you have at least a six-month supply of vitamins and medications? Is your body weight reasonable? If your answer to any of these is no, then get busy.

With careful preparations, even if you have a modest budget you will have an advantage over the average suburbanite. Your knowledge and training alone—what is between your ears—will ensure that.

A Call to Action

If you are serious about preparedness, then it is time to get out of your armchair and start training and preparing. It will take time. It will take some sweat. It will take money. But once you've prepared, you can sleep well, knowing that you've done your best to protect and provide for your family, regardless of what the future brings. Don't get stuck in the rut of simply *studying* preparedness. Unless the shelves in your pantry and garage are filling with supplies, and unless you are growing muscles and calluses, you are not preparing.

Learn the crucial skills for self-sufficiency and self-defense. Once you've mastered them, share them with others. Future generations need to learn these skills. Raise your children to be God-fearing, practical, and thrifty. That will be a lasting legacy.

If and when challenging times do arrive—whether natural or man-made—you'll be ready and able to be part of the solution. You can help to put the workings of the Big Machine back in motion, give charitably, and restore law and order. Without folks like you and me, the lights of civilization may go out for a very long time. Are you up to the challenge? I pray that you are.

Appendix A

GLOSSARY

1911: *See* M1911

4WD: Four-wheel drive

AC: Alternating current

ACP: Automatic Colt pistol

ALICE: All-purpose lightweight individual carrying equipment

AM: Amplitude modulation

AR-15: Semiauto civilian variants of the U.S. Army M16 rifle

AUG: The Austrian army's 5.56mm "bullpup" infantry carbine. Also issued by the Australian Army as their replacement for the L1A1.

Ballistic wampum: Ammunition stored for barter purposes (term coined by the late Jeff Cooper)

BLM: Bureau of Land Management, a U.S. federal government agency that administers public lands

BOB, BoB, or B-o-B: Bugout Bag: Synonymous with G.O.O.D. kit

Camo: Slang for camouflage

CAR-15: *See* M4

CB: Citizens band radio. A VHF broadcasting band that requires no license for operation in the United States. Some desirable CB transceivers are capable of single-sideband (SSB)

operation. Originally twenty-three channels, the citizens band was later expanded to forty channels during the golden age of CB, in the 1970s.

CC&Rs: Covenants, conditions, and restrictions

CCW: Carrying a concealed weapon (typically in reference to a permit)

Channelized areas: In the context of this book, the most likely routes that the Golden Horde will take WTSHTF. Also called refugee lines of drift. *See also*: Golden Horde *and* WTSHTF.

CLP: Cleaner, lubricant, protectant. A mil-spec lubricant, sold under the trade name Break-Free CLP.

COMSEC: Communications security

Conex: A continental express shipping container. The standard steel or aluminum international shipping containers used on trucks, rail packs, and ships. Usually manufactured in twenty-, thirty-, and forty-foot lengths.

CPAP: Constant positive airway pressure (some sleep-apnea patients require a CPAP machine at night)

CPR: Cardiopulmonary resuscitation

CQ: Charge of quarters

CRKT: Columbia River Knife and Tool

Crunch, the: *See* WTSHTF

DC: Depending on context, direct current or District of Criminals

Deep-larder concept: A pantry stocked with foods and essential oils for a family for two or more years

DMA: Daily moving average

E85: A gasoline/ethanol blend, 85 percent ethanol, 15 percent gasoline

EMP: Electromagnetic pulse

EMT: Emergency medical technician

ER: Emergency room

FDA: Food and Drug Administration (U.S. federal government agency)

FEMA: Federal Emergency Management Agency (U.S. federal government agency)

FFV: Flex-fuel vehicle

FIFO: First in, first out

FM: Depending on context, field manual or frequency modulation

G.I. or GI: Depending on context, general inductee (draftee), Government Issue (equipment specifications), or gastrointestinal tract. *See also*: U.S.G.I.

Glock: The popular polymer-framed pistol design by Gaston Glock, of Austria. Also derisively known as combat Tupperware by its detractors, because it was the first maker to ship its pistols in a plastic box with a snap lid.

Gold Cup: The target version of Colt's M1911. Has fully adjustable target sights, a tapered barrel, and a tighter barrel bushing than standard M1911s.

Golden Horde: In historical contexts, the Mongol horde of the thirteenth century, but in the context of this book, the anticipated large mixed horde of refugees and looters that will pour out of the metropolitan regions WTSHTF. *See also*: WTSHTF.

G.O.O.D.: Get Out of Dodge, a generic term for leaving the big city in a hurry WTSHTF (acronym coined by JWR). *See also*: BOB, WTSHTF.

GPS: Global positioning system

Grid down: An extended period of time when the power grid is nonfunctional

Grid up: A situation in which the national power grids stay functional except for brief interruptions

HDPE: High-density polyethylene, used in milk, juice, and water containers in order to take advantage of its excellent protective-barrier properties. *Most* five-gallon food-grade buckets are made from HDPE. *See also*: LDPE.

HEPA: High-efficiency particulate air (filter)

HF: High frequency

HK: Heckler und Koch, the German gunmaker

HMMWV: High Mobility Multipurpose Wheeled Vehicle, commonly called a Humvee

IBA: Interceptor body armor, the current U.S. military-issue Kevlar body armor. The base vest weighs six pounds. The front and rear trauma plates are an additional six pounds each. Additional shoulder armor and groin protectors add even more weight.

In-town retreat: A retreat inside or adjoining town limits that depends on some local infrastructure. *See also*: Isolated retreat.

Inverter: A device that converts DC electricity (anywhere from twelve to six hundred VDC) to AC electricity (typically 120/240 VAC)

IR: Infrared

Isolated retreat: A privately owned stronghold designed to be almost entirely self-sufficient and self-contained. Also often called a remote retreat. *See also*: In-town retreat.

JWR: James Wesley, Rawles

KW or kW: Kilowatt

L1A1: The British and Australian "inch"-measurements versions of the metric FAL rifle. Also known as the SLR (self-loading rifle).

LDPE: Low-density polyethylene, used in grocery shopping bags and trash bags. Not all LDPE is food grade. *See also*: HDPE.

LDS: The Latter Day Saints, commonly called the Mormons

LED: Light-emitting diode

Lines of drift: *See* Channelized areas

LP/OP: Listening post/observation post, usually the same position, used for observation in daylight hours and for listening and use of starlight devices at night. *See also*: Starlight

LR: Long rifle

LSD: Low self-discharge

M14: U.S. Army–issue 7.62mm NATO selective-fire battle rifle. These rifles are still issued in small numbers, primarily to U.S. Army–designated marksmen and as U.S. Navy deck rifles. The civilian semiauto-only equivalent is the M1A.

M16: U.S. Army–issue 5.56mm NATO selective-fire battle rifle. The current standard variant is the M16A2, which has improved sights and three-shot burst control. The civilian semiauto-only equivalent is the AR-15.

M1911: The U.S. military's standard-issue semiauto pistol, chambered in .45 ACP, that was issued for more than seventy years. It was replaced by the Beretta M9, 9mm Parabellum.

M4: U.S. Army–issue 5.56mm NATO selective-fire carbine. It is essentially a shortened and lightened M16, with a collapsing stock.

M4gery: (pronounced "em forgery") Civilian semiauto-only version of the U.S. Army–issue 5.56mm NATO carbine. Typically with a 16-inch barrel instead of the military-issue 14.5-inch barrel (to meet the U.S. 16-inch minimum-rifle-barrel-length requirement) and a collapsing stock.

Mag: Depending on context, short for magazine or Magnum

MIL-SPEC or mil-spec: Military specification. A product made to the demanding standards of military organizations.

MRE: Meal, Ready to Eat (U.S. Army field rations), aka "Meals Rarely Eaten" and "Three lies for the price of one"—viz., "It isn't a meal, it's not ready, and you can't eat it."

NATO: North Atlantic Treaty Organization

Night vision: *See* Starlight

NiMH: Nickel-metal hydride, a type of rechargeable battery

NRCS: National Resources Conservation Service (formerly called the Soil Conservation Service), part of the USDA. *See also*: USDA.

Off grid: Not connected to the power grid (as in a home that is typically powered by phovoltaics, wind power, micro-hydro generators, or gas/diesel/propane gensets)

OPSEC: Operational security

POTS: Plain old telephone service

PV: Photovoltaic. PV power panels convert energy from sunshine to DC electricity.

PVC: Polyvinyl chloride (white plastic water pipe)

Rawles Ranch: The full-time home/retreat for the Rawles family, in an unnamed western state

Refugee lines of drift: *See* Channelized areas

Remote retreat: *See* Isolated retreat

RF: Depending on context, radio frequency (radio waves) or rimfire

Rule 303/Rule 308: Civilian law enforcement, post-TEOTWAWKI (Rule 303 in Canada and Oz; Rule 308 in the Americas)

RV: In the context of nuclear weapons, a reentry vehicle—a method of delivering a nuclear weapon. In the context of survival retreats, a recreational vehicle.

SCADA: Supervisory control and data acquisition.

Schumer: A euphemism for the stuff that the septic-tank pumper truck hauls away

Schumeresque: Intolerably bad (post-TEOTWAWKI) living circumstances. *See also*: WTSHTF.

SHTF: Schumer Hits the Fan. *See also*: WTSHTF

Spec: Specification(s)

Starlight: An electronic light-amplification technology that was first developed during the Vietnam War. A starlight device literally amplifies low ambient light by up to one hundred thousand times, turning nighttime darkness into daylight—albeit a green and fuzzy view. Starlight scopes are critical tools for retreat security, especially in a grid-down situation. Note: Starlight is also the name brand of a manufacturer of heavy-duty mil-spec gun cases.

Steyr: Steyr-Daimler Puch, an Austrian firearms and military-vehicle maker. *See also*: AUG.

S&W: Smith and Wesson, an American gunmaker

TA-1/TA-312: U.S. military hardwired field telephones

TEOTWAWKI: The End of the World as We Know It (acronym coined by Mike Medintz)

The Crunch: *See* WTSHTF

Trijicon: A maker of tritium-lit sights and rifle scopes

Tritium: A glowing radioactive gas (a hydrogen isotope) with an 11.2-year half-life

Truck farming/Truck crops: Farming crops that are not processed before selling and that are directly used or sold fresh, such as lettuce, celery, and flowers

TSHTF: The Schumer Hits the Fan. *See also*: WTSHTF.

USDA: United States Department of Agriculture

U.S.G.I. or USGI: United States Government Issue equipment specifications

USGS: United States Geological Survey

UV: Ultraviolet (commonly called black light)

VDC: Volts, direct current

VHF: Very high frequency

WAPI: Water pasteurization indicator

WTSHTF: When the Schumer Hits the Fan. Synonymous with

TEOTWAWKI, the Crunch, worst case, and the old military saying "when the balloon goes up." *See also*: Schumeresque and TEOTWAWKI.

YOYO: You're on your own. When government ceases to provide essential services such as fire and police-department protection, and when utilities no longer provide water, sanitation, electricity, and phone service. Acronym coined by David Weed.

Appendix B

BOOKS AND ONLINE RESOURCES

There are more than seven thousand archived articles and letters on family preparedness available at the author's blog site, SurvivalBlog.com.

The author's book and DVD recommendations can be found at survivalblog.com/bookshelf.html.

The author's recommended Web sites for preparedness supplies, trainers, and further research can be found at survivalblog .com/links.html.

Appendix C

PROTECTING YOUR FAMILY FROM AN INFLUENZA PANDEMIC

The emerging threats of the H1N1 ("swine") flu and the still-present Asian avian flu virus bring into sharp focus the vulnerability of modern, highly mobile and technological societies to viral or bacterial infectious diseases. The last major flu outbreak (H2N2 in 1957, which killed 69,800 people in the United States) took five months to reach the U.S. With the advent of global jet travel, it is now clear that highly virulent disease strains can be transmitted to population centers around the world in a matter of just a few days.

You can take measures to protect yourself and your family from the next great pandemic. Although the likelihood of H1N1 mutating into a more virulent strain is relatively low, the potential impact if this were to occur is devastating. The current strain of the virus has a low lethality rate for humans, but even if H1N1 turns out to be a nonevent, in the next few decades there is a very high likelihood that some other disease will emerge. Influenzas have a tendency toward antigenic shift. Because influenzas are viral and are spread by casual person-to-person contact, the majority of the world's population could be exposed in just a few weeks or months.

Here are the key things that you need to do to protect yourself and your family, and to help restore order during a pandemic:

Raise Your Immune Response

There are two philosophies regarding fighting off influenza viruses. The first and most prevalent is to raise the body's immune response. The other is to maintain normal immune response to prevent a collapse caused by over-response—hypercytokinemia, commonly called a "cytokine storm." Hyper cytokinemia is an immune-system overreaction to infection in which a feedback loop develops between cytokines and ostensibly helpful immune-system cells, such as T-cells. Once this feedback loop develops, cytokines rapidly build up to very high levels. Effectively, the body's immune system overreacts, and begins to attack healthy tissue.

While opinion is divided on this issue, I tend toward keeping the means at hand to trigger a strong immune response—particularly if combating a highly virulent illness.

To increase your resistance to disease it is important that you stop smoking. If you are a smoker you are much more susceptible to respiratory infections, and you are at high risk to develop complications.

Get plenty of exercise, eat healthy foods, drink alcohol only in moderation, get plenty of sleep, and use top-quality vitamin supplements.

If you are overweight, you need to alter your diet to get down to within five pounds of normal body weight. Unhealthy foods weaken your immune system. Cut out refined sugar. Avoid candy, junk foods, soft drinks, and any processed foods with preservatives, artificial sweeteners, or MSG. Avoid store-bought meat, which is often tainted by the hormones and antibiotics used in commercial livestock feeds. Wild game or home-raised livestock is much healthier.

Lastly, pray. Why? Anxiety is a form of stress that weakens the immune system, and prayer is a proven way to relieve anxiety and stress. And more important, as a Christian I believe that it is crucial to pray for God's guidance, providence, and protection.

Be Ready to Fight the Illness

Know thy enemy: Flus typically cause fever, chills, achy feeling (malaise), headaches, and extreme fatigue. Cold symptoms are usually restricted to the upper respiratory tract, while flu symptoms tend to involve the entire body.

Influenzas kill most of their victims in two ways: dehydration and lung congestion. Even the avian flu, which is a respiratory infection, typically starts with stomach-flu symptoms. Stomach flus usually induce diarrhea, which rapidly dehydrates the victim. To fight dehydration, you need to stock up on both anti-diarrhea medicines (such as Imodium AD, an antispasmodic) and electrolyte solutions such as Pedialyte. The latter is available in bulk through large chain warehouse stores. The various sports-type drinks (such as Gatorade) can be used as oral rehydration solutions (ORSes) too. However, I prefer to dilute them about 50 percent with water; they have a lot of glucose in them, which will exacerbate diarrhea symptoms.

If commercial ORSs are not available, I have read that you can make an emergency solution as follows:

- ½ teaspoon salt
- 2 tablespoons honey, sugar, or rice powder

- ¼ teaspoon potassium chloride (table-salt substitute)
- ½ teaspoon trisodium citrate (can be replaced by baking soda)
- 1 quart clean water

Imodium is a trade name for loperamide. It can be purchased generically for relatively low cost. The generic or house brands are just fine. Stock up on acetaminophen (Tylenol) and ibuprofen (Motrin) as well—for treating fevers. Have a traditional glass thermometer on hand for each person, or a digital thermometer with lots of disposable sleeves. The thermometers are a couple of bucks at most drugstores. The sleeves are a dollar or so per hundred. Don't cross-contaminate your patients.

Because influenzas are viral rather than bacterial, most antibiotic drugs (antibacterials) are useless in combating them. If you suspect that you are coming down with influenza, get bed rest. Too many people ignore their symptoms because that project at work just has to get done. Not only do they risk their own health, but they put their coworkers at risk for infection as well. Liquids help ease congestion and loosen phlegm and are of course crucial to rehydration. A fever alone can double your body's dehydration rate.

Note: There is a difference of opinion in medical circles about suppressing a fever with a nonseasonal influenza. It all depends on the particular strain. Before using aspirin (for adults) or acetaminophen (for children and adults), check the literature on the current flu strain. If there are widespread reports of cytokine-storm reactions, then suppressing a fever might be a good thing. As always, you should consult a medical professional before taking any medications.

Statistically, the largest group killed by the 1918 flu was sixteen- to twenty-five-year-olds—those with the strongest immune systems. Those patients often died because their bodies fought the virus too vigorously in a cytokine storm. Aspirin can help suppress the response that leads to a cytokine overreaction. Again, there is still considerable debate in medical literature over the issue of fever suppression versus the risk of cytokine overreaction in treating influenzas.

Respiratory flus such as the swine flu and Asian avian flu kill mainly via congestion. Buy a steam-type vaporizer. Stock up on expectorants containing guaifenesin as the main ingredient.

You will need to watch carefully for any symptoms of pneumonia. These include difficulty or painful breathing, a grunting sound when breathing (quite distinct from the wheezing of bronchitis or the "barking" of croup), extremely rapid breathing, flaring nostrils with each breath, or coughing up rust-colored phlegm. Pneumonia can be a deadly complication of the flu and is the main cause of flu-related death. It is important to note that pneumonia is typically a coinfection that can be either viral or bacterial. In case of a bacterial pneumonia, antibiotics are crucial for saving lives. If it is viral, there is not much that can be done. While antibiotics can clear infection, they cannot remove secretions. The patient must cough them all the way back up the respiratory tract. Do not use cough suppressants—anything with active ingredients like dextromethorphan or diphenhydramine. A wet cough that produces phlegm is a *good thing*. Your doctor might recommend expectorants, such as Robitussin. These are also available as generics, which are quite cheap, so stock up. You should also read up on postural drainage and percussion techniques for chest secretion clearance.

Avoid Exposure

Even though the chances of a full-scale "nation-busting" pandemic are small, the possibility definitely exists. A full-scale pandemic that starts taking lives on a grand scale may quite reasonably cause you to take some extreme measures to protect the lives of your family members. You can cut your chances of infection significantly if you prepare to live in isolation (a strict "self-quarantine") for an extended period of time. You need to be ready to avoid all contact with other people during the worst of the pandemic.

History has shown that infectious diseases do their worst in urbanized regions, so if you can afford to, make plans to move to a lightly populated region, soon. Where? You can go to my blog (SurvivalBlog.com) for some detailed recommendations, but in general, I recommend moving west of the Missouri River (because of much lighter population density) to a rural, agricultural region. For more details on ideal retreats, see Chapter 3.

Aside from being actually coughed on or sneezed upon by an infected person, the most common way to catch the flu is by touching something that has been coughed on or sneezed upon by said infected person. For instance, the person who used the shopping cart before you might have had the flu. If he covered his mouth with his hand when he coughed and then used that very hand to push the cart around the store, you could catch an infection if you rubbed your eye or nose, introducing the virus to your most vulnerable point of infection.

To protect yourself (at least marginally) from infected spittle, wear wraparound goggles and buy or fabricate surgical-style masks, in quantity. Note that even an N100 gas-mask filter will not stop an airborne virus, since the viruses are too small, but a cloth mask will give you some protection from virus-laden spittle. Once the pandemic breaks out in your region, you won't look out of place wearing these, even on a trip to the post office. Stock up on disposable gloves. Note that some individuals are allergic to latex, so do some extended-wear tests before you buy gloves in quantity. Wear gloves whenever away from your retreat, and wash your hands frequently, regardless. Keep your hands away from your nose and eyes at all times, since your mucus membranes are some of the most sensitive to infection. Stock up on soap and bottles of disinfecting hand sanitizer and use them often, especially when using public restrooms. (Don't forget to cover the doorknobs with a paper towel on your way out!)

Stockpile Key Logistics

To make long-term self-quarantine effective you will need to buy a large quantity of long-term storage food. (See Chapter 5 for details.) You will also need fuel. (See Chapter 6 for details.) In the event of a worst case, you may have to repel looters by force of arms. (See Chapter 11 for details.)

With the consent of your doctor and his prescription, you should stock up at least moderately on antibiotics such as penicillin and ciprofloxacin ("cipro") to fight coinfections. But they should be used only if it is abundantly clear that a coinfection has set in. (Again, watch for pneumonia symptoms.)

There are a few drugs that have been clinically proven to be useful in lessening the symptoms of viral influenzas and shortening the duration of illness. These include Relenza (zanamivir), Tamiflu (oseltamivir phosphate), and Sambucol. These drugs are used immediately after the onset of flu symptoms. Of the three, Sambucol—a nonprescription tincture of black elderberry—is probably the best. I predict shortages of these drugs in coming months, so stock up while they are still readily available.

Be Prepared to Dispense Charity from a Safe Distance

It is important to lay in extra food and medication to dispense as charity. I cannot emphasize this enough. Helping your neighbors is biblically sound and builds trustworthy friendships that you can count on. To avoid risk of infection, you need to be prepared to dispense charity from a safe distance—without physical contact. Think planning, teamwork, and backup. While your family's food storage can be in bulk containers (typically five- to seven-gallon food-grade plastic pails), your charity storage food should mostly be in smaller containers. Or at least buy some extra smaller containers that you can fill and distribute to refugees. Also be sure to lay in extra gardening seed to dispense as charity. Non-hybrid (heirloom) varieties that breed true are available from several vendors including the Ark Institute (arkinstitute.com). By dispensing charity you will be helping to restore order and reestablish key infrastructures. You'll be part of the solution rather than part of the problem.

For further research, I highly recommend that you read Dr. Grattan Woodson's monograph *Preparing for the Coming Influenza Pandemic,* available for free download at my blog site (survival blog.com/AvianFlu.pdf).

Index